Quizzical Eye

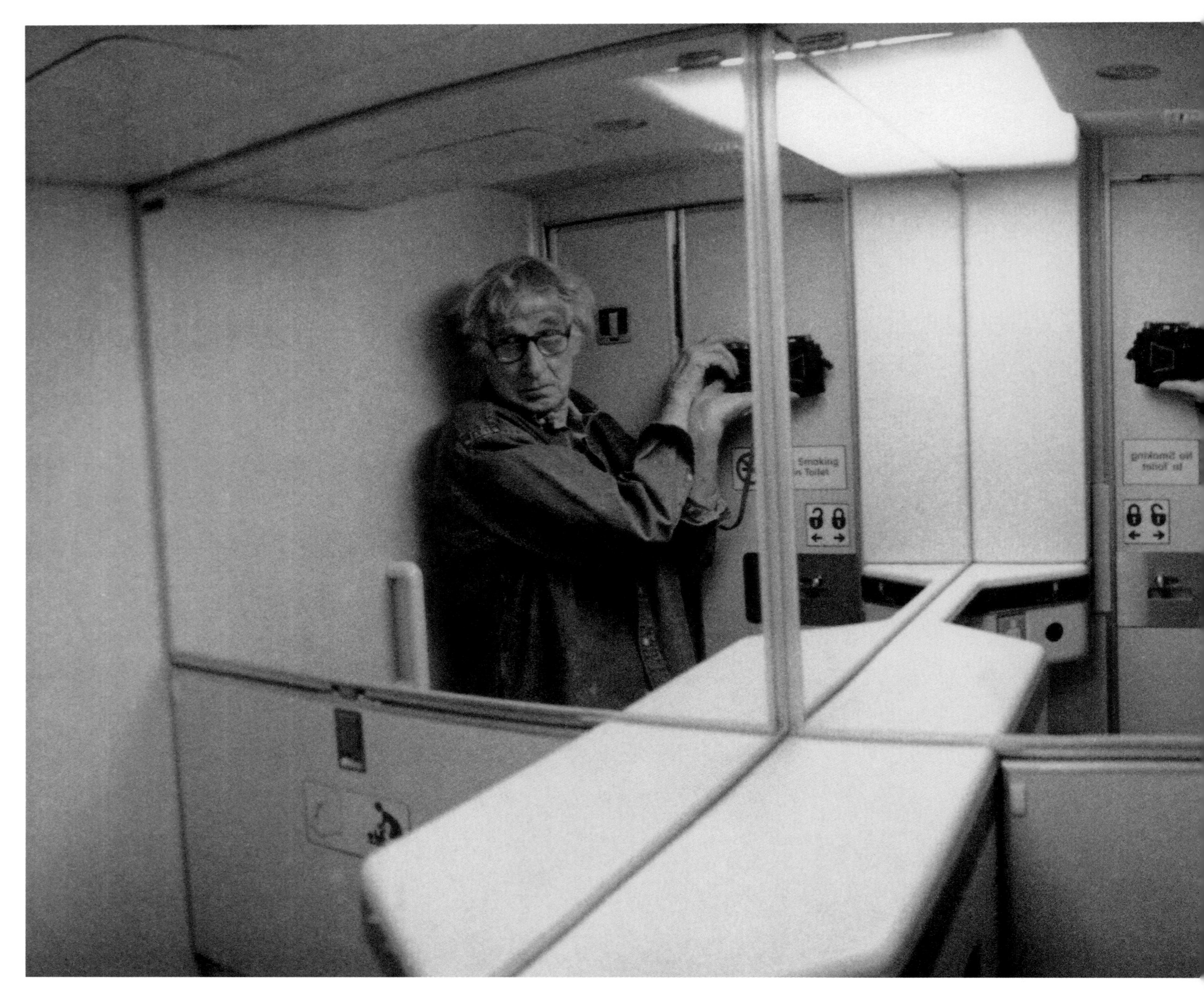

Quizzical Eye

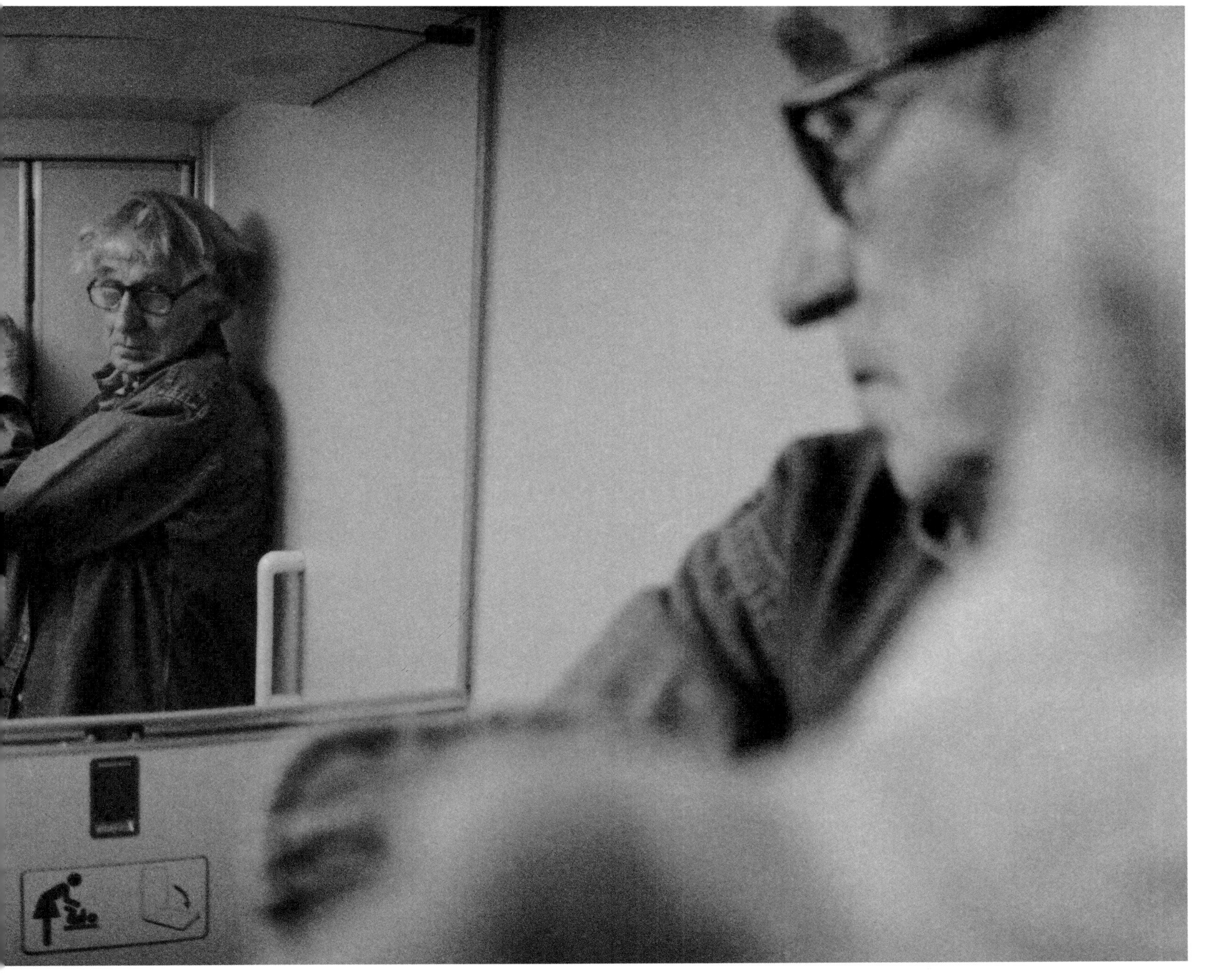

THE PHOTOGRAPHY OF
Rondal Partridge

ELIZABETH PARTRIDGE & SALLY STEIN

California Historical Society Press
San Francisco, California

California Historical Society Press is a collaboration between the California Historical Society and Heyday Books. California Historical Society Press is supported by grants from The William Randolph Hearst Foundation and The Mericos Foundation.

Library of Congress Cataloging-in-Publication Data
Partridge, Elizabeth.
  Quizzical eye : the photography of Rondal Partridge / Elizabeth
  Partridge and Sally Stein.
      p. cm.
  ISBN 1-890771-56-2 (hardcover) — ISBN 1-890771-57-0 (pbk.)
    1. Photography, Artistic. 2. Partridge, Rondal, 1917- . I. Partridge, Rondal, 1917- .
II. Stein, Sally. III. Title.
  TR654 .P337 2003
  779'.092—dc21   2003010258

Cover photograph: "Rondal Partridge," 1978 by Annette Kaplan
© 2003 by Annette Kaplan
Back cover photograph: "Judy Dater," 1978 by Rondal Partridge
Plate 1 (title page): "Airplane Bathroom," 1999 by Rondal Partridge

Cover and book design: John Hubbard
Produced by Marquand Books, Inc., Seattle
  www.marquand.com
Separations by iocolor, Seattle
Printing and binding: CS Graphics, Singapore

Orders, inquiries, and correspondence should be addressed to:
  Heyday Books
  P.O. Box 9145, Berkeley, CA 94709
  (510) 549-3564, Fax (510) 549-1889
  www.heydaybooks.com

10 9 8 7 6 5 4 3 2 1

For Elizabeth Woolpert Partridge,
who makes all of this possible

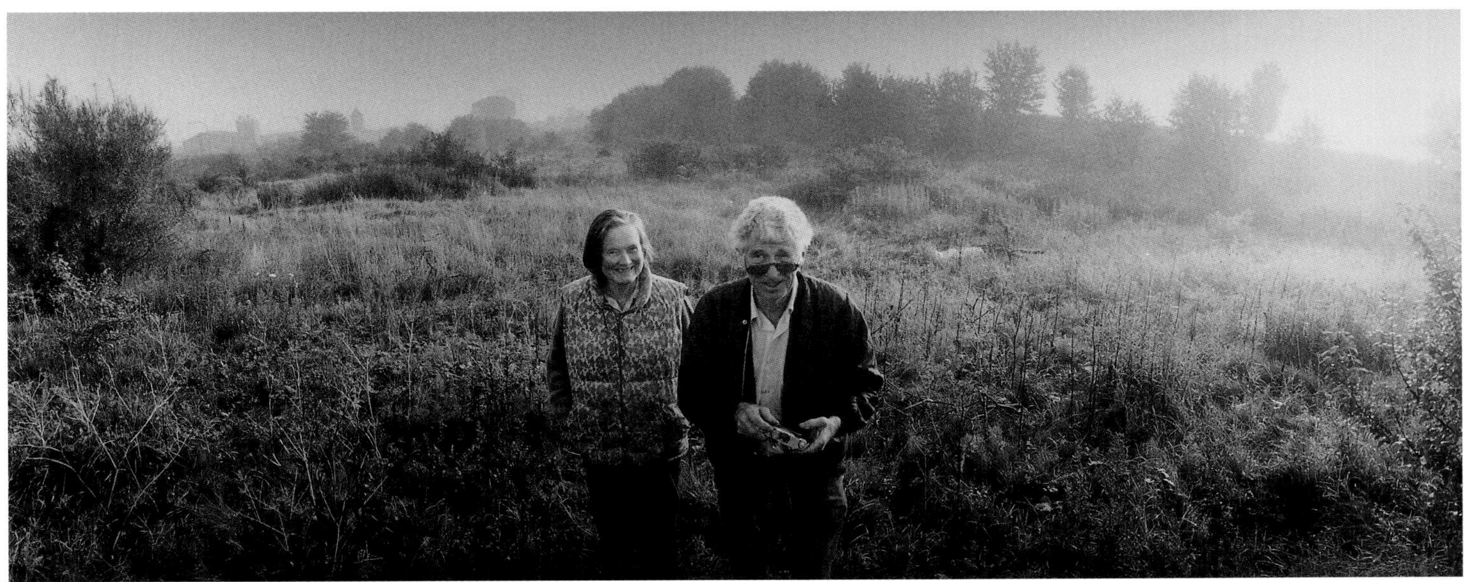

Elizabeth W. and Rondal Partridge. Arhus, Denmark, 1989
(Photograph by Paul Erick)

Acknowledgments

For their diverse contributions in support of this publication, the authors gratefully acknowledge Stephen Becker and the incredible staff at the California Historical Society; Malcolm Margolin, Jeannine Gendar, Rebecca LeGates, and indeed the whole Heyday staff; John Hubbard; Drew Johnson; Lucia Woods Lindley; Ed Marquand; Tom Ratcliff; Allan Sekula; Elizabeth Whipple; and Elizabeth Woolpert Partridge and the rest of the Partridge clan—Joan, Josh, Meg, and Aaron.

—EP and SAS

Contents

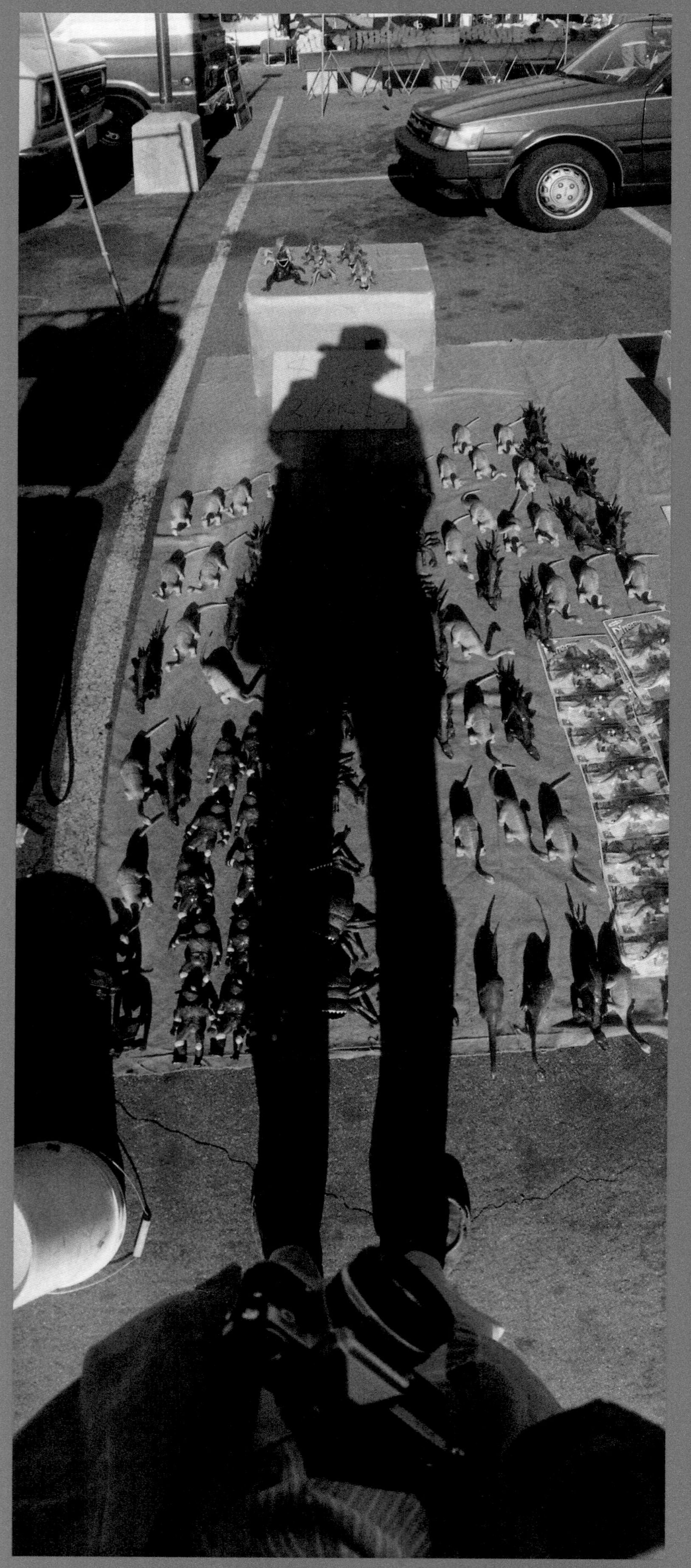

DANIEL DIXON

FOREWORD | # The Last Man Standing

At least once a week, early in the morning, a rangy, angular man with a tangle of ginger-white hair scrambles out of bed, gulps a quick mug of coffee, drapes a camera around his neck, jumps into his van, and drives from his home in the Berkeley hills to the Oakland flea market. It's a pilgrimage he's been making for twenty years. The journey takes him only half an hour, but it plunges him into a jumbled universe of arts and crafts, housewares, clothing, tools and implements, books, electronics, food, musical instruments, cameras, antiques, jewelry, and just plain junk—things to see, touch, appreciate, appraise, and maybe to photograph. *Click* goes the camera. *Click, click, click.*

The regulars there at the flea market know this photographer well. So do I. "Hi, Ron!" somebody shouts. That's what I call him, too, as I have for seventy years.

"Ron" may sound commonplace, but his full name—Rondal Partridge—has a wild Celtic resonance that vividly suggests a singular man, an irrepressible man, a valiant man, a man who is anything but ordinary. His children have their own eloquent description of him. "He's the last man standing," they declare. I wish my own daughter felt the same way about me.

Ron has now edged into his eighties and is beginning to feel it. "I'm finally getting old," he concedes. But climbing a steep hill, he can still reduce his juniors to gasping laggards. His muscles are like knotted cables and his eyes, like his mind, are sharp and inquisitive. "He's interested in everything," a friend told me recently. "A photographic magpie. No wonder he's so fascinated by the flea market."

Interested in everything? So it seems. But Ron Partridge is a whole lot more than just *interested* in photography. I've known and worked with many different photographers over the past fifty years, and I doubt that any of them ever loved photography as Ron Partridge loves it. That includes my mother, Dorothea Lange, with whom he worked as her assistant before he was able to vote, and also *his* mother, Imogen Cunningham, whose passion for the art was almost equally intense. Ansel Adams was likewise, in his

Shadow as Substance 2, late 1990s

9

own way, as ardent. But in my experience, Ron's feeling for photography is unique and incandescent.

To begin with, he loves the *craft* of photography. Many of his fellows wince at darkroom drudgery. But Ron exults in probing a possibility, in testing a technique, in devising a process, in solving a problem, in making a print that even he may think is just about perfect.

Craft inevitably involves tools, and Ron loves equipment—tripods, easels, light meters, lenses, gadgets, gizmos. He collects photographic paraphernalia as some connoisseurs collect books or paintings or porcelains. Much of it was acquired at the flea market. His rambling old house is only partly a dwelling. Home, offices, darkroom and laboratory, library, archives and files have all been merged into one sprawling environment. The contents leak out of their assigned spaces into the living and dining rooms. Cameras are everywhere, ubiquitous as tables and chairs.

"Cameras!" Ron exclaims. "Let me show you my family of cameras." He owns about fifty of them, all sorts and sizes. The most exotic were designed and constructed by himself. Some are venerable relics, lovingly restored to working condition. Each has its own personality and purpose.

Ron photographs every day on one project or another, and always with delight. He usually has several projects in progress at the same time. The volume of his work is prodigious, and so is its immense variety. No horizon is too distant for Ron Partridge to explore, and no detail too intimate.

Consider the images. Portraits that search out the elusive truth that's hidden in every face. Uncompromising visual documents—the testimony of a witness under oath. Impressionistic visions of people and places and objects, of atmosphere and emotion. Mysterious abstractions that ask rather than answer questions—that make you wonder rather than understand. The themes go on and on, developed in an astounding profusion of techniques.

Many of these photographs are beautiful to behold, but others shock the eye. A close-up of an inert squirrel, one in a disturbing series, is shot in a way that seems almost obscene. To look at it makes you itch and wiggle. The discomfort is caused not only by the image, but by the photographer's intention. What you see here is deliberately extreme.

And that's no accident. Ron himself is often deliberately extreme. He savors irreverence and provocation. He likes to make some noise. He doesn't shrink from the spotlight. Some people perceive him simply as a gifted, raucous, ribald, amusing, and sometimes annoying caricature.

They're wrong. Behind his antic facade, Ron Partridge is both a very serious man and a significant artist. Nobody who has taken the trouble to view and review his work can have much doubt about that.

And if you know him as I do, you've learned that he's also a gentle and sensitive man. Ron rarely makes any Hollywood display of hugging and kissing, especially of rosy rear ends. If he did, he might be more heralded today than he is. But when he likes and respects you, he may just give you a photograph. Several years ago, soon after our wedding, Ron sent my wife and me an unexpected present. No note—only a framed image of two fragile vines. I'm looking at it right now. The tendrils yearn toward each other, their delicate tips inter-twined. "Marriage," reads Ron's one-word caption, though my wife thinks even that brief explanation is unnecessary. "I knew what it meant the moment I saw it," she says.

More recently, Ron decided to drop me a postcard. One side of it was occupied by what I think may be the best photograph of me ever taken. I'm studying some of his mother's extraordinary self-portraits, which makes Ron's comment especially meaningful. "To look is not an art," he writes with a bold, black, felt-tip pen. "To see is."

That portrait was taken without my being aware of it, but my brother and I once shared a different kind of experience with Ron. He asked us to come and be photographed. The

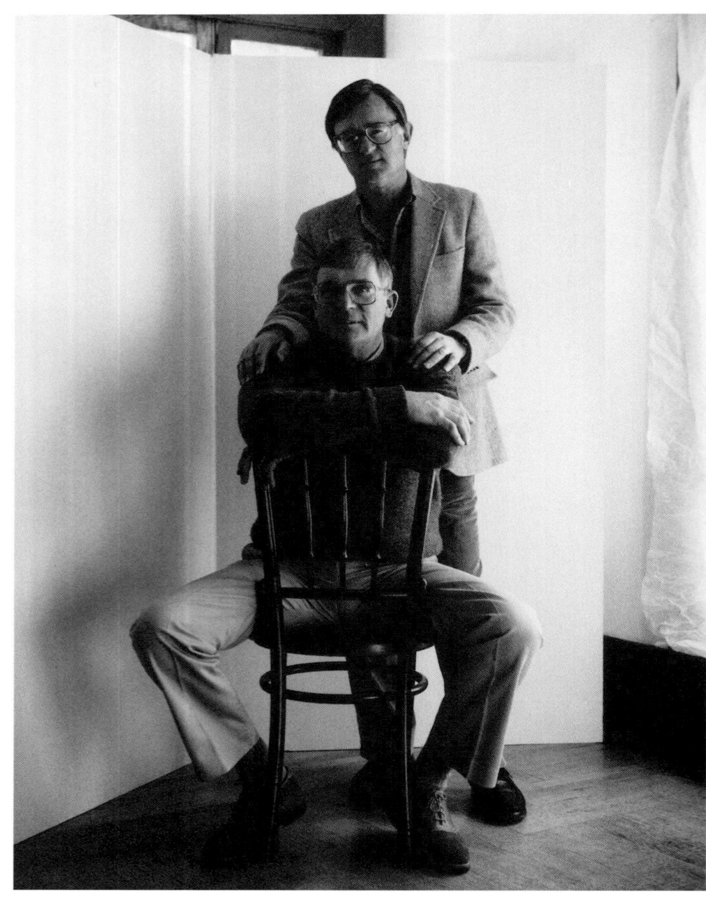

1   *Daniel and John Dixon,* 1985

invitation was uncommonly formal, and the sitting was treated as a special event. We weren't instructed to dress for the occasion, but I nevertheless wore a jacket. Ron arranged us before his most massive view camera—a huge old veteran with bellows and glass plates and a rubber bulb that actuated a shutter that sounded like the snap of a crocodile's jaws. My brother and I composed ourselves for the time exposures. It was as though we were preparing for immortality. We didn't blink. We didn't breathe. There we sat, congealing, as solid and solemn as two Tammany Hall aldermen. I learned later that this was another of Ron's projects—that he was photographing a select circle of friends and associates in the same way and with the same camera. I've never seen the whole portfolio, though I think the portraits of the Dixon brothers are remarkable. They are quiet and concentrated; each of us is distilled to an essence (fig. 1). And I wonder—did the other subjects react as we did?

I've said that Ron loves photography in all its guises and disguises. That's not quite true. He doesn't derive much pleasure from the buying, selling, and promotion of photography. These days he's managed to delegate most of the burdensome paperwork and commercial negotiations, but he believes that the business itself is poisoned by hypocrisy and manipulation. Beyond that, he disdains the highbrow hokum dispensed by many critics, curators, and historians. "Don't get intellectual with *me!*" he recently admonished one authority who

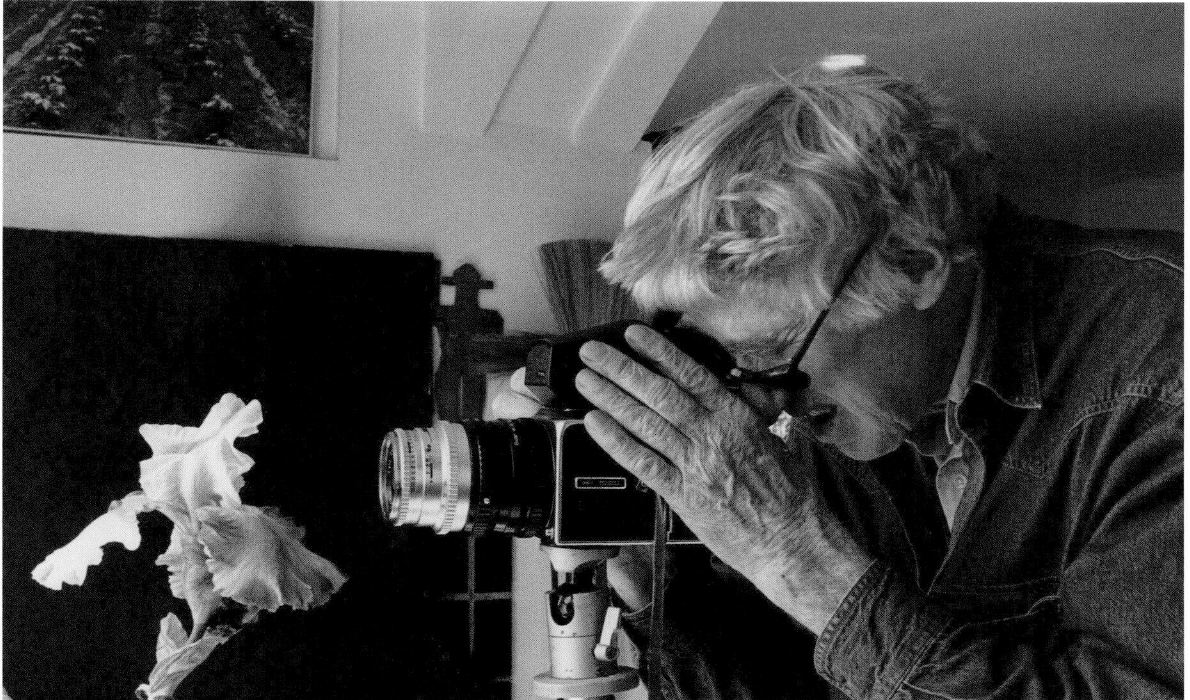

had rashly attempted to impose a fancy psychological theory on the simple act of making an exposure. And when he was interviewed by the producers of a television special on Ansel Adams, his comments were so pungent that not a word was aired. "They were just worshipers," Ron says. "They thought I was farting in church."

Ron's church isn't built of stone and steeples. It's built of light. Light seems sacred to him. It summons him as the devout are summoned by bells. One day, as a group of us were having lunch, he suddenly stopped in the middle of a conversation. Then he rose from the table and moved away. He didn't excuse or explain himself; he simply went to where one of his cameras was positioned in a pool of light at a window overlooking his garden. He was focused on a still life, and now the luminous glow it required had arrived. For the next fifteen minutes he was totally, silently absorbed in the joy of his work. But slowly the light dimmed, and he finally rejoined his guests as though he'd never been away.

When I told one of his daughters about this incident, she laughed. "Oh, that's typical," she said. "He does that all the time."

All the time, for all of his life, Rondal Partridge has followed the light. You can see it in his work. You can sense it in his spirit. Sometimes his hand has started the flame. There it is, as clearly to be seen as a candle in the dark. His children might be right. As a man and as a photographer, he may be one of the last still standing.

2 Rondal Partridge Photographing an Iris, 1995 (Photograph by Meg Partridge)

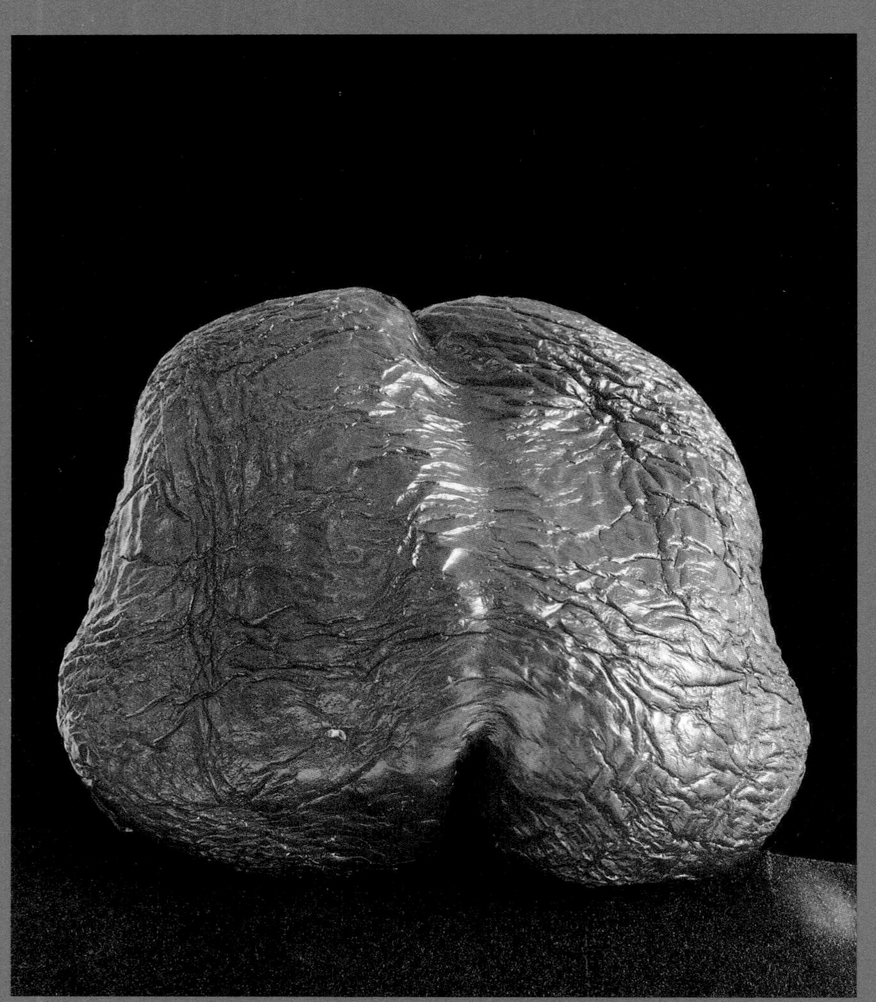

SALLY STEIN

"EVERYTHING BUT THE GRAND GESTURE" | Tradition and Irreverence in the Photography of Rondal Partridge

I first came upon photographs by Rondal Partridge two decades ago, while researching the records of the National Youth Administration (NYA) for an exhibition of government-sponsored Depression-era photography called *Official Images*.[1] I had nearly lost hope that anything graphically significant might be uncovered when I encountered a set of photographs so stunningly fresh they more than justified plowing through the archives.

The portraits had remarkable self-assurance and, as impressive, so did the most impoverished portrait subjects. A pretty young woman dressed for work in the fields seemed accustomed to her agricultural labor but not resigned or stooped by it (Plate 18). At a 1940 Berkeley student rally, one demonstrator denounced the prospect of a wartime draft with the posture and rhetoric of militant class conflict (Plate 19). Maybe the most memorable photograph showed a young hobo looking simultaneously lost and still eager for the next adventure—a cross between James Dean and Jack Kerouac (Plate 20). Even these admittedly anachronistic allusions underscore the ways this vision departed from conventional Depression iconography. For all the subjects' sense of privation and social pressure, there was attitude to spare.

The distinctive name attached to this outstanding set of pictures helped me identify the photographer as one of the sons of California etcher Roi Partridge and the celebrated photographer Imogen Cunningham. Tracking him down by telephone in the San Francisco Bay Area, I was eager to learn how Partridge had come to make these exceptional Depression photographs that rippled with a current of rebellious alienation.

From initial conversations I sensed how much the youthful hobo picture contained the photographer's quite personal investment. The caption, which reveled in the fact that this young man had just left a kitchen job after blowing up at the cook, was not dissimilar from Partridge's own teenage work history: by his early twenties when he made this portrait, the young photographer had experienced his own share of bumming around.

Pepper Butt, 1998

speaking his own mind, and on occasion getting fired. Born in 1917, Ron—the abbreviated name he mostly goes by—had been nearly the same age as the California teens that he photographed in the late 1930s and early 1940s, which is one reason they look so different from most documents of New Deal youth. But even in his teens, Partridge was making photographs that were far more deliberate than the typical juvenile snapshots.

If he was something of a photographic prodigy, he had a definite head start. The son of two artists, he grew up in a fairly bohemian household, albeit one that maintained traditional gender roles. His father held a regular teaching position at Mills College, while his mother produced innovative photographs at home while raising three sons. Among the close friends of the family were some of the most important U.S. photographers of the twentieth century, including Ansel Adams, Edward Weston, and Dorothea Lange.

Just based on these illustrious names, one could say that he grew up in the lap of photography. But there's more. If photography might be considered the art of replication, Ron experienced the strange magic of exact duplication from the start of his life. He is an identical twin. In one early photograph Imogen made of her two younger sons, she ingeniously doubled the story of Narcissus by arranging these lovely naked boys around a large mirror she had placed, pond-like, on the floor (fig. 1). But, resisting pushing the metaphor to extremes, she depicted them in slightly different positions. Likewise in her raising of these sons, she was quite committed to cultivating their differences, even resolving to send one or the other twin away to live with relatives and friends for periods of time in order to ensure individuality in these self-same brothers. Most frequently it was Ron who was dispatched because, as he recalls, he was by far the more rebellious of the two, frequently provoking his father's wrath. So much did Imogen esteem such signs of independence that she assured him it was preferable to spend time away than face harsh reprisals at home.[2]

Imogen's unwavering support for Ron's development as an individual left its mark. In his teens, though he had already made remarkably skillful portraits of other students (fig. 2), Ron almost failed to graduate from high school, because he was determined to

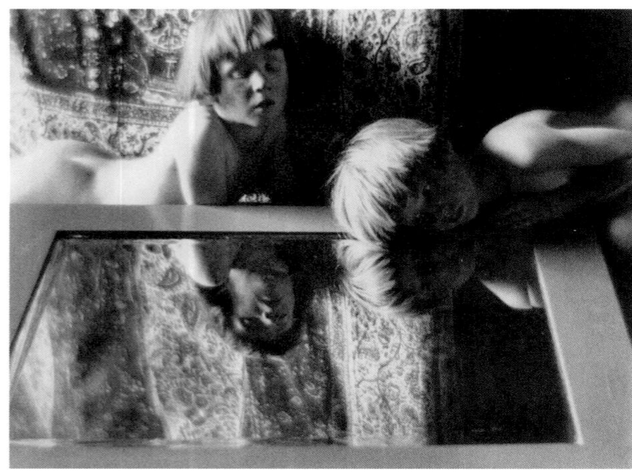

1   *Twins with Mirror 2*, 1923
(Photograph by Imogen Cunningham)

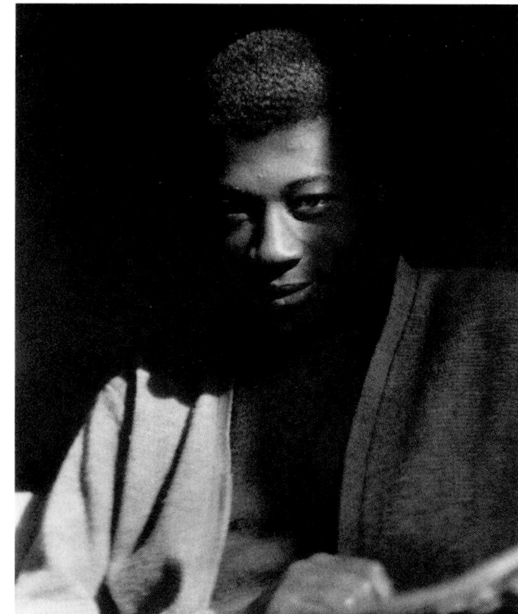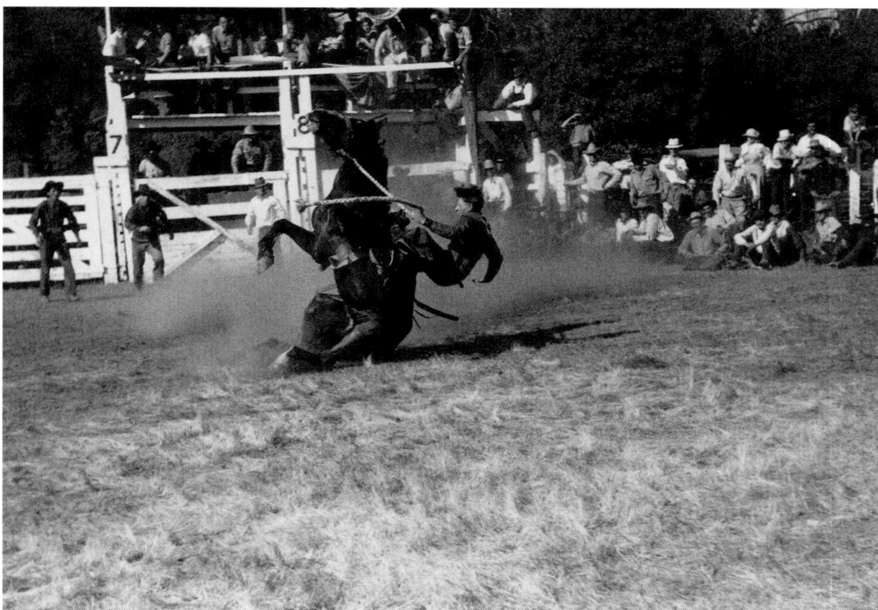

defy the edicts of a dogmatic art teacher. Following high school, he resolved to become a photographer by a combination of informal apprenticeships and the oldest if sometimes hardest teacher, practical experience. As if anticipating a challenging ride, he started out by documenting the cowboys performing on the local rodeo circuit (fig. 3). By the time he had turned twenty, Ron had apprenticed to both Adams and Lange, and indeed it was Lange, one of the celebrated Depression-era photographers of the Farm Security Administration (FSA), who helped secure his brief commission with the NYA. Lange continues to be the photographer he most reveres, yet reverence in Partridge's ethos does not mean being a follower in any simple sense. Throughout the first half of his life, he observed key members of his mother's photographic circle—Adams and Lange—balancing mutual respect with impassioned disagreements about the proper use and direction for photography. More crucial than the techniques he acquired from these eminent figures was the value each placed on personal and artistic autonomy.[3]

2   *High School Portrait.* 1934

3   *A Horse Called Sitting Bull.* 1936

I did not have the chance to visit Partridge until shortly before the Washington-based *Official Images* project was ready for exhibition and publication. By the time we met face-to-face, I was contemplating a more in-depth study of the long photographic career of this Depression-schooled documentarian. And even as photography had become increasingly established as an art form in the subsequent half-century, he had sustained a single-minded passion for the medium while inexplicably avoiding the spotlight. However much these romantic preconceptions had some basis in fact, this first meeting was destined to be a classic crash of image and reality.

Gregarious rather than hermetic, the lanky Partridge though he was already pushing seventy had energy enough for both of us. He was brimming with so many stories that I had trouble following any to the end. His pictures also abounded and the effect was nearly as diffuse. I had come wanting to see more documentary photographs from, and spawned by, the Depression era. He assured me there were many more but not many immediately at hand, for that was so long ago and since then he had done so many other kinds of things. As evidence he showered me with pictures of 1950s family life in what seemed a premature back-to-the-land hippie style, with his wife and children mingling with snakes, horses, eagles, and chickens—at least that was the impression from the quick succession of photographs. Then there were pictures of increasing pollution in the San Francisco Bay interspersed with portraits of anybody who had wandered into his house and agreed to sit before his antique view camera. Plus puzzling compositions involving multiple prints of the same semi-abstract details jigged together in different directions to fan out or interlock. Nearly as disorienting was the sheer multitude of self-portraits snapped over seven decades whenever, it seemed, he was moved by his reflection—ranging from deadpan head-on mirror views to one phantasmagoric scene of a child poised to use a toaster with the photographer's face floating in the chrome surface above a slice of bread (fig. 4).

Maybe the oddest grace note for me were his recent close-up views that oscillated between the gorgeous and the grotesque. The loveliest of these nature studies manifested the most kinship with his mother's photography. And like some very old Cunningham prints from the early years of the twentieth century, they were printed in platinum—a painstaking print process of soft gradations, only revived in the 1970s and not only conspicuously archaic but the stylistic antithesis of 1920s machine-polished modernism and the 1930s no-frills sensibility of documentary culture. Overall, the contradictions seemed enormous, but Ron took such pleasure in the jaggedly eclectic whole I was unsure whether they were his or, alas, mine. Feeling overwhelmed by my inability to place him in the familiar neat categories, I said farewell after a few hours and headed straight for a drugstore to buy some aspirin.

For over a decade, I worked on more manageable research projects before attempting a second time, this time with his daughter as guide, to make sense of this extraordinary lifetime of photography. Child of a celebrated photographer, Partridge was immersed in the conventions of photography from infancy while his upbringing encouraged him to break these conventions or bend them distinctly to his purposes. In its chronology and diversity, his committed exploration of this medium over the course of seven decades spans and even makes an idiosyncratic weave of the contrary poles of photography: between old-style softly expressive Pictorialism of the pre-WWI era and hyper-sharp Precisionism that followed WWI, a movement that in the Bay Area photographic circles came to be known as *f.64*; between dispassionate straight photography of the 1920s and social documentary

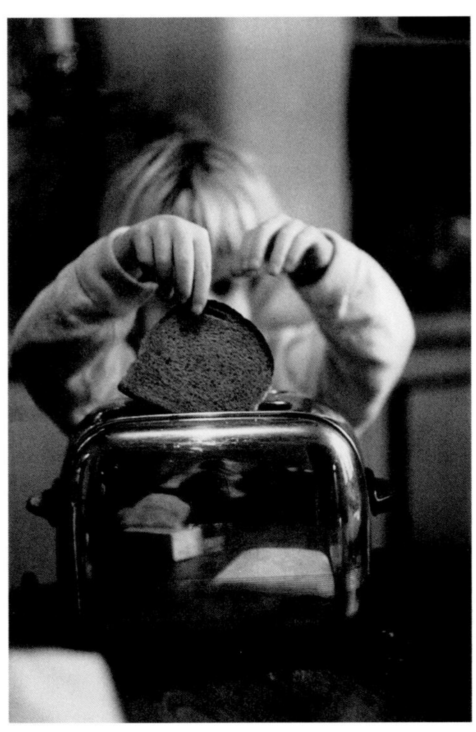

4 *Self-portrait in Toaster.* c. 1956

of the 1930s; and even between largely masculinist notions of masterful photographic modernism and rather recent postmodern subversions of the notion of absolute originality.[4] With all its tensions, that mix pervades his work, imbuing it with its dazzling, even dizzying, range.

In the last years of her life, Dorothea Lange longed to resist all inessential activities and devote herself to "a visual life."[5] For years I was uncertain what precisely she meant by that phrase, though it was clearly linked to a notion she had promulgated earlier that photography should focus on the familiar with at least as much intensity as was usually directed to documenting the extraordinary and newsworthy.[6] Studying Partridge's archives has given me a better sense of what living the "visual life" might mean, for this early protégé of Lange treated photography from the outset as a means of exploring all manner of experience in his immediate world.

There may be a biographical logic for taking this humble path of using photography to chronicle the quotidian. We tend to want our artists to spring directly from the mysterious sources of genius.[7] Such radical self-invention was impossible for the son of Imogen Cunningham. Moreover, as committed as Imogen was to her family, her especially close interweaving of photography with child-rearing doubtless had unusual consequences.[8] Ron claims his first memory of photography was "burning negatives"—just the opposite of exalted appreciation. His mother, he explains, was an especially inconsistent technician, so what else was there to do with the exposures she judged inadequate but let her sons dispose of them in the fireplace and watch the nitrate film start to melt, sizzle, then crackle into flame?[9] Though he is indebted to his father for a lifelong interest in ecology, "waste not, want not" was never part of Ron's artistic lexicon.[10] Savoring the process, even indulging in repetitions born of failure, was always more enjoyable than staying fixed on the end result, the artistic product.

Integral to Partridge's apprentice years as a photographer were numerous pictures expressing some of the ideas he still maintains about the practice and malpractice of photography. As much as he has had a lifelong love of the medium, he was deeply skeptical from childhood about those who postured as photographic masters. Excepting Dorothea Lange and maybe also Edward Weston, none of the remarkably successful photographers he grew up knowing held special power over him. His response to Ansel Adams and his heroic mode of nature photography seemed always to combine deep respect with nose-thumbing mirth. At one well-oiled gathering, Adams was attempting to perform some trick with a handkerchief while balancing an apple on his head when Ron caught him on his knees, appearing to genuflect before a miniature, snow-capped sierra (fig. 5). In a quite different context, during one of the regular mountain hikes when Ron carried Ansel's

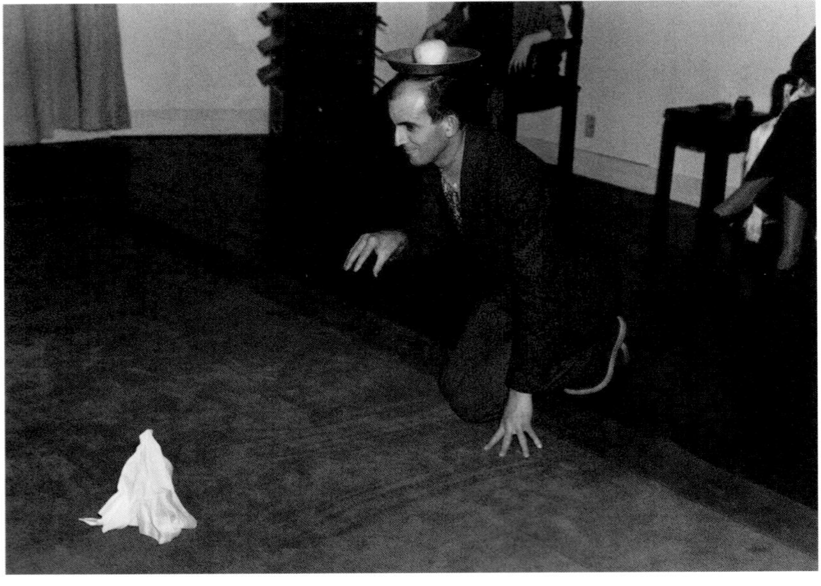

5 *Ansel Adams' Party Trick.* late 1930s

heavy equipment, the assistant made one exposure of the master photographer striving for the heights of expression, and the now-famous results show Adams framed vertically against a background of rock and snow, like a lone pine above the tree line (Plate 6). But the mule also could not resist giving a kick, for this exposure is matched by a variant framing that is far less honorific, with Adams resembling a deranged outlaw intent on capturing, or hiding, ill-gotten gains (Plate 9).

As for nude photography, Partridge occasionally has asserted that he has never done it. Strictly speaking, that's not true, as this book demonstrates. But nudes are not his habitual subject, and an early picture he made of his mother draped in black while crouching

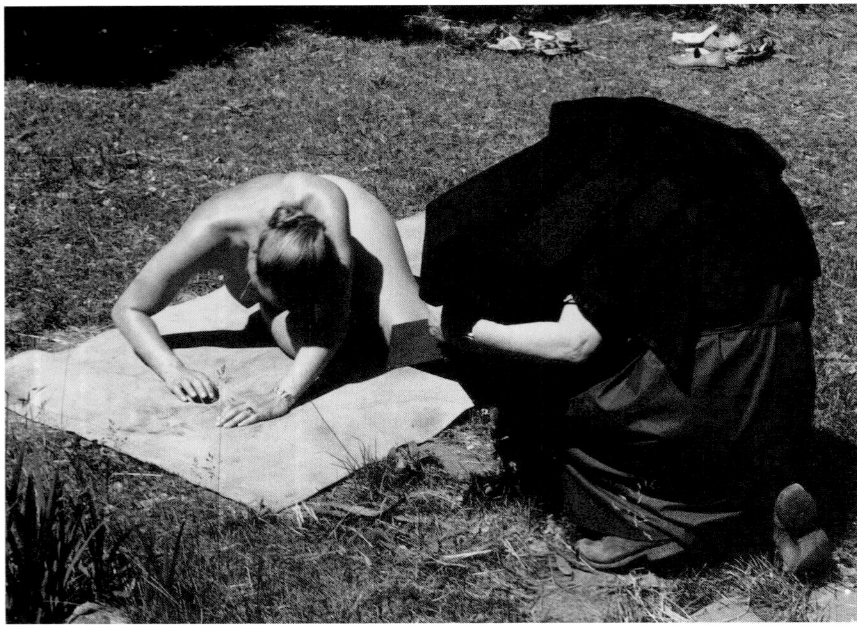

6 *Imogen Cunningham Photographing Olympic Fencer Helena Meyer.* c. 1935

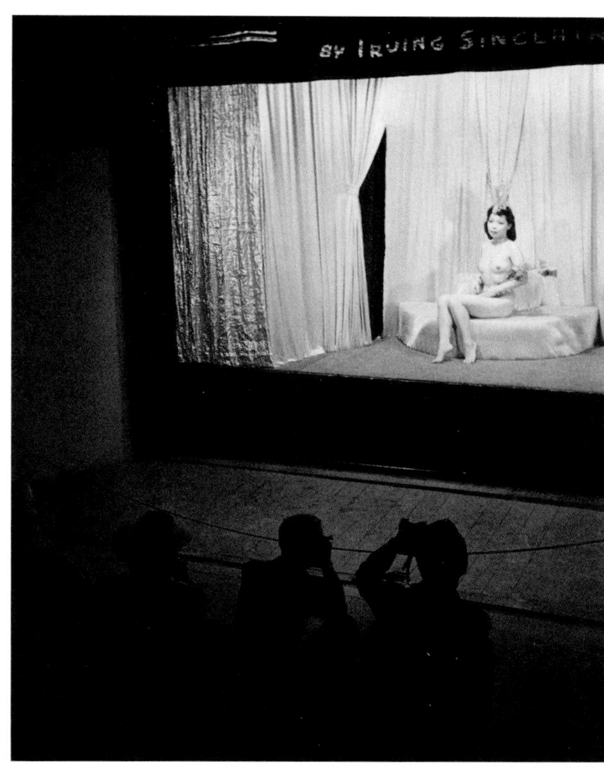

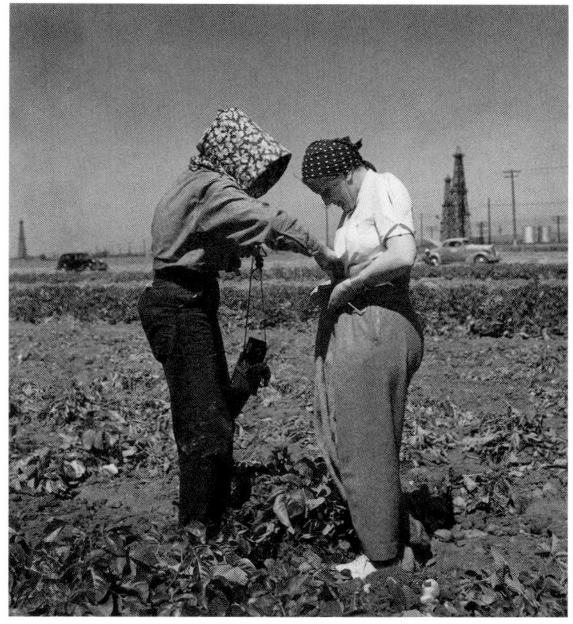

beside a more elegantly crouching naked female suggests that he could think of better things to do with such opportunities (fig. 6). Even more hilarious is the photograph he made inside a "live model" sideshow at the San Francisco World's Fair of 1939: with the comic's perfect timing, he caught the moment when a row of male silhouettes seated in near darkness were raising their cameras toward a lone naked female decorously posed on a stage (fig. 7).

If many of Partridge's early photographs on the subject of photography are satiric, his photographs of Dorothea Lange from the mid-1930s to the 1960s consistently express admiration and often awe. In a fairly recent commentary, he noted the unusual degree of collaboration between Lange and her subjects: "Together they said what they had to say."[11] One might wonder if the representational playing field was so level as all that, but the photographs he made of Dorothea attest to her spontaneous interactions with strangers, including moments when the roles were nearly reversed and the subject had taken charge—in one instance showing Lange how to tie on a gunnysack, in the process taking hold of the camera in order to free the photographer's hands for this alien lesson in the details of stoop labor (fig. 8). It was this sort of thoroughgoing transformation of roles as well as vision that Ron sought with his own photography.

7 *Live Model Session.* San Francisco World's Fair. 1939

8 *Dorothea Lange Being Shown How to Tie on a Potato Sack.* 1937

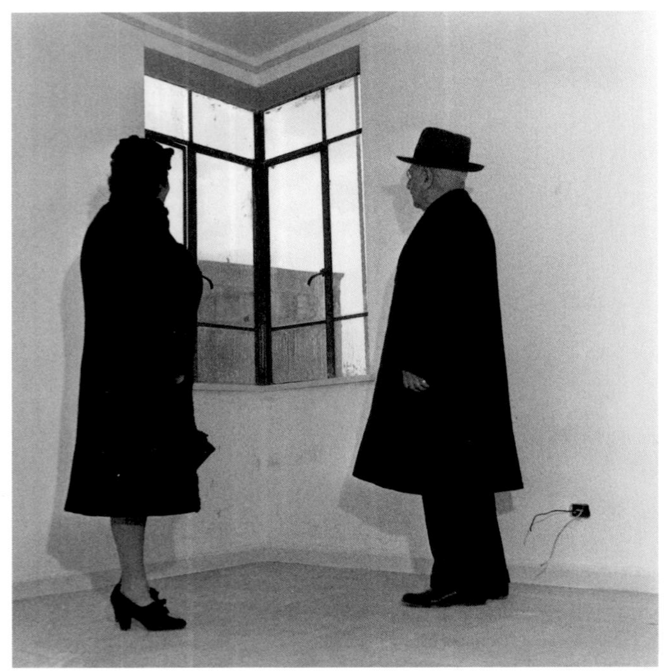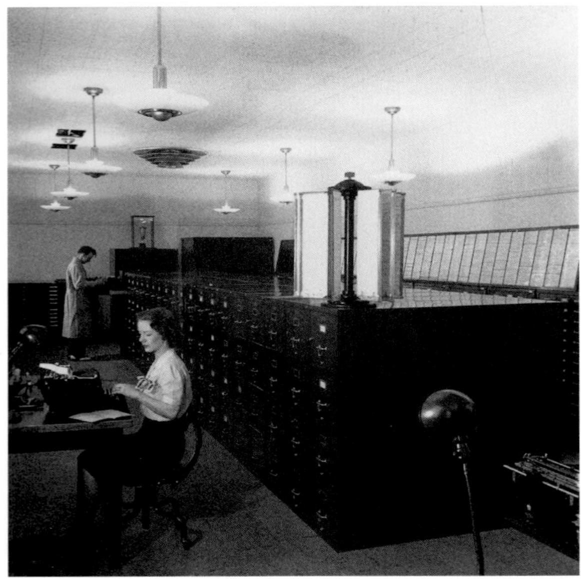

For a few years in the early 1940s, Partridge tried taking his photography to New York. Based on the remarkable series he had prepared for the NYA, he was offered a contract with one of the leading photo agencies—Black Star—that regularly supplied pictures to major magazines like *Fortune* and *Life*. Even had U.S. entry into World War II not interrupted this career move, it is doubtful that the initial excitement of big-time media work would have sustained him. For one interior shot of a barely finished luxury apartment in Manhattan, Partridge made a claustrophobic mockery of the prized corner view; as for the supposedly glamorous Black Star agency, his interior view makes it look like a police morgue tidied up by Edward Hopper (figs. 9, 10). His wartime service in the Navy only convinced him beyond a doubt that he wanted no permanent part in any organization.

On getting discharged from the Navy at the end of the war, Partridge made a half-hearted return to New York, where the story assignments reminded him of rote military orders. No sooner had he arrived than he packed up, heading back to the still-rural hills behind Berkeley and Oakland with dreams of raising a family with his wife while living close, very close, to the land. (One series of pictures documents a prized pig definitely out-scaling the slender Partridge, followed by pictures of buckets of pig parts.) In 1959 the family moved to a large home in Berkeley proper.

With the San Francisco Bay Area as his permanent base, Partridge has ranged widely over the varied terrain of California and the West. In the field of photography, he has roamed even more widely in terms of subject matter, genre, and style. As for hardware, "eclectic" barely covers his range of equipment, from top-of-the-line precision instruments to a hodgepodge assortment of used cameras and lenses that Partridge adopted for periods

9   *Manhattan Real Estate*, 1940

10   *Black Star Photo Agency*, New York, 1940

of time because he was intrigued to see how they might serve his purposes, particularly when the price was irresistibly low. "Imo hip-hopped around like a flea in a hot skillet," is the colorful way he recalls his mother's ever-experimental approach to photography.[12] It describes at least as aptly his own attitude to both photography and cooking—another specialty he practices daily. Whatever is around is worth trying before the camera or on the stove; or even better, subjected to both forms of savoring.

With camera or saucepan, Ron is unlikely to stick to recipes. Just as he turned his back on magazine work in New York, he also turned down a position in the 1950s as West Coast staff photographer for *Look*, the reason being that such work would have involved following pre-scripted story assignments. He opted instead to eke out a living for himself, his wife, and ultimately five children through a combination of jobs for local architects and sporadic freelance magazine work, supplemented with weekend stints photographing weddings for extended family and friends.

No matter that these choices made for chronic insecurity. Partridge's distrust of photography turned formulaic for the sake of efficiency and good business is best expressed in his close-up of the interior of a desk drawer crammed full of one photographer's collection of proprietary rubber stamps (fig. 11). In the nineteenth century, Charles Baudelaire launched a broad attack on photography as a supreme expression of "industrial madness."[13] Partridge of course does not share this wholesale antipathy, for he has always believed in photography's capacity for personal expression. But Baudelaire might have relished his sly commentary that photographic work-for-hire risks becoming as standardized and predictable as the stamps themselves. In sum, though Partridge has supported himself as a professional photographer for most of his life, he is, or styles himself as, the consummate unprofessional.

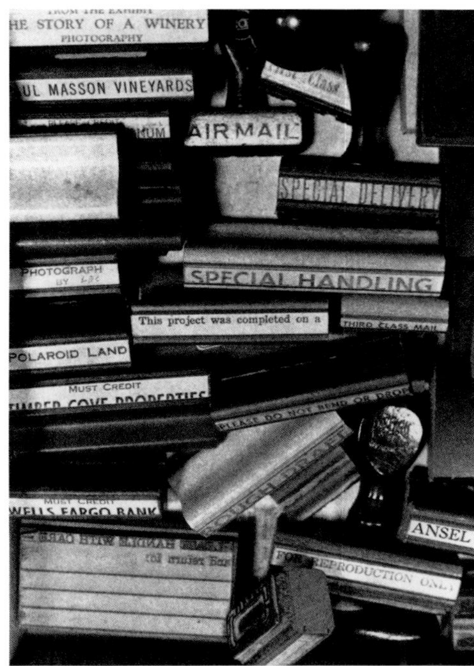

11   *Special Delivery*, 1997

Private family photographs are the sideline of most working photographers. But Partridge's have a different quality than most, for he never treated them as anything other than a core concern. Consider one photograph that on first viewing is dreamily sensual: recalling classic odalisques, his wife reclines on a bed while turning to nurse her infant, which affords the viewer ample opportunity to appreciate the smooth curved planes of body. But the kick here is that if one lingers any length of time, one discovers that the process of looking has not been unidirectional. The mother is otherwise occupied, but in the hollowed space between her shoulder and head is the watchful eye of her nursing infant (Plate 35).

With his cyclopean camera eye, Partridge declared his own insatiable appetite to look. It is the naturalist's probing curiosity that structures even the sweetest family scenes. One photograph distills Partridge's ideal synthesis of life-into-art: while his young son Joshua works to sculpt a feline relief, the kitten serves double duty as inspiring subject and attentive critic (fig. 12). Jean-Jacques Rousseau could not have envisioned a more sympathetic mode of education. Ron wanted nothing less, or more, for his children and himself. The astounding feat is that he has maintained such an alternative vision of self-enlightenment, all the while giving this utopian ideal a greater sense of viability through photography.

Arguably the most majestic (and monumentally sentimental) of his family pictures, the one included in Edward Steichen's *Family of Man* (1955), shows a baby being offered by Ron's wife to her grandmother; yet complicating that sweet triadic grouping is the distinctly separate figure of an older child (Plate 37). Standing beneath the main action, she threatens to upstage it, with jutting elbows amplifying her wary crooked smile. Still less conventional is the series of another daughter focused at an early age on reading: with the rest of her body oriented toward a book, her legs are depicted from the knees down as they shift positions a half-dozen times, semaphoric proof of energetic self-absorption (Plates 42–47). Recorded quietly, such minor details in the long-term acquisition of independence become just the opposite: the momentous incidents of everyday life. In this attention to the everyday, Ron seems most influenced by the feminist sensibilities of both Imogen and Dorothea. As such he occupies a curious transitional position between an earlier generation of suffrage-era New Women and a contemporary sensibility that prizes the finely observed detail over the traditional masterful scenario, which he derides as "the grand gesture."[14]

Yet contradictions arise with every effort at generalization. To stress Partridge's attention to detail and domesticity should not imply that he was unmindful of a larger public landscape. Son of an ardent nature lover, early apprentice to the reigning nature photographer, he could hardly ignore these issues. But just as he rejected normative gender divisions between home and work, he likewise resisted compartmentalizing nature as a thing

12   *Joshua and Kitten.* c. 1953

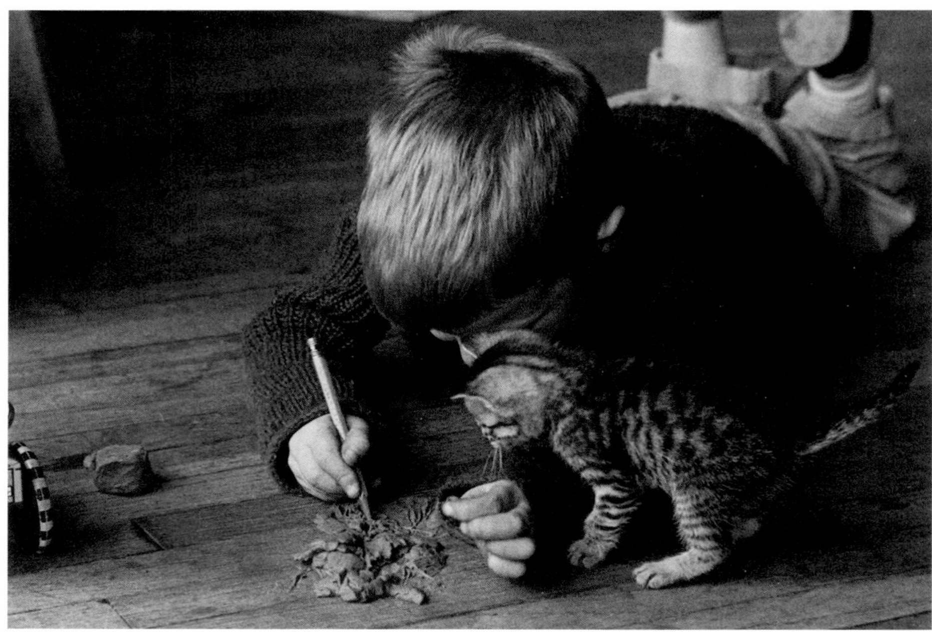

revered for its very apartness. Rather, in his view, we are part of nature and, for better and worse, it is yoked to us.

According to a number of sources, Ansel Adams did not appreciate Ron's mid-1960s independent film and photography of Yosemite.[15] The reasons are obvious enough. Partridge broke with traditional ways of framing the protected park as pristine site. Moreover, he had the audacity to make the deliberately wide-angle view when the parking lot in the foreground was bound to compete for attention, with its richly detailed display of American car models made more diverse by the addition of a lone VW and a Jaguar. While the next generation of "New Topographics" photographers would combine bits of nature and culture in a mélange that suggested love for only ironic mutation, there is something more resonant about Ron's visual mix.[16] Especially regarding his nearly halved composition of Half Dome (Plate 58), this photographer all but declares his love for both Yosemite and the garden of automotive delights. By not letting himself off the hook of conflicting desires, Partridge anticipates the famous ecological declaration of Walt Kelly's comic hero Pogo: "We have met the enemy and he is us."[17]

Partridge's Yosemite parking lot relates to a much larger body of photography in which he juggled fascination and despair over processes of environmental change. For decades following World War II he photographed the maze of power lines spreading over the California landscape. The linear patterns positively attracted the photographer even as he recognized in these designs the harbingers of an irreversible web of congestion. With the same spirit of frank ambivalence, Partridge since the 1970s has redirected his photography from increasingly despoiled wilderness to urban flea markets, in the process starting to explore the potential for complexity in the much wider format of the panoramic camera.

A recent survey of two centuries of panoramic photography attests that this rather specialized genre continues to be most attentive to the long-standing American romance with wide-open spaces.[18] Partridge has used his panoramic cameras in contrary fashion, striving to capture the dense disorder of late twentieth-century urban life. What better place than the flea market to scan the landscape with the aim of encompassing human energy at its most entropic? In these satiric studies of the curiosity seeker's paradise, he has repeatedly included himself, not in the mode of conventional self-portraiture but as marginal bits of shadow, shoes, pants, belt, and dangling camera strap (Plates 68-71). Such details implicate the photographer as active participant, while adding to the general sense of distraction and dispersal in which all are apt to lose as well as find themselves. By identifying himself as a member in good standing of the culture of scavengers, Partridge's flea market photographs extend his commentary on the subject of photography: here we are shown that nearly all possible matter is pre-owned, on haphazard display, awaiting the serendipity of being rediscovered.

Dorothea Lange claimed to be uninfluenced by others, an expression of independence she considered the mark of the true artist.[19] In words and pictures alike, Partridge has adopted the opposite view. This second-generation photographer has always viewed the issue of originality in relative terms. He has a large library of photographic books that he studies intently, thereby sustaining his own vigorous dialogue with photographers of many generations. Asked about his elegant studies of one of his family's dogs (Plates 85-87), he readily claimed familiarity with William Wegman's dog portraits, then adding a caveat: "Didn't care for them. No need to direct or dress up a dog. I wanted to show Chester just as he was—magnificent in repose."[20] Likewise, Partridge's unending series of close-ups of his own increasingly wrinkled hands may well be the literalist's response to Robert Frank's visual memoir, *The Lines of My Hand*, which featured on its cover a more generic drawn rendering of a palm.[21] Certainly Joel-Peter Witkin's melodramatic stagings have inspired Partridge to demonstrate that visceral effects might be achieved with much more economy of means: with just a pepper sliced open to disclose its skull-like resemblance, or with a block of frozen squid that has started defrosting into an oozy mass of gelatinous tentacles (fig. 13). Perhaps as a way of managing the anxiety of influence, Partridge all but proclaims the source while fashioning a visual riposte.

A few pictures are astonishing for the way they seem less to quote with a twist than to sum up a tradition and then, in the best tradition of summations, to suggest the aporia, the fundamental gap or omission in the proposition. His portrait of photographer Judy Dater, like some of his funniest self-portraits, makes emblematic the blind spot in the very idea of a commanding photographic vision (Plate 74). For here we see demonstrated that at the very moment the shutter is open (in this instance, Dater probably was still adjusting her camera before making Ron's portrait), no eye is monitoring exactly what the film records. At the moment of capture, the photographer is guided only by instinct and faith or simple curiosity about that which critic Walter Benjamin called the "optical unconscious."[22]

Just as he disdains "grand gestures," Partridge ordinarily steers clear of overarching theories. But on one rare occasion, when pressed to enunciate his philosophy of photography, Partridge began by invoking Ansel Adams' renowned theory of "pre-visualization" only to distance himself from that canonical stance by improvising a new concept of "*post-visualization*."[23] Starting in the 1930s, Adams urged all who considered themselves serious about photography to develop a more systematic relation to their craft. One should only make a photograph, Adams advised, after forming a mental picture of what the final print should look like, calculating on that basis the technical means to best achieve that end.[24]

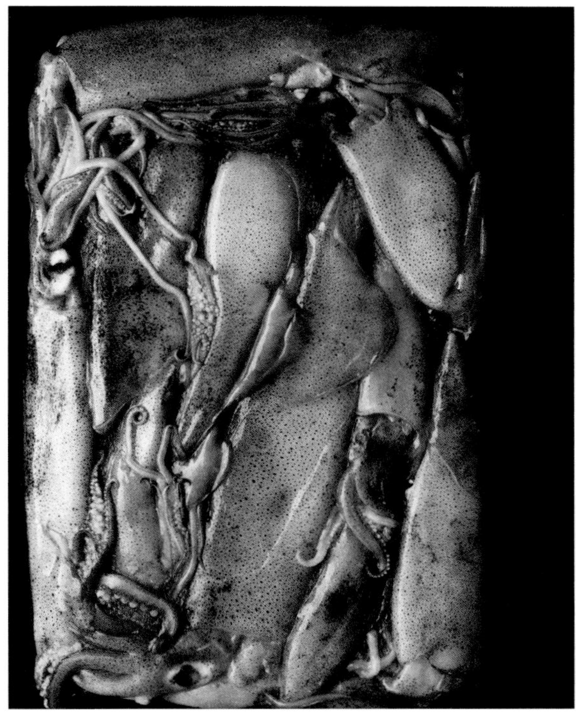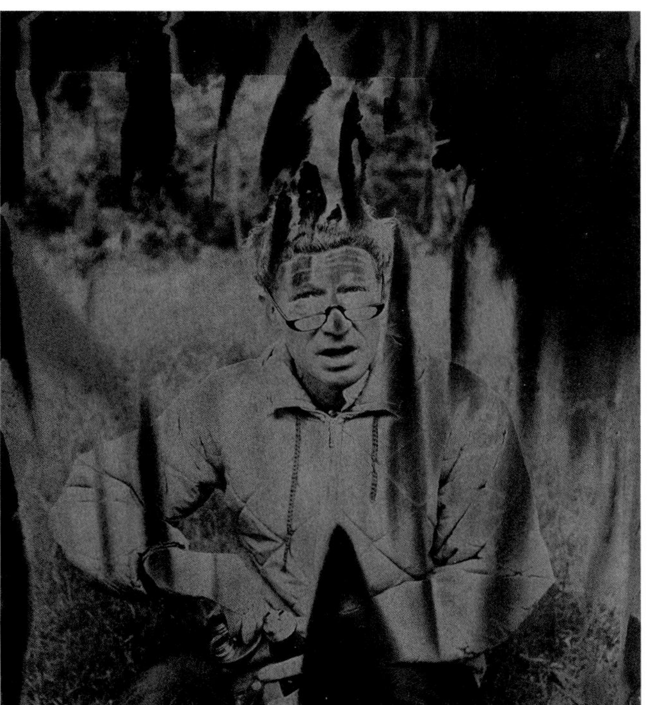

For Ron, this was far too cerebral an approach. He values having learned Adams' precise technique of exposure and development, while questioning whether the supremely rational system produced overly uniform results.[25] Which goes to show that one man's pride in consistency is another's fate worse than death.

Rather like his Beat cohorts, Partridge has preferred to surrender to some combination of impulse, intuition, and chance. His collection of self-portraits contains a number of "junk prints" with tones that are reversed, stained, or mottled, retrieved from the discard pile in his darkroom sink (fig. 14). Finding some of these to be fascinating portrait permutations, the photographer has mounted a number of uncontrolled accidents, filing them with more deliberate depictions of his changing image. Photography practiced with such a protean spirit is a fickle muse, and I doubt he would want it any other way.

Using the camera as a means of discovery requires unwavering faith in the promise of invaluable rewards. Partridge is ever eager to be surprised by what he has obtained on film, expecting in the process to learn more about what he was seeking. Only an optimist would lay claim to the notion of post-visualization, and an equally optimistic corollary is the belief that time will produce retrospective discoveries and developments. Unlike his mother, Partridge does not dispose of many negatives or prints. In his view, although photography aims to capture the moment, time just as surely alters our view of photographs. Even pictures that have gone unnoticed may at a later date find responsive viewers. Seeing himself as part of a great chain of ardent photographers, he is also confident that many of his pictures initiate ideas that will be taken up and pursued by others.[26]

13   *Squid.* 1995

14   *Solarized Self-portrait.* c. 1970

To this day, Ron raises chickens in the backyard of his Berkeley home, and one of the most quirky pictures of this eccentric photographer shows him allowing his head to serve as pedestal for a favorite rooster (photograph facing Notes on Plates). This paternal portrait made by eldest daughter Joan pairs nicely with a picture Ron made of a chicken perched on an egg (Plate 94), a photograph that more than most of his pictures seems to resolve with finality the old riddle of priority. Even if this chicken obviously came first, it can't stay resting on top of the egg for long. This might be the fundamental law of generation and generativity—all is in flux; whatever might be proclaimed as fixed, authentic, or original will necessarily be superseded.

As early as the 1930s, Partridge was photographing dead animals as part of his larger interest in documenting the changing environment. But some of his recent work has the distinct quality of funerary art. These studies in the mode of memento mori are as good a preparation as any for facing facts toward the end of a long life. But they should not be mistaken for therapeutic exercises. I am unable to shake his picture of a small dead bird suspended upside down in a wineglass (Plate 93). One might dismiss the obvious setup as lighthearted commentary on the dangers of indulging, except the wineglass is crystal clean, indicating that the bird did not succumb to alcohol. As such, it recalls an ancient story about mimesis, in which the artist Zeuxis proved his virtuosity when the birds were deceived into trying to snatch the grapes he had just painted. But in that parable of art overpowering nature, we never find out what happened to the snookered fowl. Did they get killed or knocked unconscious from darting headlong into the two-dimensional plane of representation? Has Partridge composed an allegorical self-portrait with the refracting wineglass figuring like a lens that ensnares those, inside and out, drawn to the captivating power of light and images?

No matter that the wineglass was primarily a convenient prop for this bird study, like the bowl of luminous onions that serves as bier in another mortuary close-up (Plate 92). Partridge readily acknowledges his addiction to photography, and he has no desire to wean himself of the daily habit of exposing and developing film and making his now customary platinum prints. Though he still prowls the flea markets each weekend, since the mid-1980s he has made an increasing number of his photographs on a crowded table in one light-filled corner of his spacious living room. Of these tabletop compositions, some are quite classical and others rather weird. It may start with flowers collected while still in bloom that then sit around, past the normal time of discard, as decay sets in. He likes observing those stages most often banished from view—kept off-scene, literally considered *obscene*—convinced he is discovering something new in that over-ripeness which then may turn brittle. Among other things, it permits him an ongoing dialogue with Edward Weston, who made such exquisite studies of shells and peppers and women's bodies, all at the peak of their conventional beauty or formal perfection. With stunning graphic rhetoric, these recent photographs propose that the aftermath of bloom is just as worthy of our attention.

In this work one may find oblique commentary not only on canonical photographs but also on the very notion of "still life," arguably the quintessential oxymoron in the vocabulary of representation. In contrast with this Anglo-Saxon terminology, which made it easy to evade the morbid aspect of stillness, "nature morte" (dead nature) is the more frank label that gained currency in French.[27] Quite a number of Partridge's recent studies take the jester's pleasure in jabbing at our polite evasions by placing dead things unapologetically on display.

In the early years of photography, the depiction of the dead was a popular staple of this new form of representation. But even if, as some have argued, death is photography's truest subject, most today resist that calling.[28] Characteristically, this photographer exhibits no such inhibitions. Among the fairly recent additions to his archives, there is even a super-wide rendering of the family meeting to discuss a new protocol in the culture of longevity: living wills. For a few decades, he has used the panoramic camera to document many annual gatherings of his extended family. In typical Partridge fashion, these elongated family scenes look happily unruly—indeed, just the opposite of the strictly ordered holiday events that his daughter Elizabeth recalls Dorothea Lange used to orchestrate annually.[29] It is only natural that the encyclopedic chronicler of everyday incidents would want to record this more sober meeting, where all try to attend to the matter at hand—except Ron, who is completely focused on staring down the camera as it makes its circuit.

It seems he has already decided on his own living will: end all forms of life support when the last camera breaks or the supply of film runs out. Until then, he invites us to share his abiding love of photography's illusory power to stop time so that we may look closely, marvel, and maybe even reflect upon that which too often passes unnoticed.

NOTES

1. See my essay "Figures of the Future: Photography of the National Youth Administration," in Pete Daniel, Merry A. Foresta, Maren Stange, Sally Stein. *Official Images: New Deal Photography* (Washington, D.C.: Smithsonian, 1987), including ten photographs and extended captions from Partridge's 1939–1940 series on California youth.

2. Biographical information gleaned from extended conversations with Rondal Partridge in the winter of 2002. I am grateful to both Ron and his daughter Elizabeth for their multifaceted hospitality while this book and the related pair of exhibitions were being prepared. (Among many other unforgettable experiences, this collaborative project provided me with my first up-close encounter with chickens!)

3. An extended study of the multi-decade dynamic between Lange and Adams has yet to be written. Significant aspects of that relationship have been examined by Karin Becker Ohrn in a comparative analysis of their photographic work on the Japanese American imprisonment during World War II in *Dorothea Lange and the Documentary Tradition* (Baton Rouge: Louisiana State University Press, 1980), pp. 115–157; and by David L. Jacobs in a careful review of their collaborative and ultimately contentious work on a story for *Life*, "Three Mormon Towns," *Exposure* 25:2 (Summer 1987), pp. 5–25. See also Therese Heyman's interview, "Ansel Adams Remembers Dorothea Lange," in Elizabeth Partridge, ed., *Dorothea Lange, A Visual Life* (Washington, D.C.: Smithsonian, 1994), pp. 153–159. On the culture and community of Bay Area photographers in the era following World War I, see my essay "Starting from Pictorialism: Notable Continuities in the Modernization of California Photography," in the catalog edited by Drew Heath Johnson to accompany the Oakland Museum of California's exhibition *Capturing Light: Masterpieces of California Photography, 1850 to the Present* (New York: Norton, 2001), pp. 121–143.

4. For an overview of this rich period of rapid transition in California photography, see my essay "On Location: The Placement (and Replacement) of California in 1930s Photography," in Stephanie Barron, Sheri Bernstein, Ilene Susan Fort, eds., *Reading California* (Berkeley and Los Angeles: University of California, 2000), 153–177.

5. These words by Lange open the 1966 documentary film on Lange, *The Closer for Me*, produced by Phillip Greene and Robert Katz of KQED; transcript in the Dorothea Lange Collection of the Oakland Museum of California.

6. Dorothea Lange and Daniel Dixon (the photographer's elder son), "Photographing the Familiar," *Aperture* I:2 (1952), pp. 5–15.

7. For a survey of origin myths of the artist, see Ernst Kris and Otto Kurz, *Legend, Myth and Magic in the Image of the Artist* (New Haven, Conn.: Yale, 1979).

8. For an overview of Cunningham's life and work that, like the artist, strives to interweave these elements, see Richard Lorenz, *Imogen Cunningham: Ideas without End* (San Francisco: Chronicle Books, 1993).

9. The most extensive interview with Partridge was conducted over several days in mid-April 1995 by daughters Elizabeth (a writer) and Margaret (a filmmaker), joined by cinematographer and long-time family friend Dyanna Taylor; in the rough transcript of the interview (hereafter referred to as RPT), reference to this memory appears twice, on pages 9 and 15. (I am indebted to Elizabeth for sharing the transcript of this invaluable interview.)

10. "I inherited one thing from my father, and he had it strong . . . he was a great ecologist, because he never went to school, and he brought himself up in the woods, and he had great reverence for nature and for preserving the woods and for cleaning up our landscape, you know, in the twenties. Forty or fifty years before ecology became a buzzword, he was doing it, which was amazing." RPT, p. 5.

11. RPT, p. 18.

12. From an informal interview conducted in late January 2002 by Elizabeth Partridge and me, excerpts of which were transcribed by Elizabeth Partridge, who titled them "Ronisms."

13. Charles Baudelaire, "The Modern Public and Photography," in Alan Trachtenberg, ed., *Classic Essays on Photography* (New Haven, Conn.: Leete's Island, 1980), p. 89.

14. RPT, p. 70.

15. The anthropologist and photographer David Sapir recently recalled hearing this from his friend and colleague, the late John Collier Jr. Partridge confirmed that Adams was not favorably disposed toward his 1960s depictions of Yosemite.

16. "New Topographics" was coined by curator William Jenkins in 1975 for the eponymous exhibition at George Eastman House of a

new generation of mainly U.S. photographers of the western landscape:
Jenkins' introduction to the exhibition is reprinted in Thomas F.
Barrow et al., eds., *Reading into Photography* (Albuquerque: University of New Mexico Press, 1982), pp. 51–56.

17. The oft-quoted line by cartoonist Walt Kelly was published to
coincide with the first Earth Day (April 22, 1971), accompanying a
comic strip showing Pogo on a camping trip in junk-cluttered woods.

18. Jennifer A. Watts and Claudia Bohn-Spector, *The Great Wide
Open: Panoramic Photographs of the American West* (London:
Merrell, 2001).

19. "I'm sure that artists don't influence artists," Lange insisted in the
extended oral interview conducted in 1960 and 1961 by Suzanne
Reiss, published as "Dorothea Lange. The Making of a Documentary
Photographer" (Berkeley: Regional Oral History Office, Bancroft
Library, University of California, Berkeley, 1968), p. 145.

20. From personal notes scribbled during a wide-ranging conversation with Ron one weekend in February 2002.

21. Robert Frank, *The Lines of My Hand* (New York: Lustrum, 1972).

22. "It is a different nature which speaks to the camera than speaks
to the eye: so different that in place of a space consciously woven
together by a man on the spot there enters a space held together
unconsciously. While it is possible to give an account of how people
walk, if only in the most inexact way, all the same we know nothing
definite of the positions involved in the fraction of a second when
the step is taken. Photography, however, with its time lapses, enlargements, etc., makes such knowledge possible. Through these methods
one first learns of this optical unconscious, just as one learns of the
drives of the unconscious through psychoanalysis." Walter Benjamin
(P. Patton, trans.), "A Short History of Photography" [1931], *Classic
Essays on Photography*, pp. 202–203.

23. RPT, pp. 21, 33.

24. I examine in greater detail Adams' early theory and practice of
visualization in "On Location," pp. 174–177.

25. RPT, p. 33.

26. In his inimitable thoughtful-but-loose fashion, Partridge develops
and intertwines these ideas in the extended 1995 interview that
resulted in a transcript of over a hundred pages; see especially RPT,
p. 39.

27. For this comparative etymology, I thank my colleague George C.
Bauer for steering me directly to the relevant section of Charles Sterling,
Still Life Painting. From Antiquity to the Twentieth Century, 2nd ed.
(New York: Harper & Row, 1981), pp. 63–64.

28. Roland Barthes offers a philosophical meditation on this topic in
Camera Lucida: Reflections on Photography (New York: Hill & Wang,
1981); Jay Ruby explores the culture of postmortem photography,
especially for nineteenth-century U.S. history, in *Secure the Shadow:
Death and Photography in America* (Cambridge, Mass.: MIT, 1995).

29. In the introduction to *Dorothea Lange. A Visual Life* (pp. 2–11),
Elizabeth Partridge vividly recollects her childhood impressions of the
holiday gatherings Lange carefully organized.

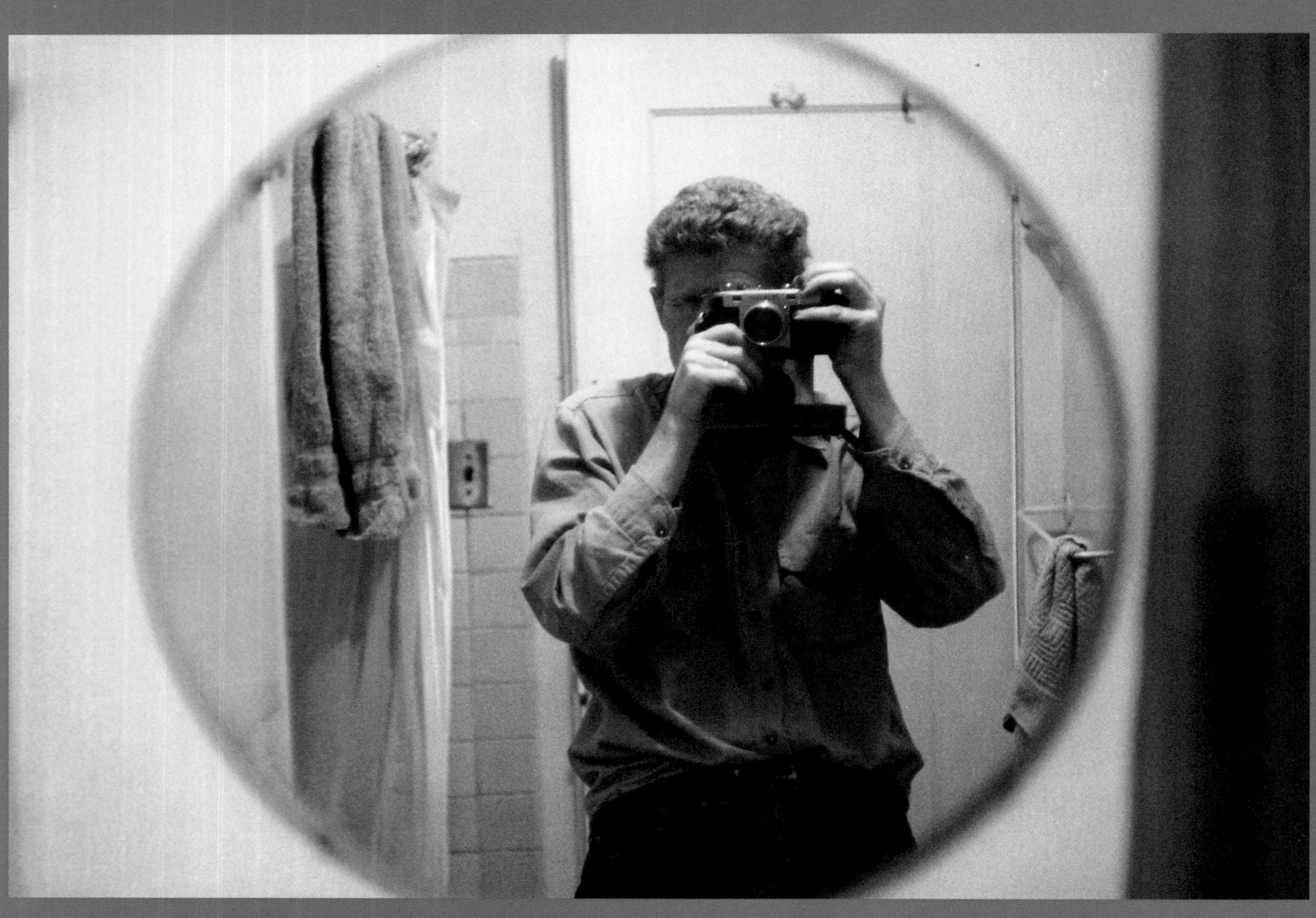

2 *Self-portrait in Bathroom Mirror.* 1953

Plates

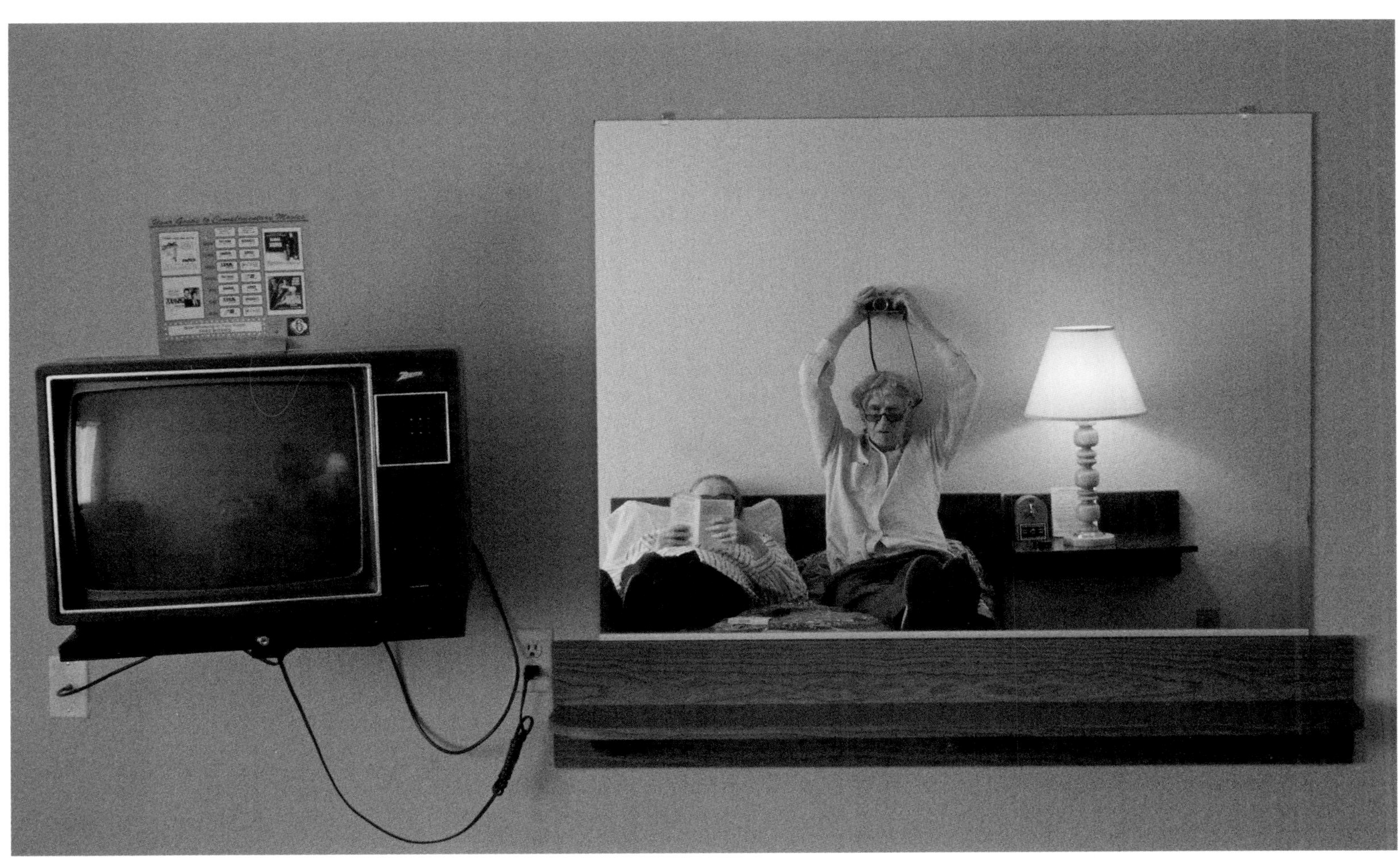

3   *Self-portrait in a Motel. Anywhere. USA. mid-1980s*

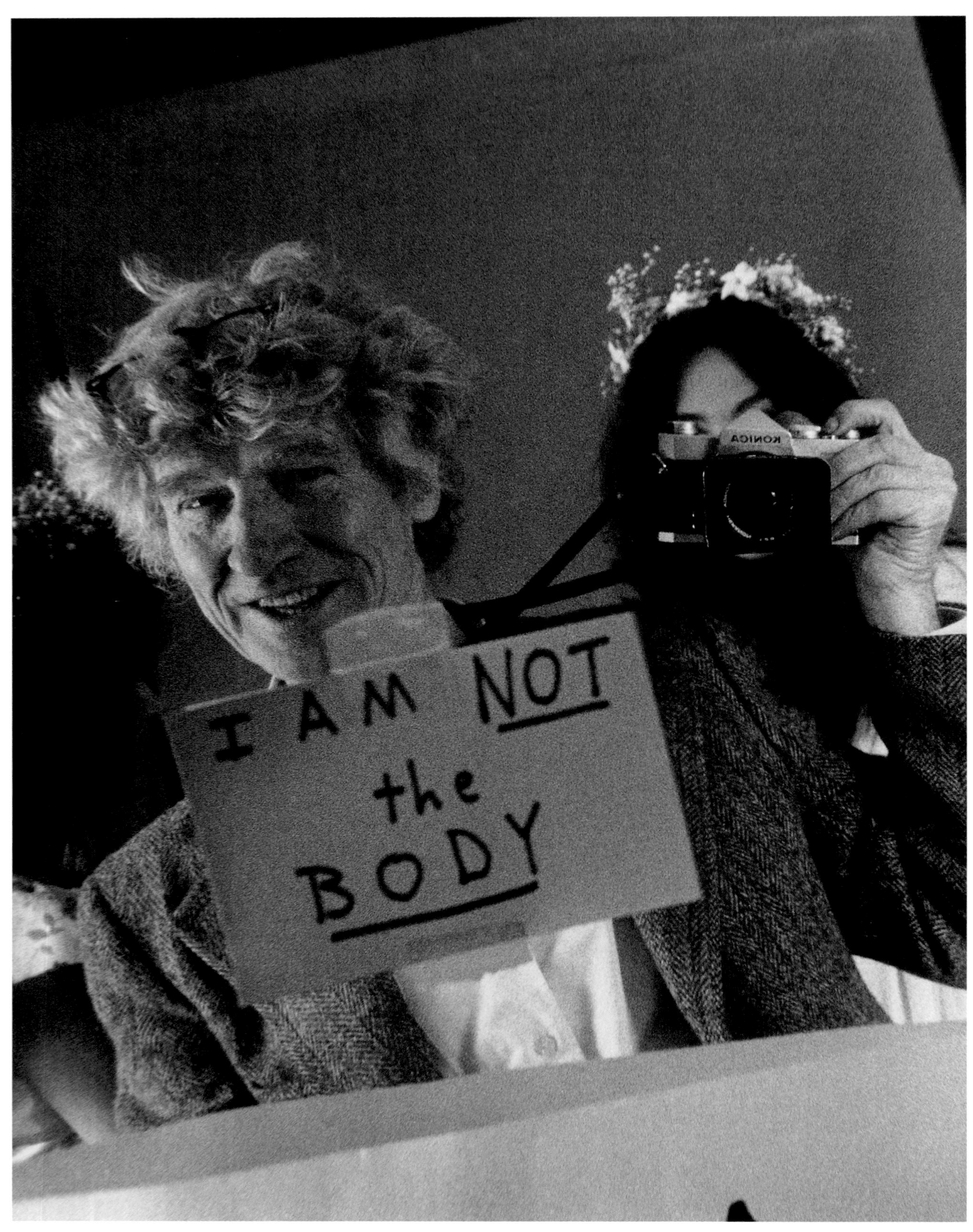

4 *Self-portrait with the Bride.* mid-1970s

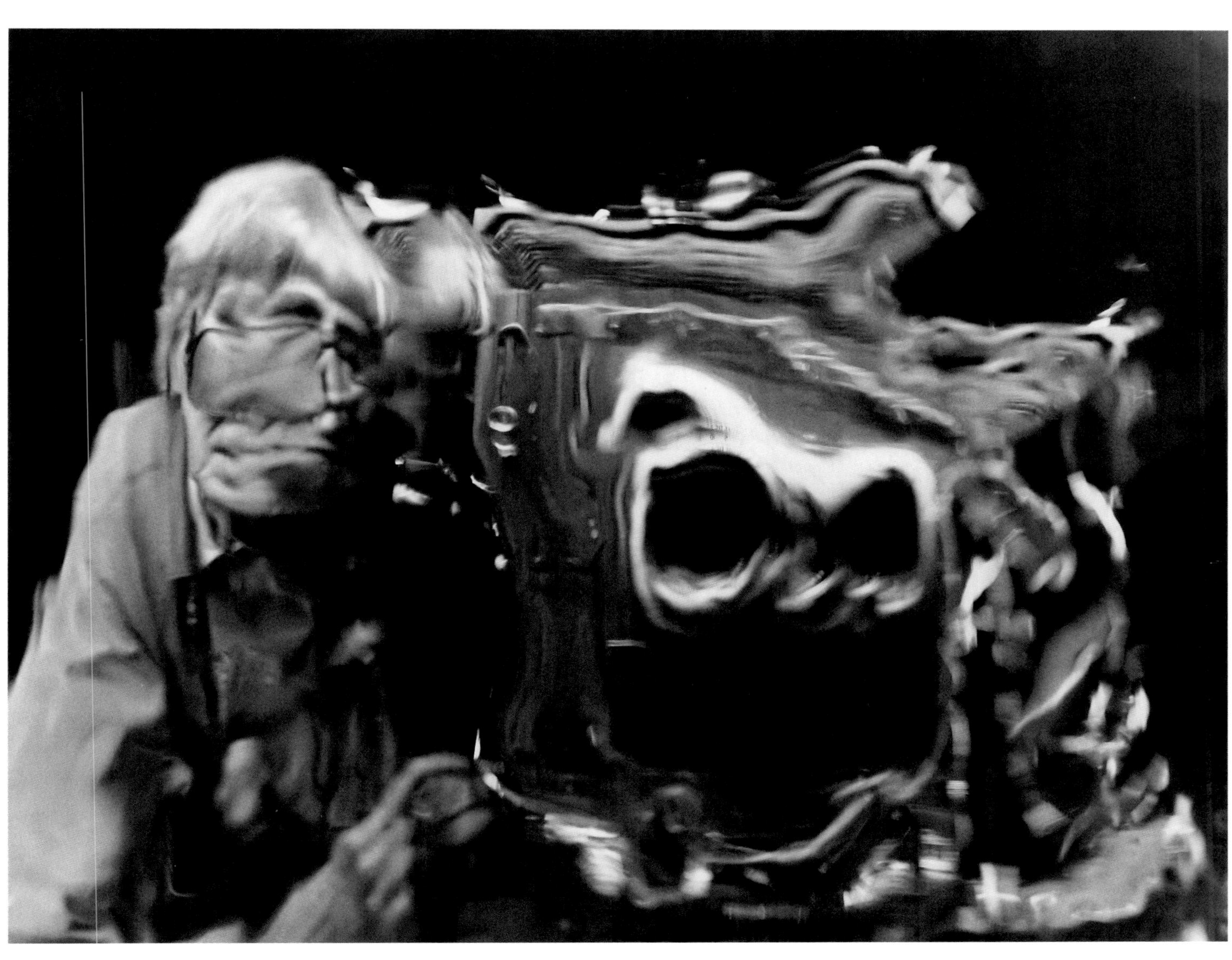

5 *Old Photographers Never Die.* 1994

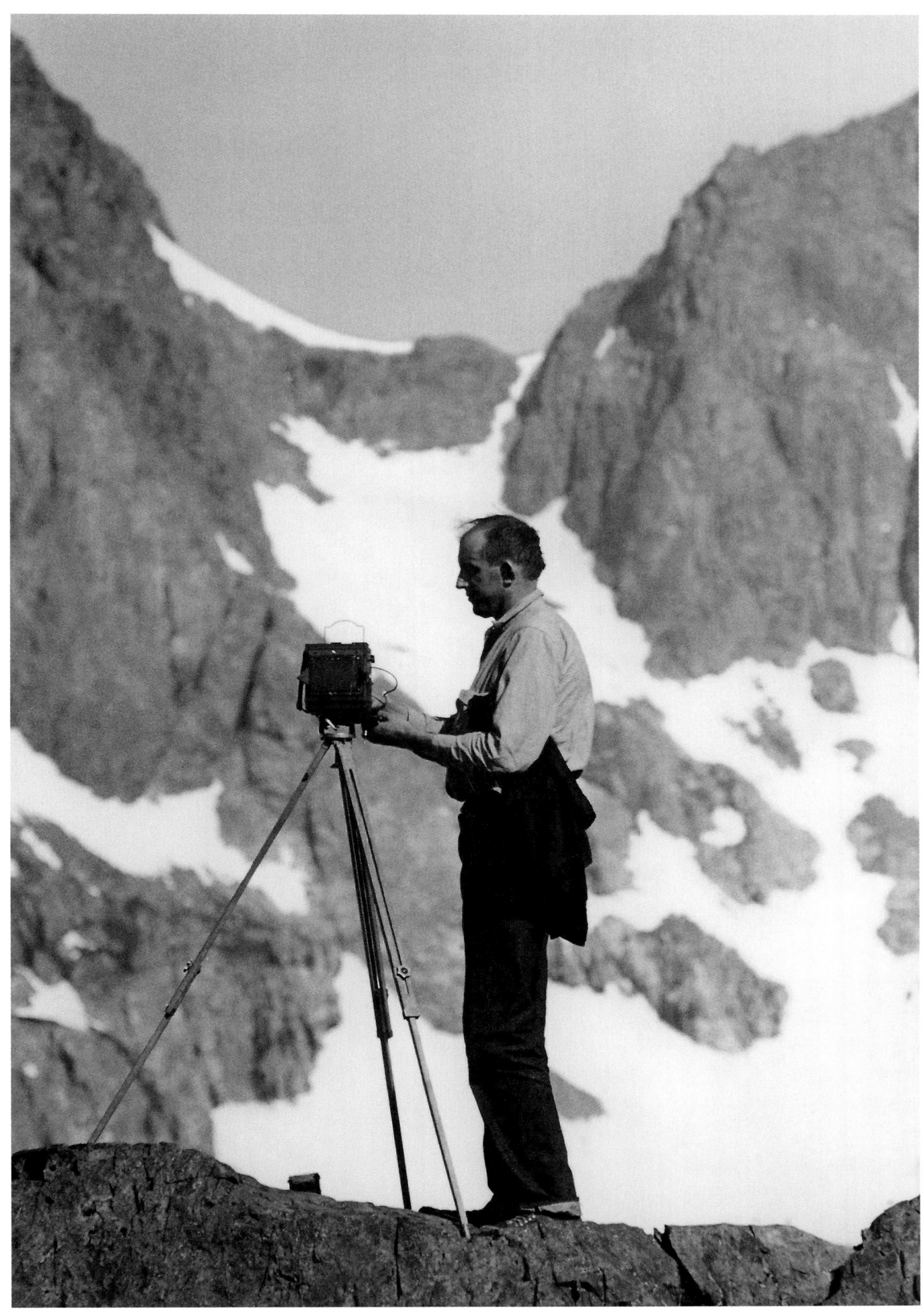

6 *Ansel Adams in the Sierra,* late 1930s

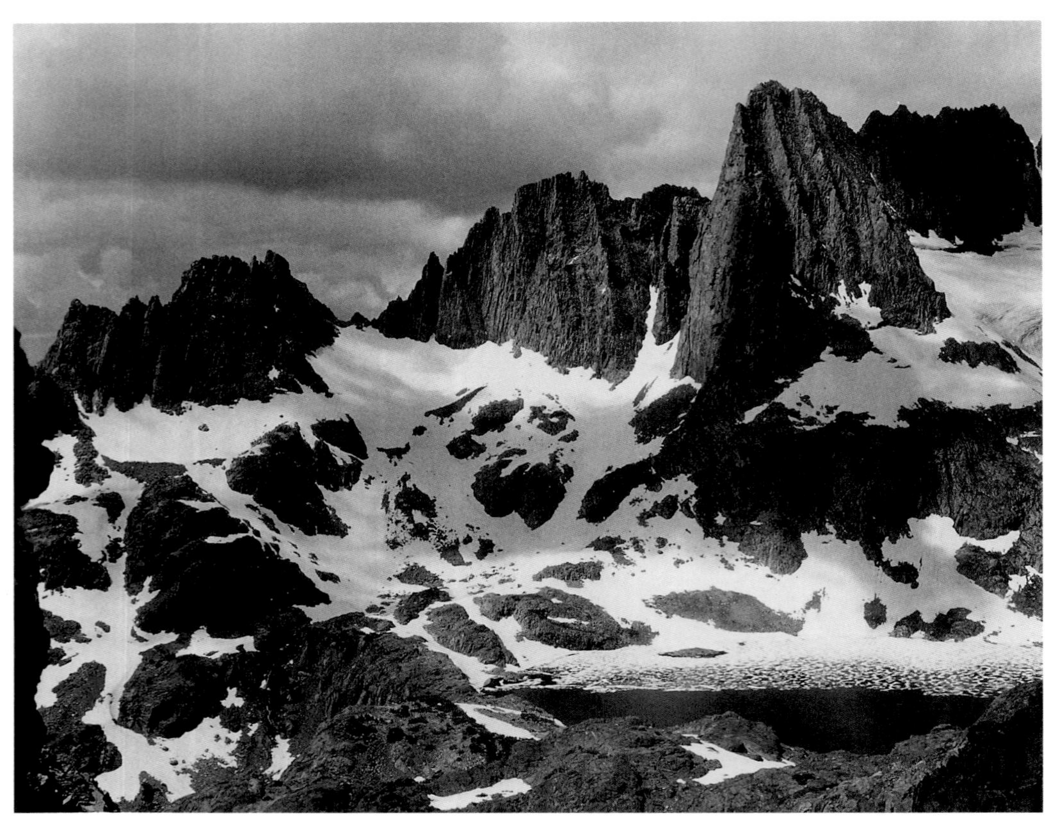

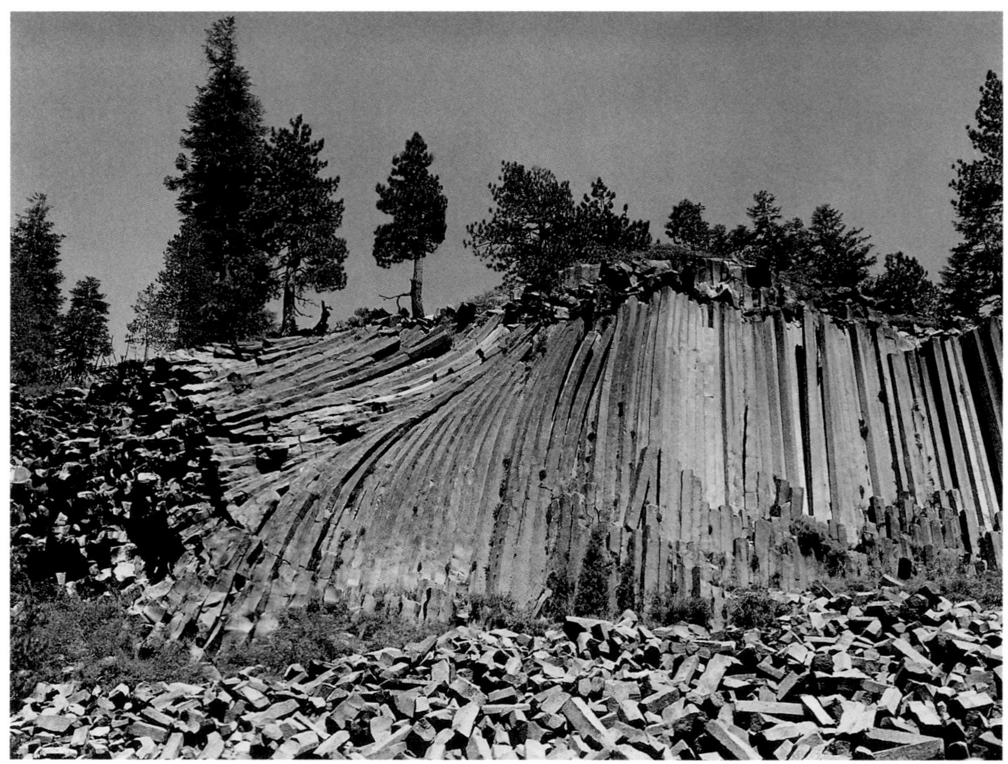

7 *High Sierra,* late 1930s / **8** *Devil's Postpile,* late 1930s

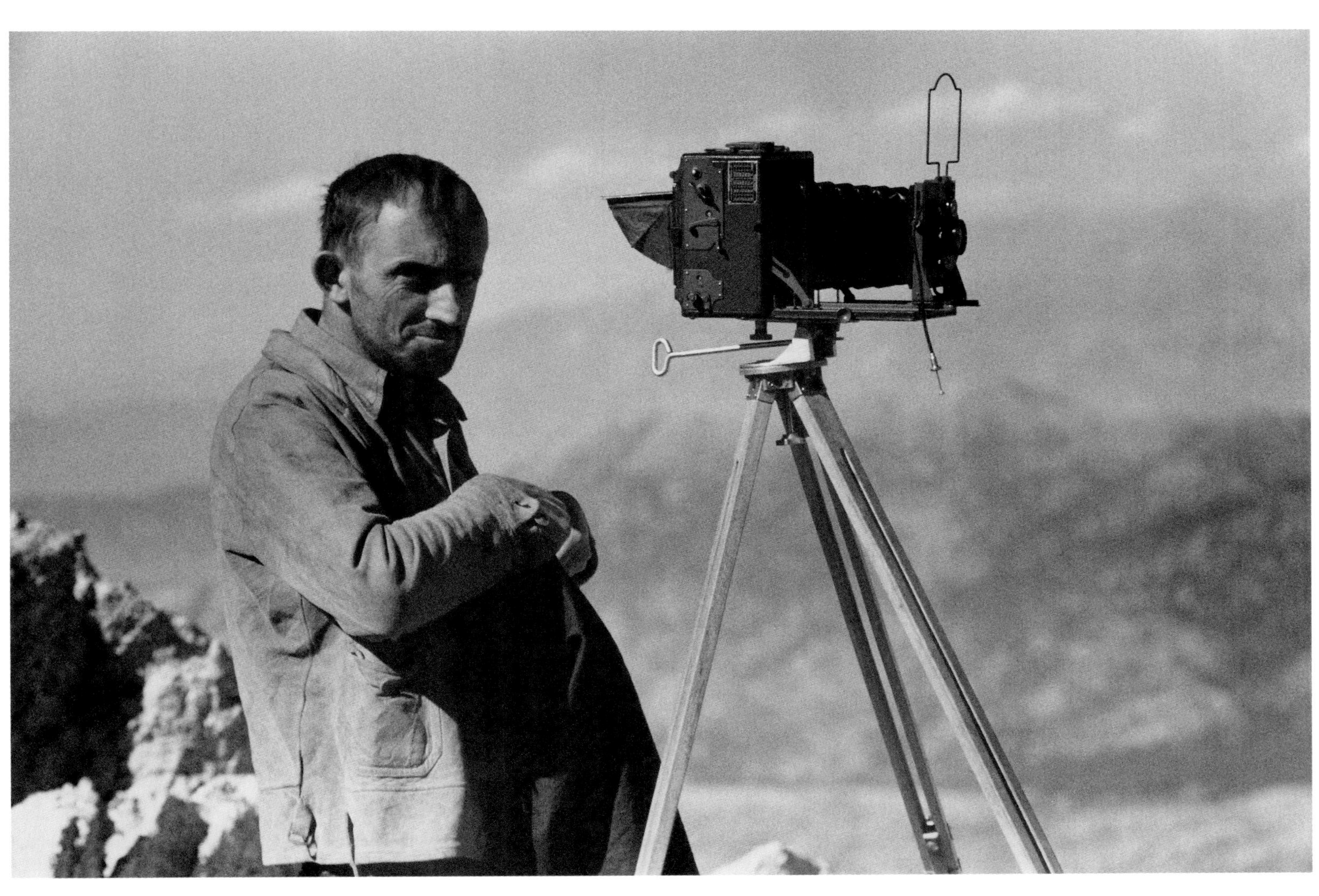

9 *A Different View of Ansel, late 1930s*

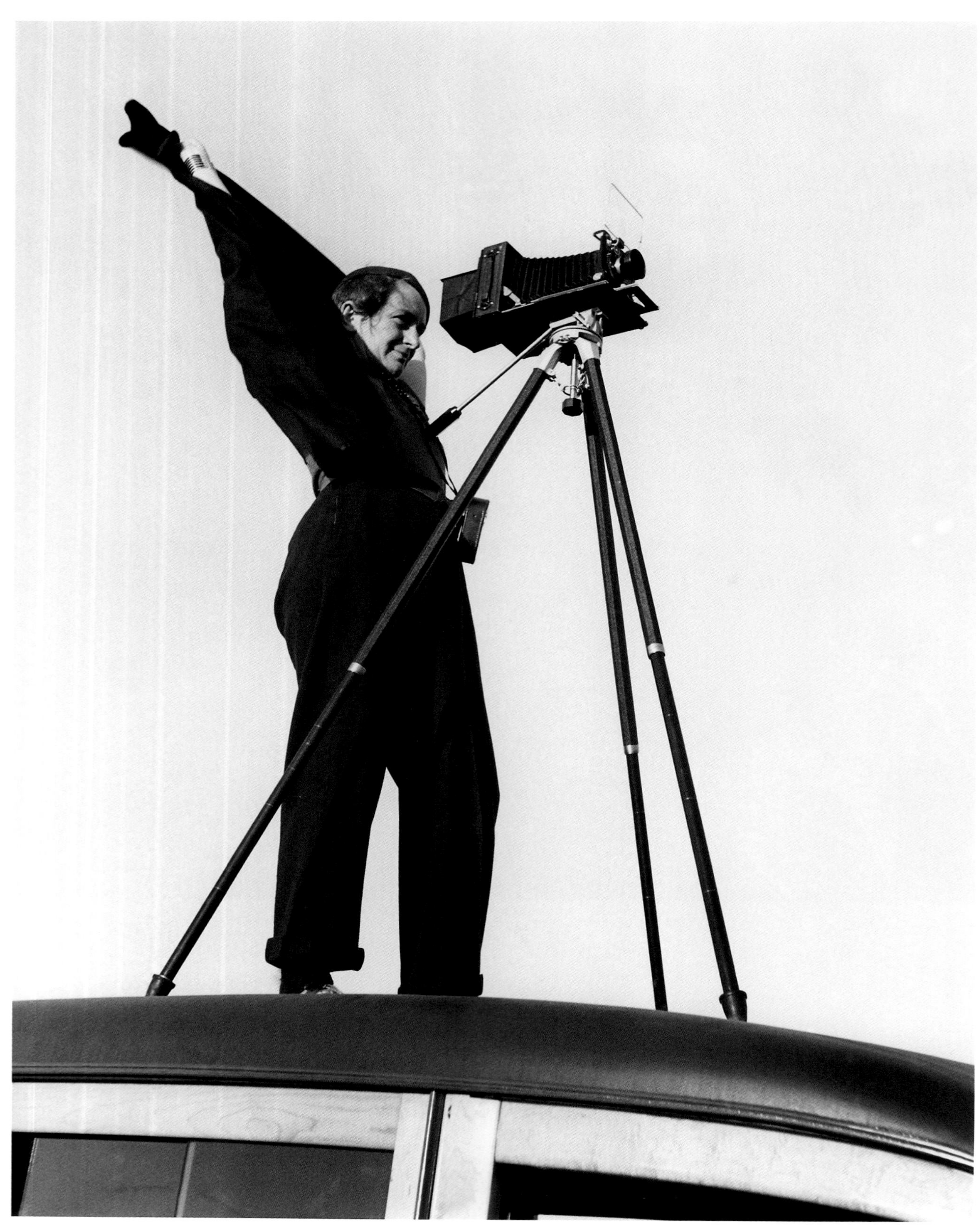

10   *Dorothea Lange and the Zeiss Jewell Camera.* 1937

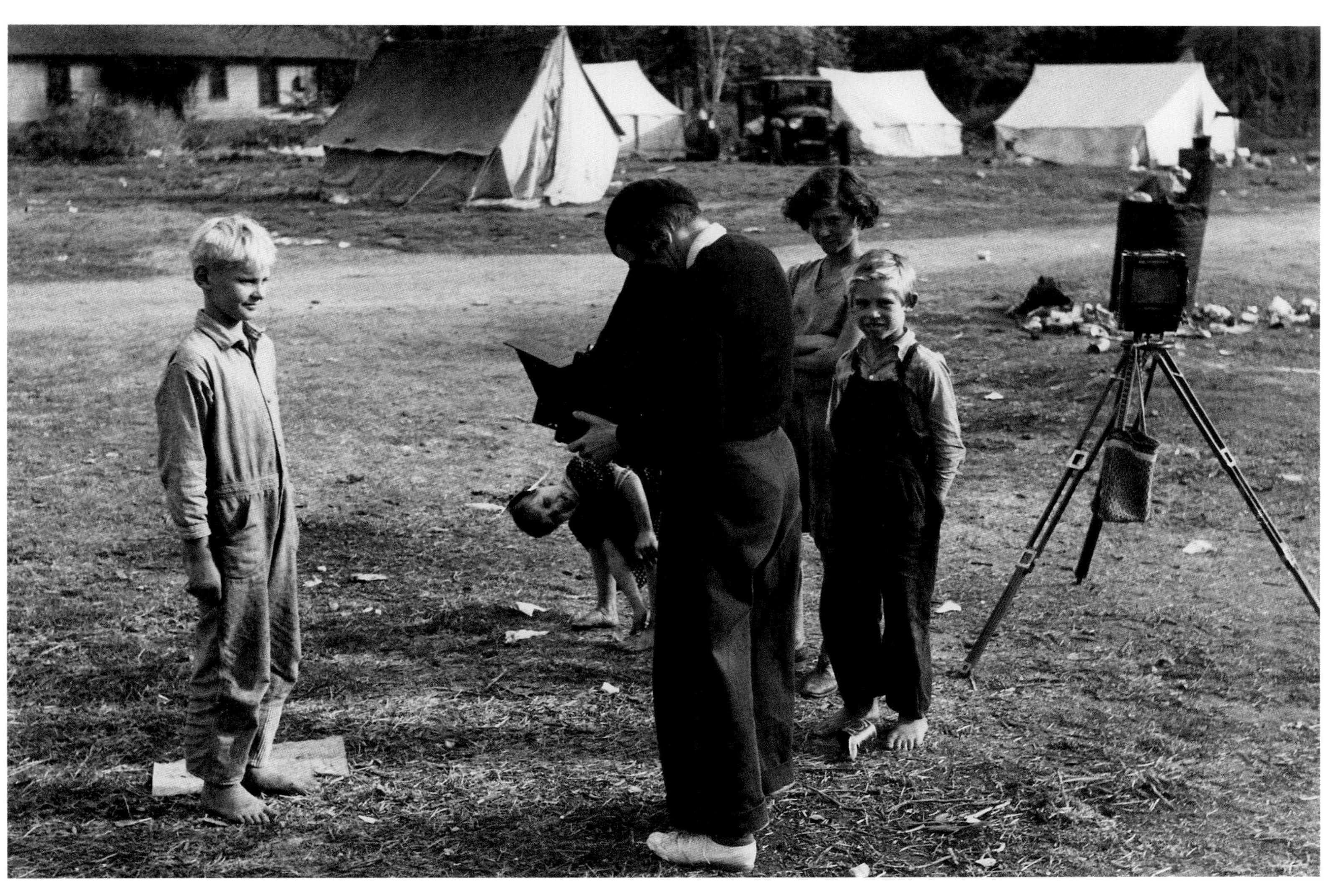

11   *Dorothea Lange in the Field.* 1938

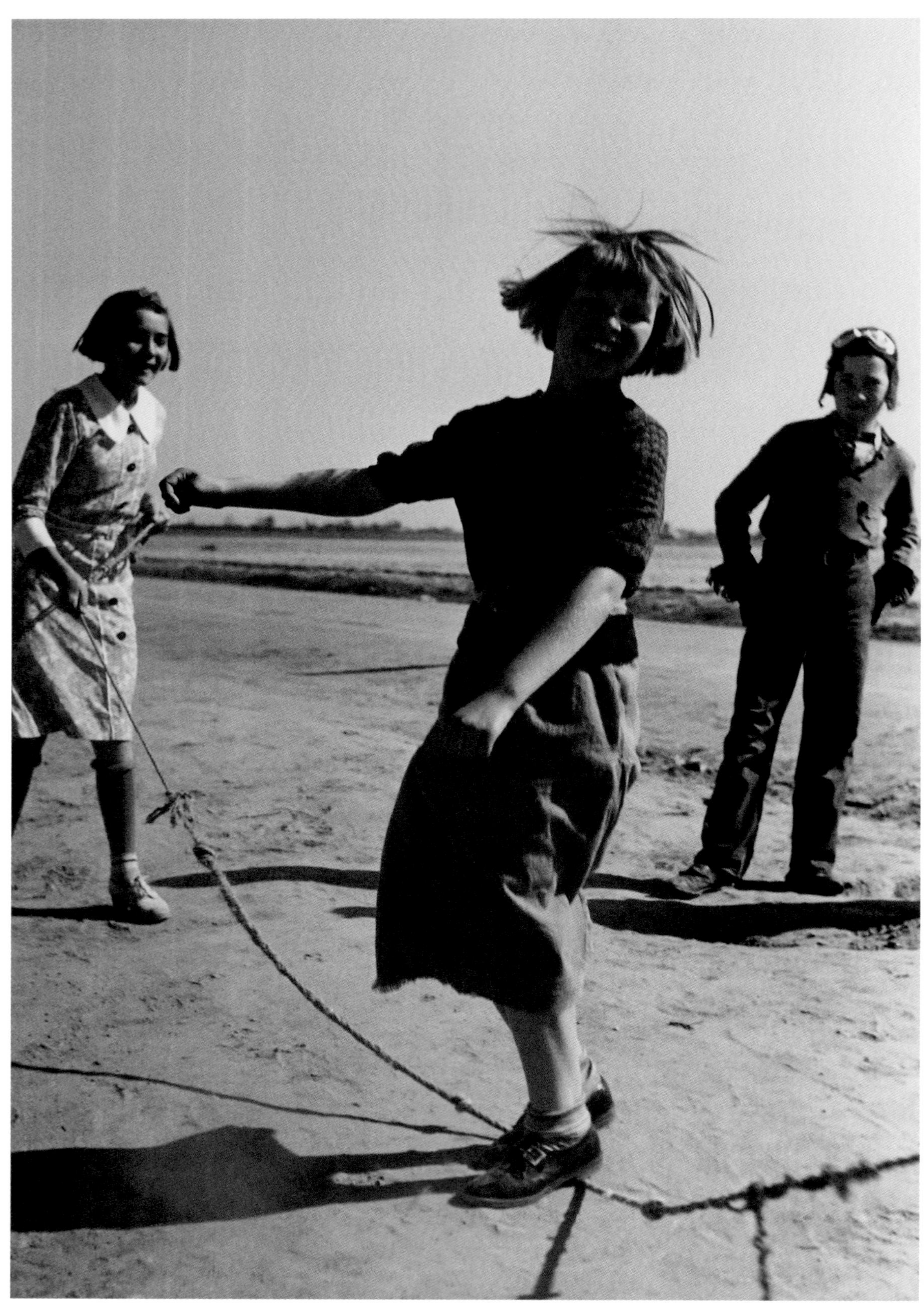

12 *Migrant Kids Jumping Rope.* Arvin camp. California. 1938

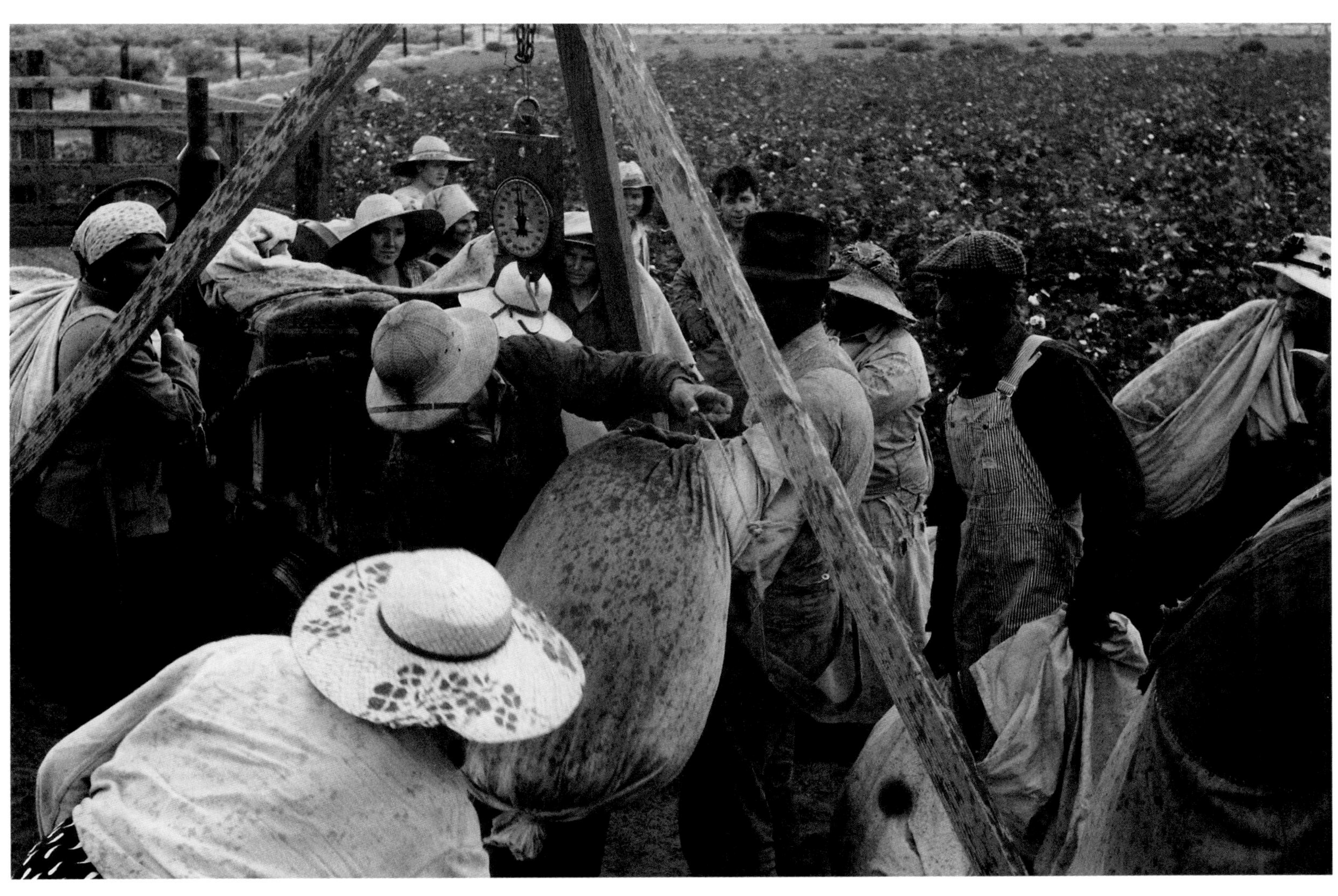

13 *Weighing Cotton*, Central Valley, California, late 1930s

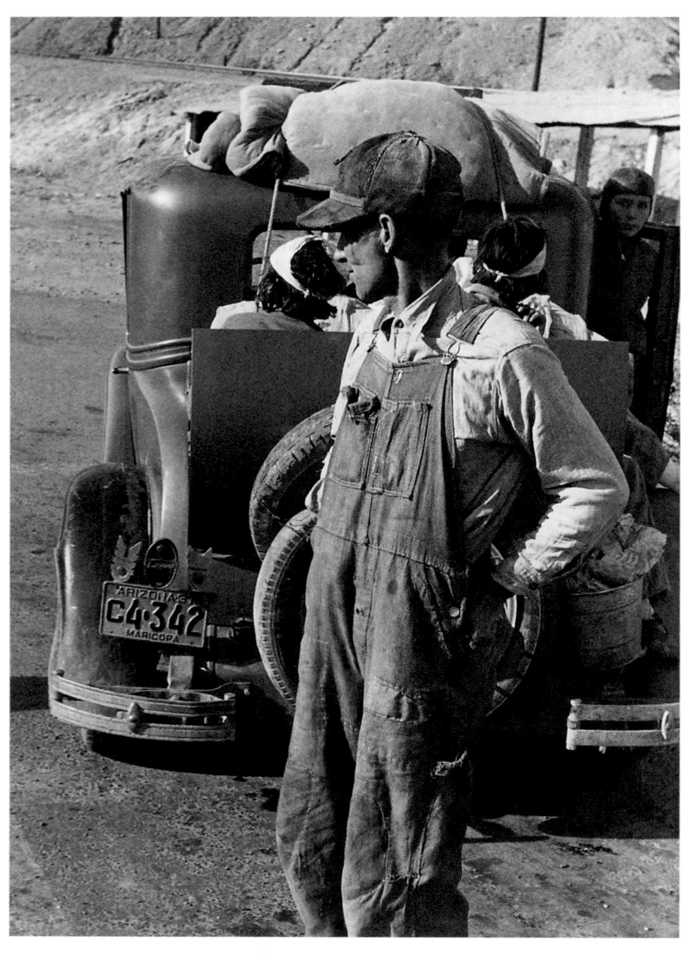

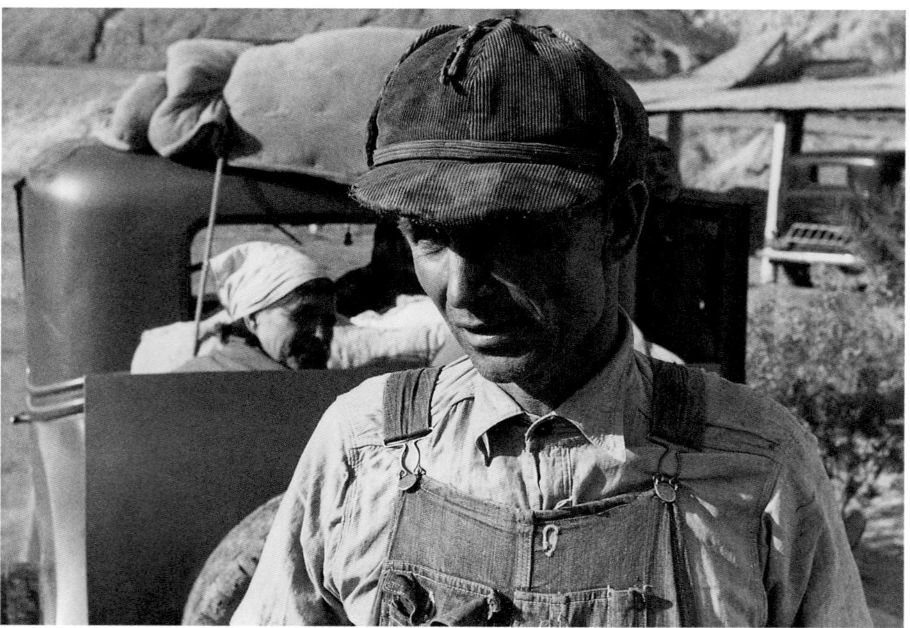

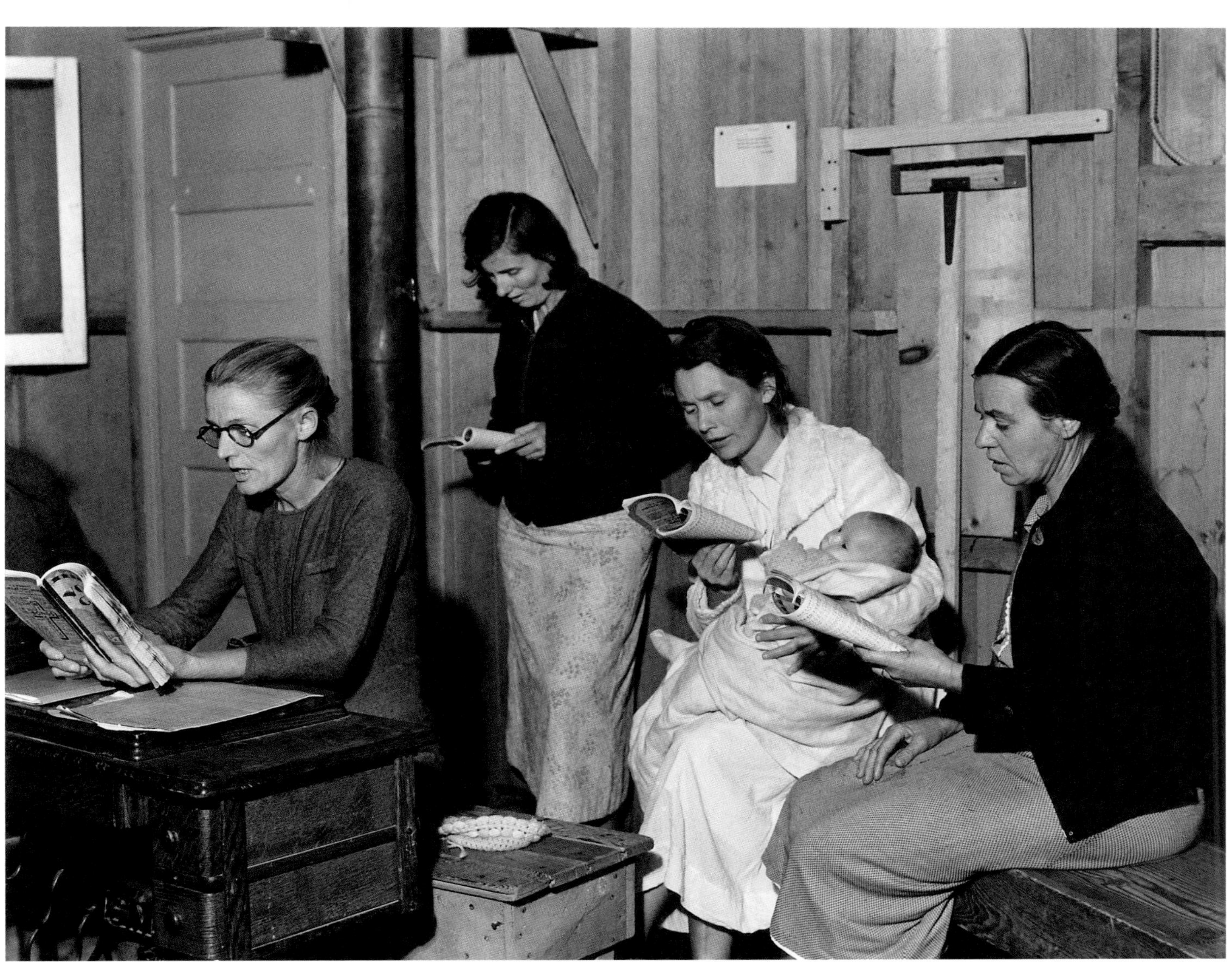

16 *Hymn Singing.* Arvin camp. California. 1938

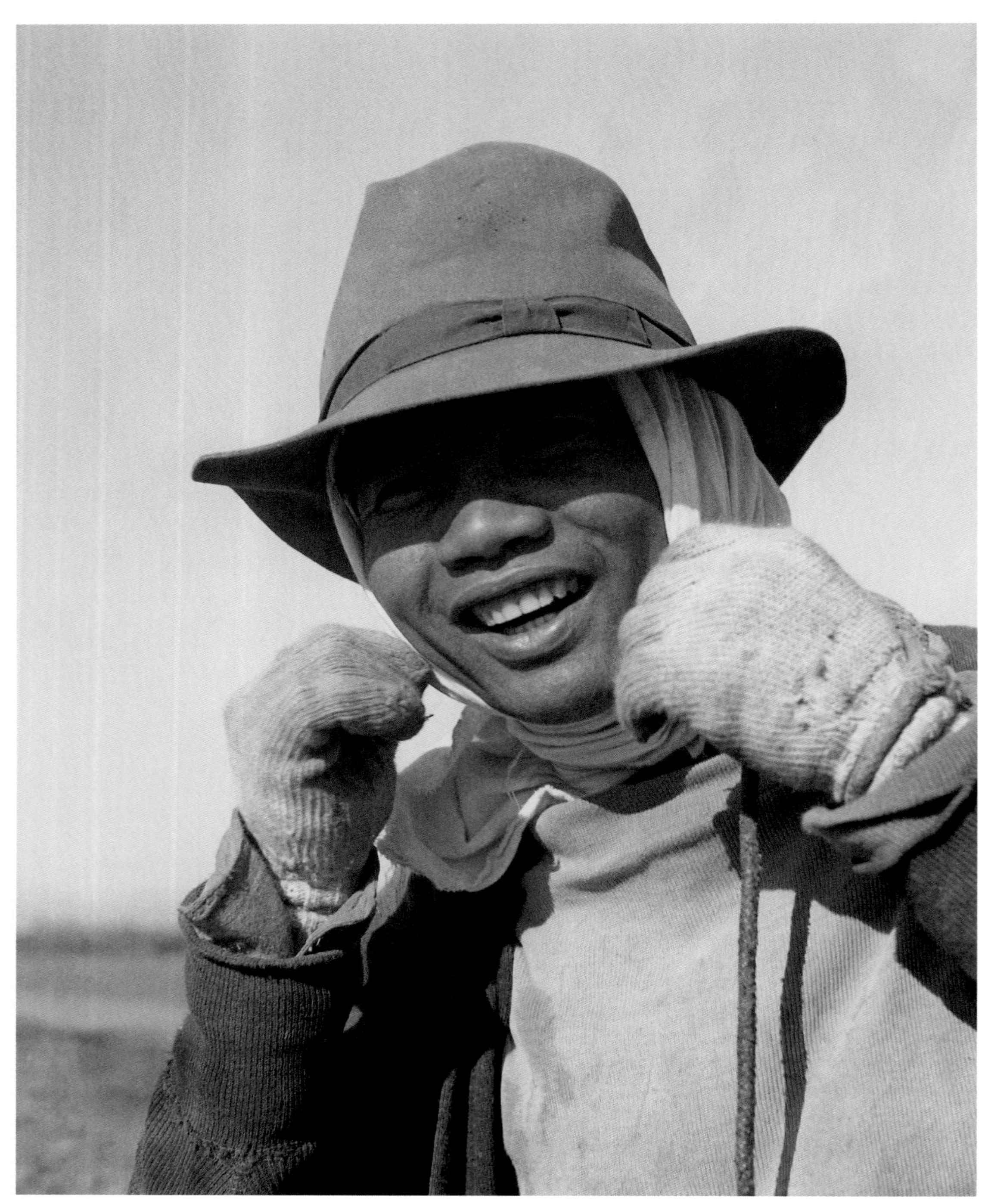

17 *Asparagus Worker.* Sacramento River Delta. California. 1940

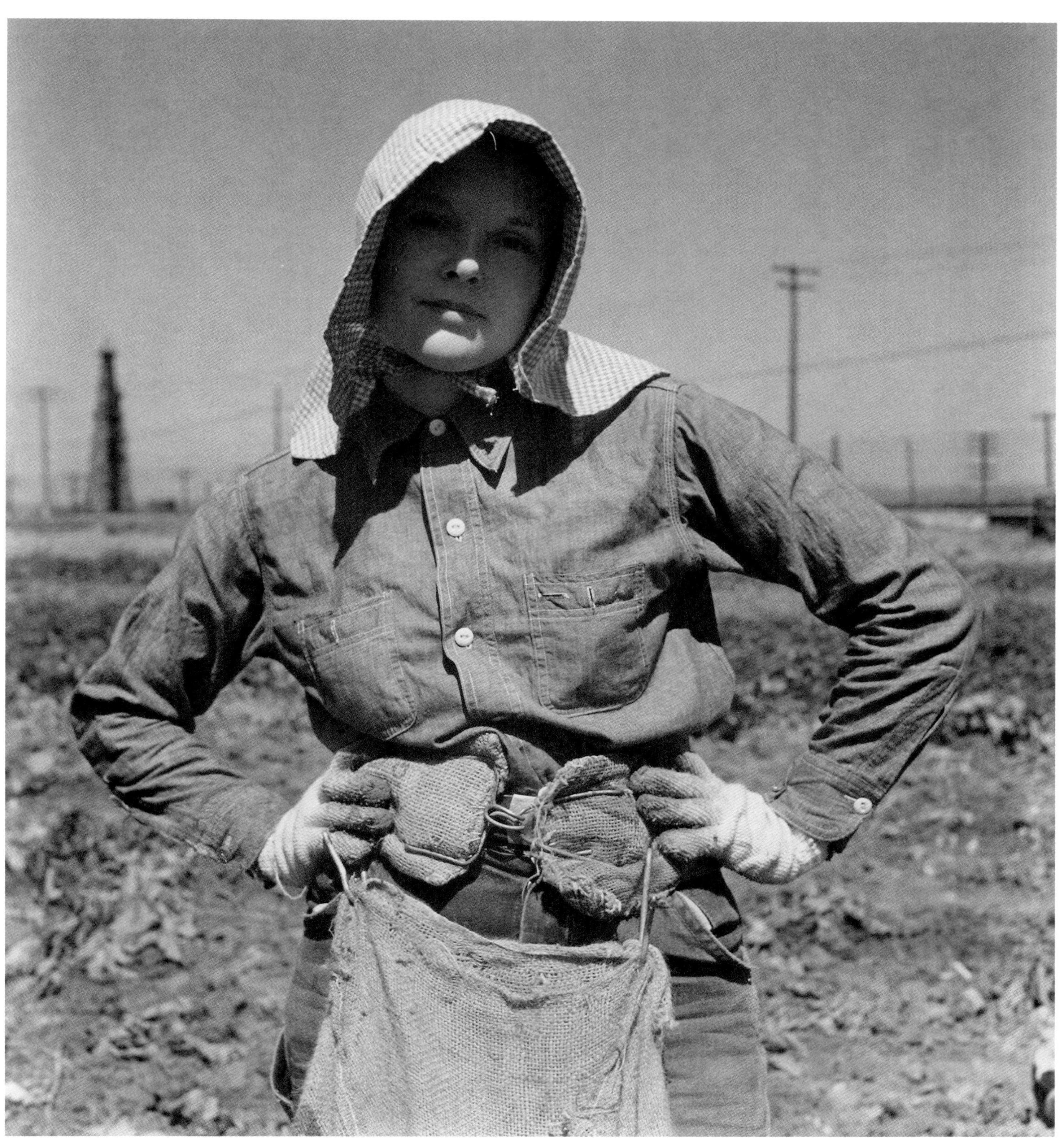

18 *Potato Field Madonna,* Kern County, California, 1940

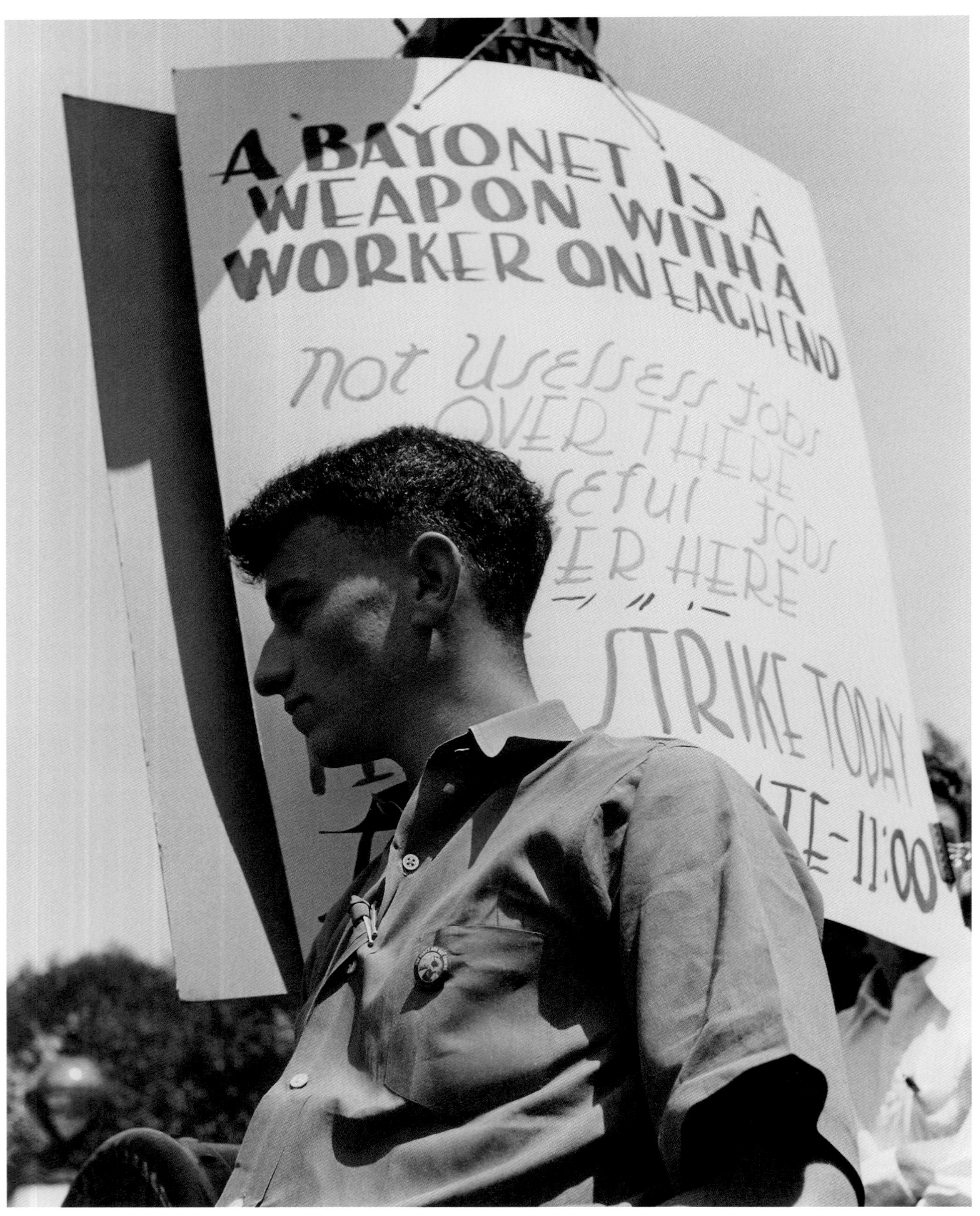

19   *April Peace Strike*, University of California, Berkeley, 1940

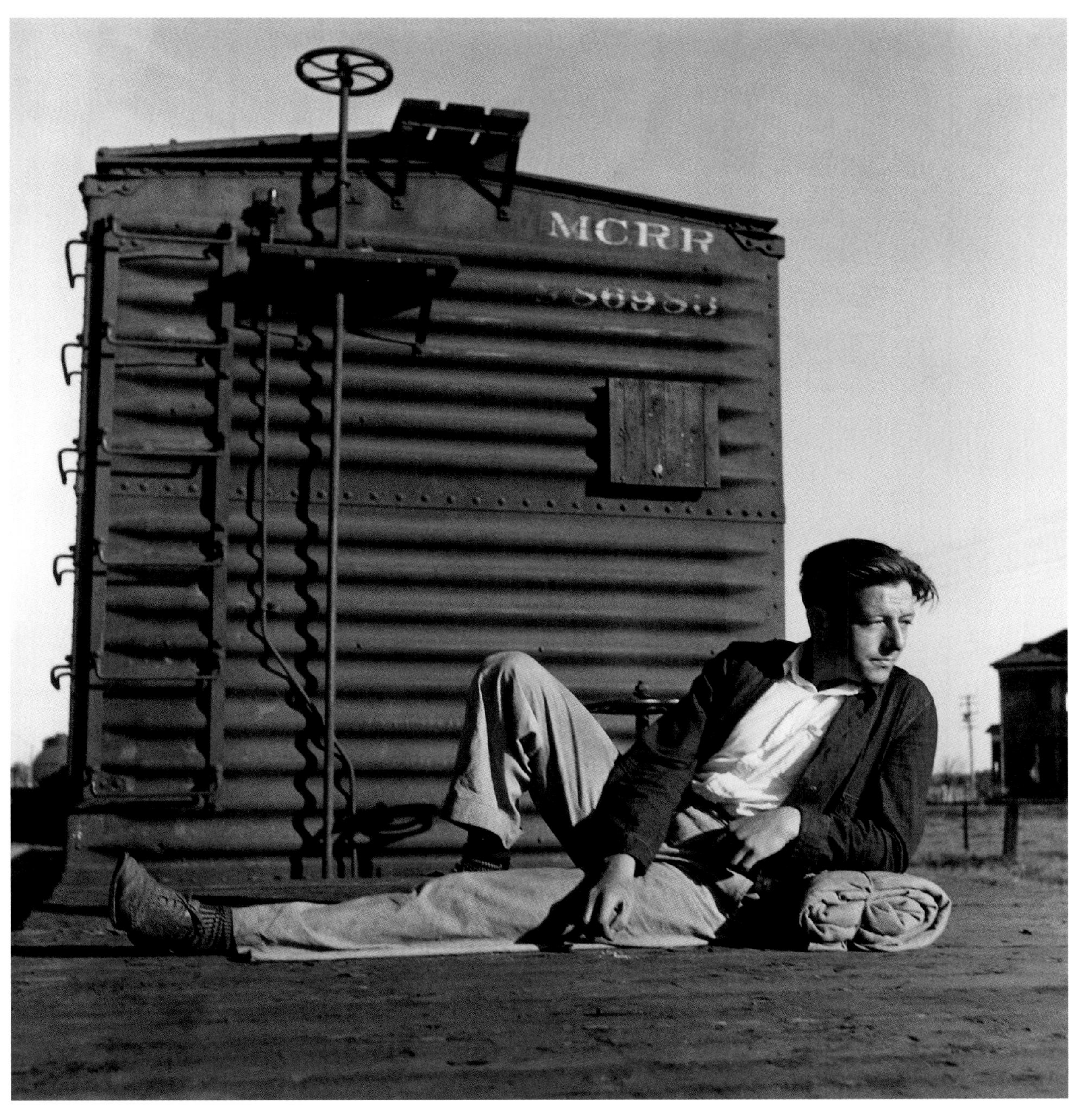

20   *Riding the Freights*, Yuba County, California, 1940

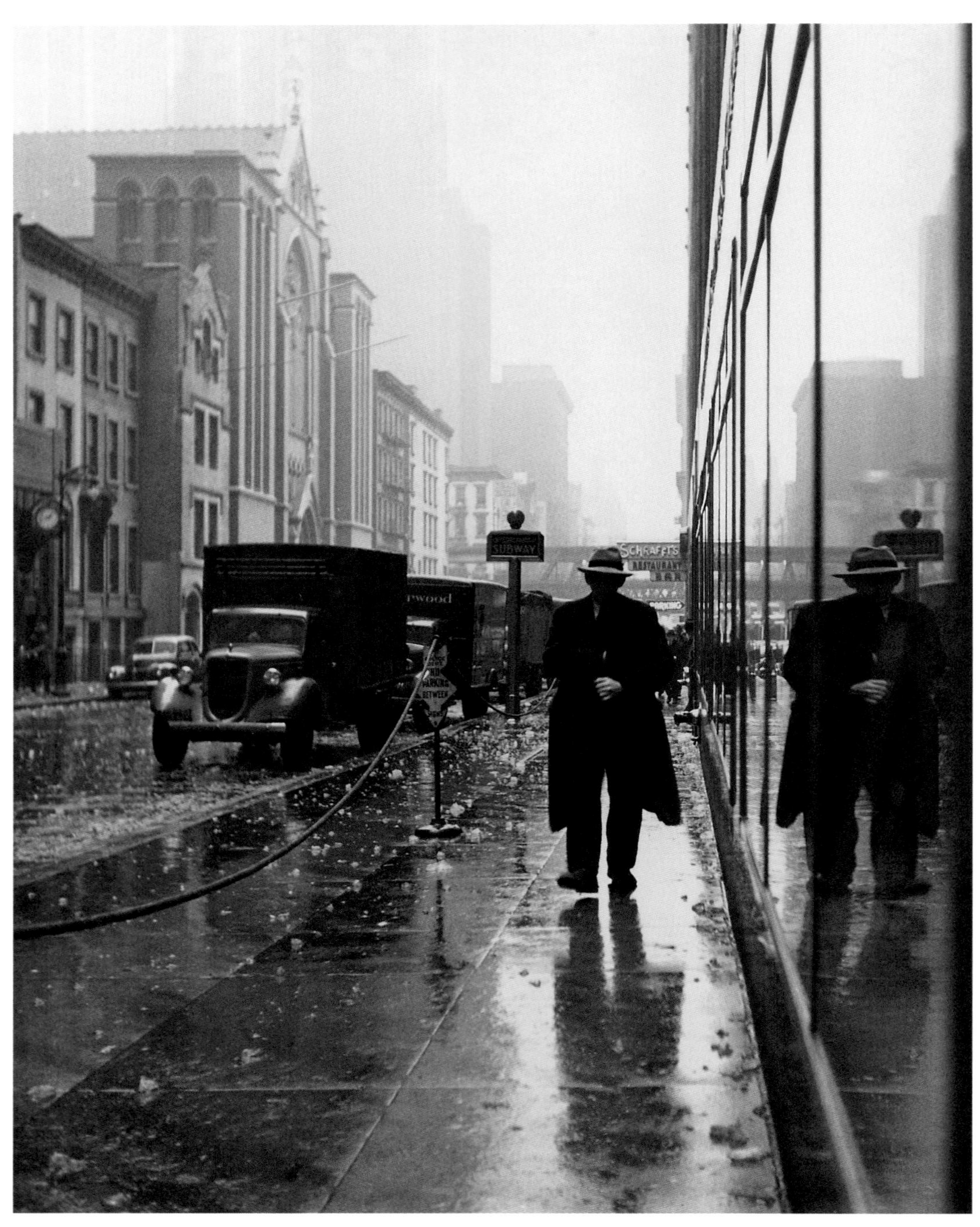

21 *Falling Ice.* New York City. 1940

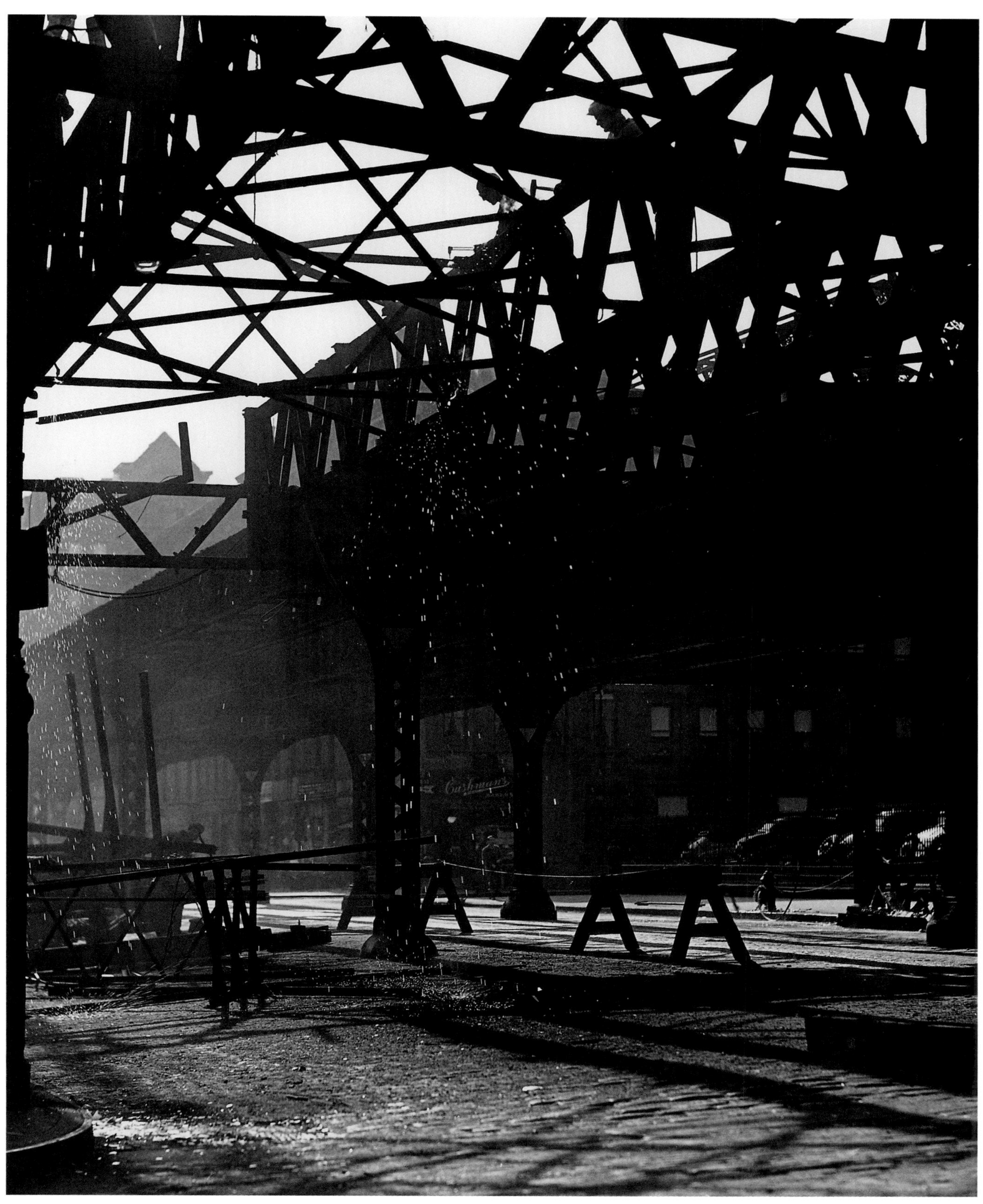

22 *Taking Down the Sixth Avenue El Train Tracks.* New York City. 1940

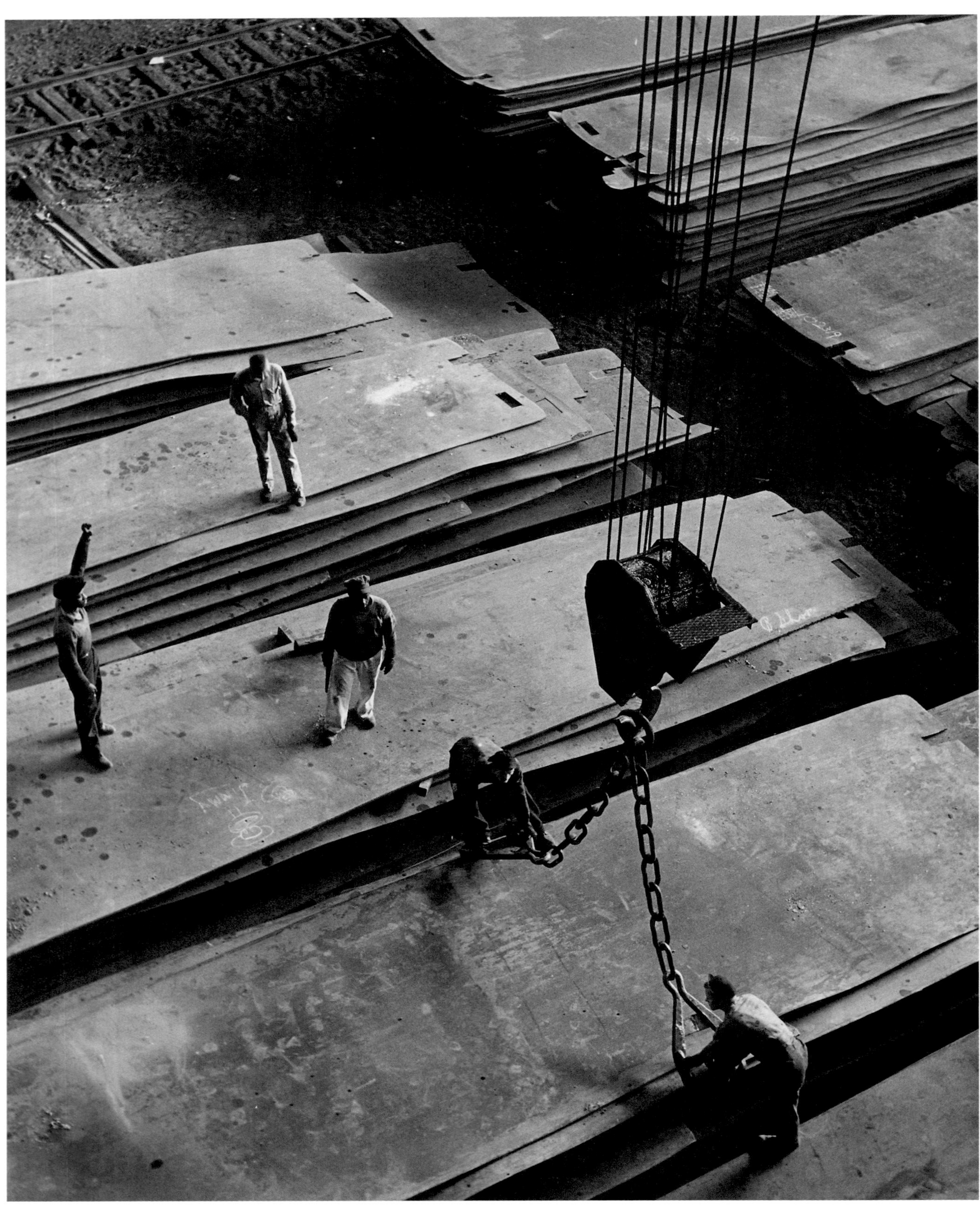

23   *Preparing Sheets of Steel to Make Battleships. Pennsylvania. 1940*

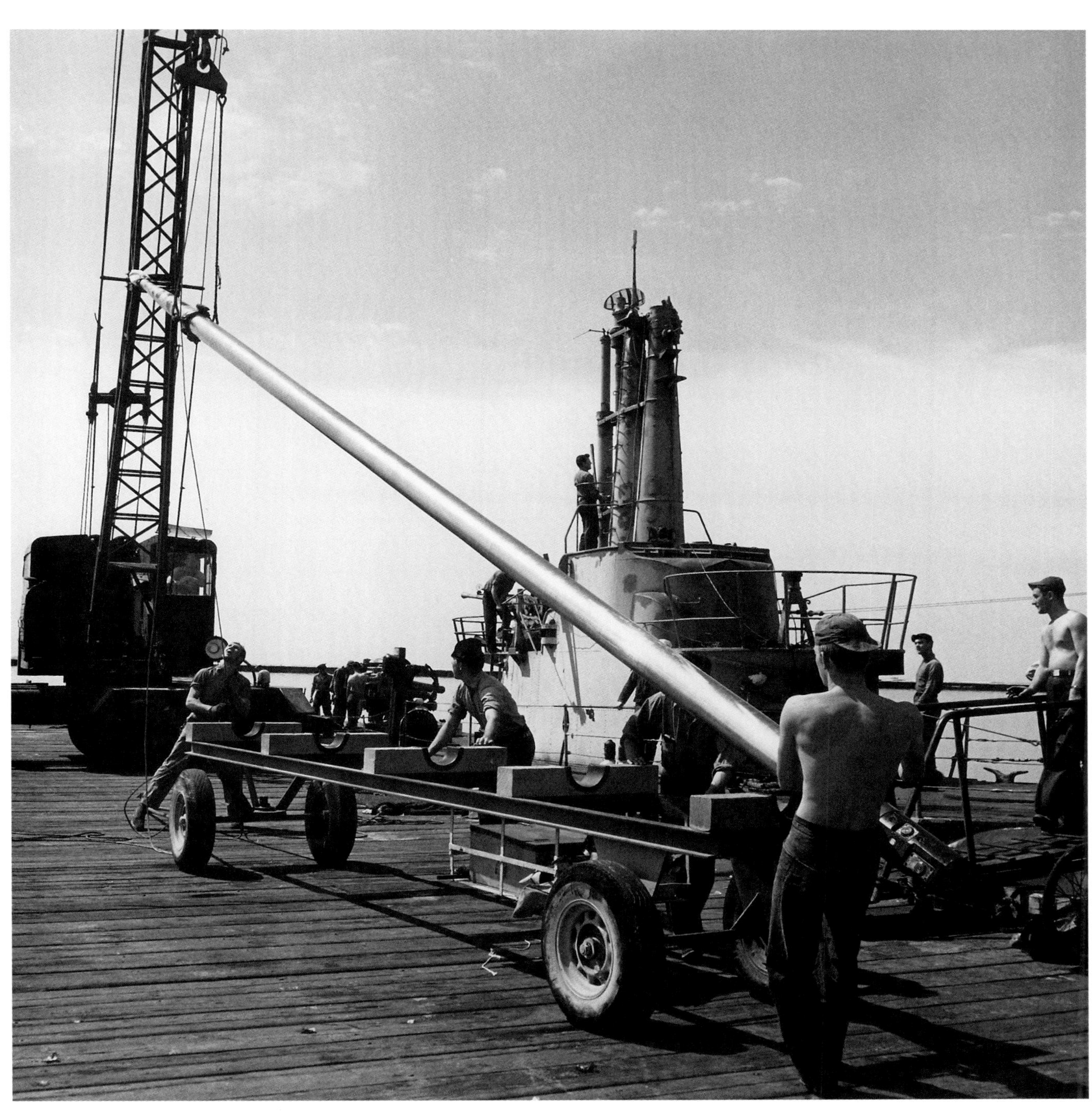

24 *Installing a Periscope*. Pearl Harbor. 1945

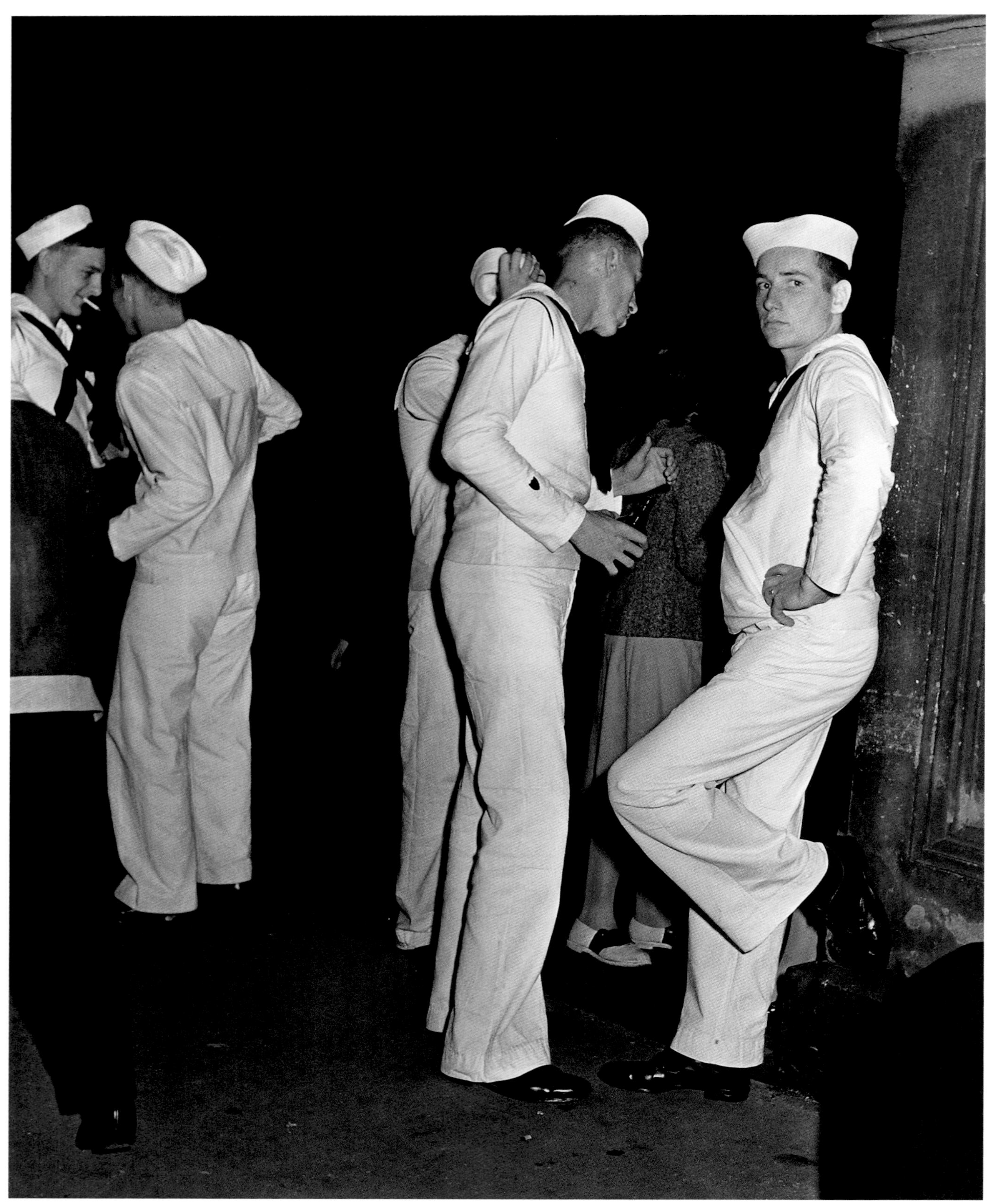

25   *Sailors in Central Park*, New York City, 1940

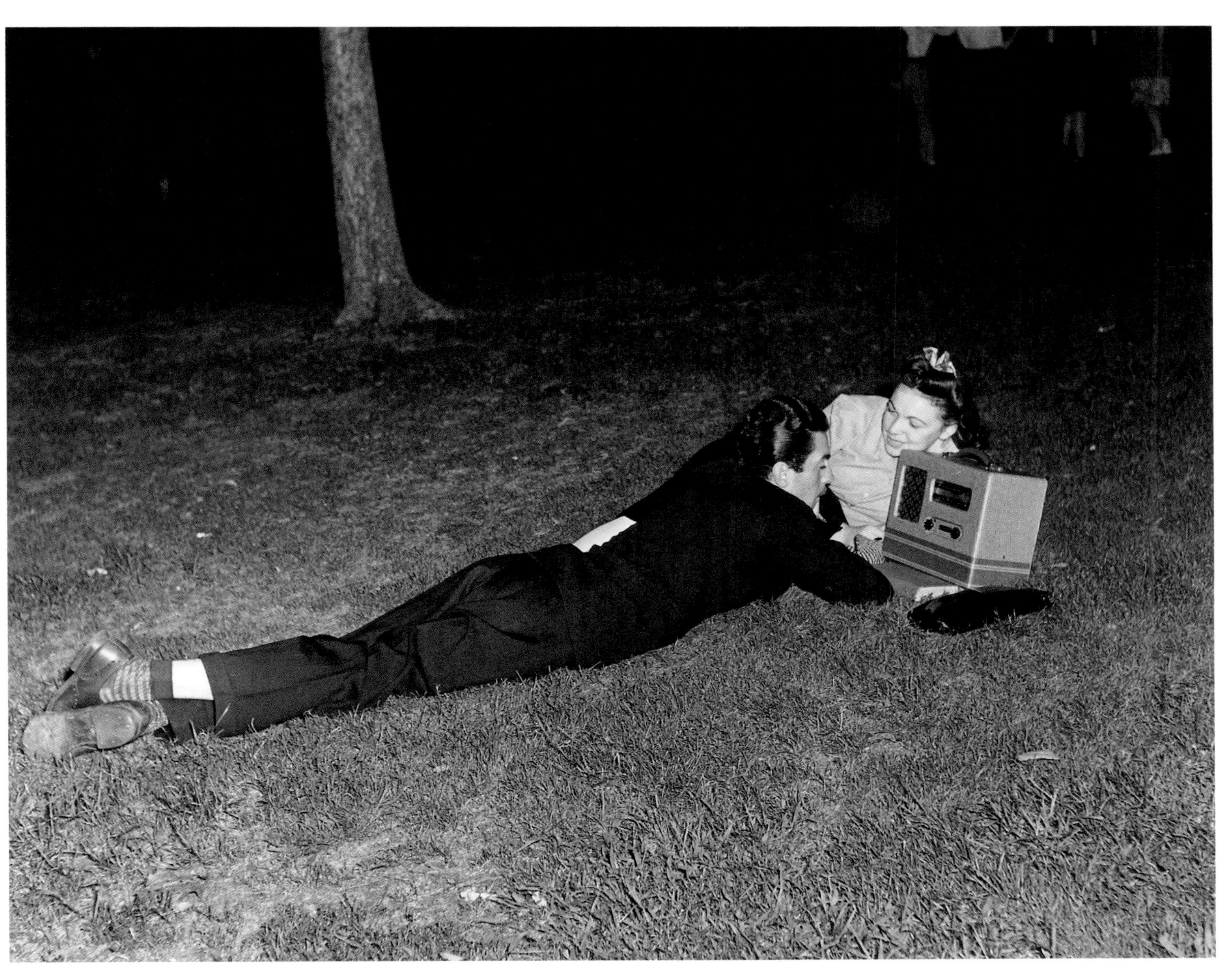

26 *Couple in Central Park. New York City. 1940*

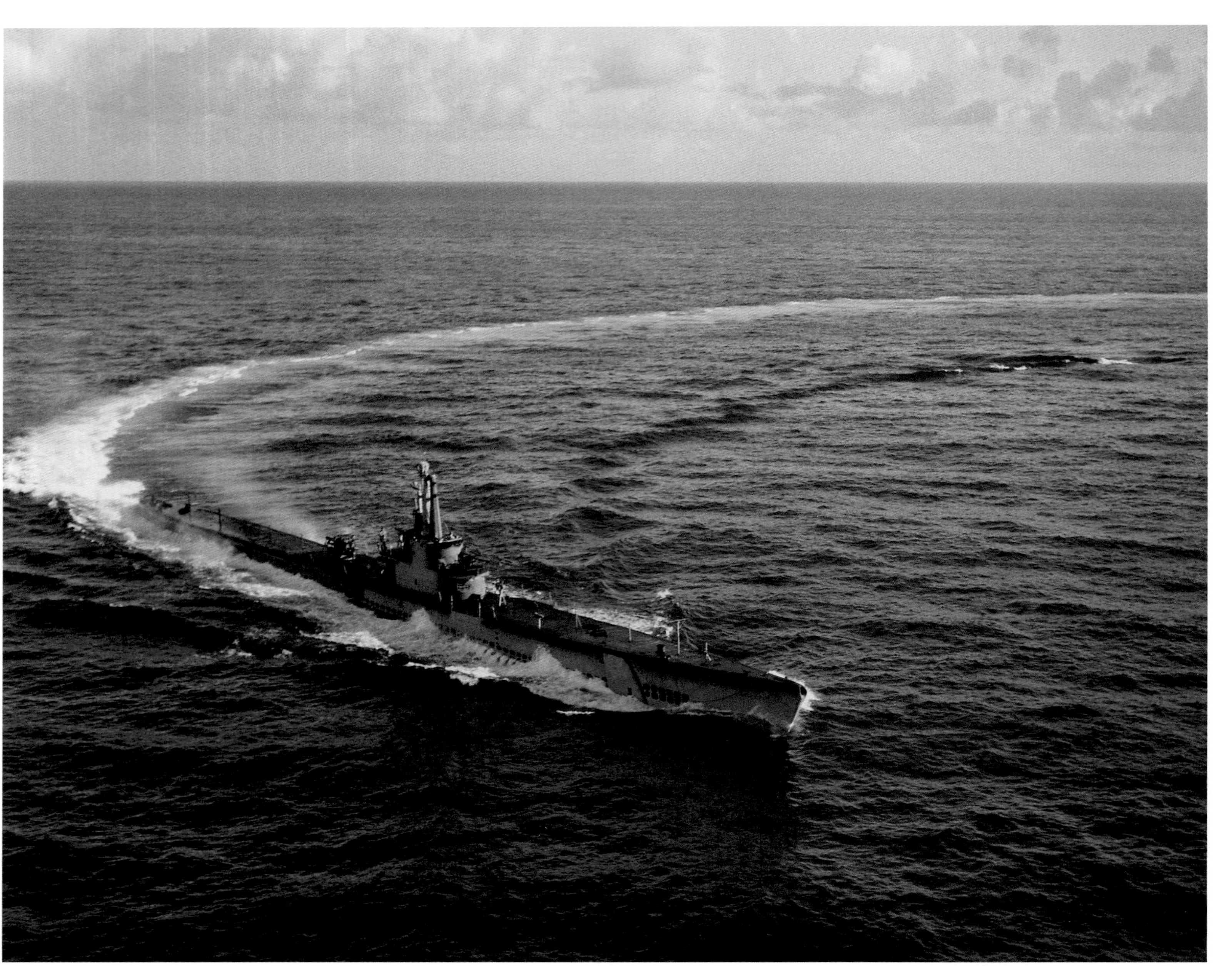

27 *Testing an Overhauled Submarine.* Midway Island. 1945

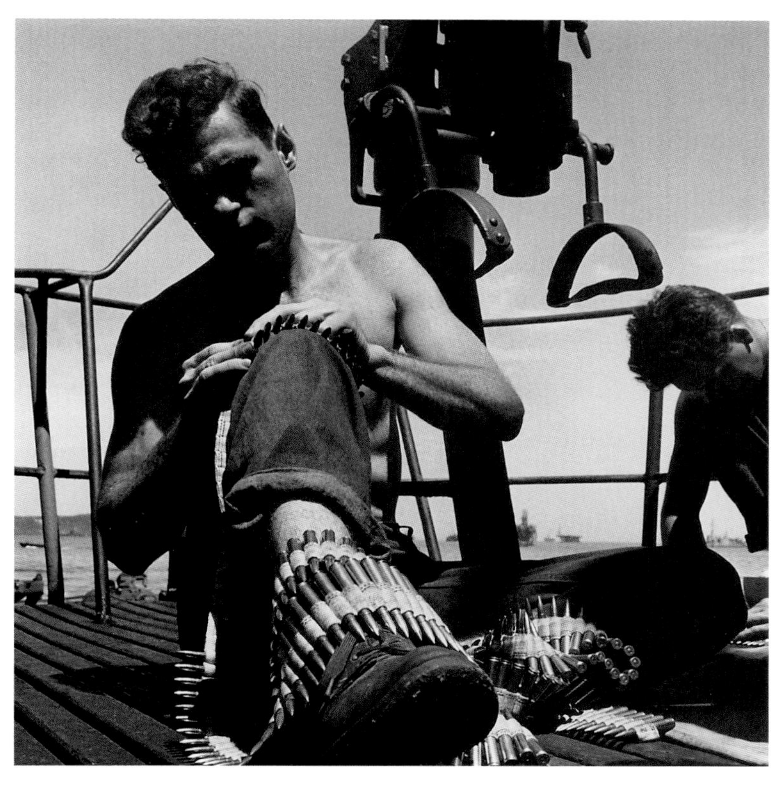

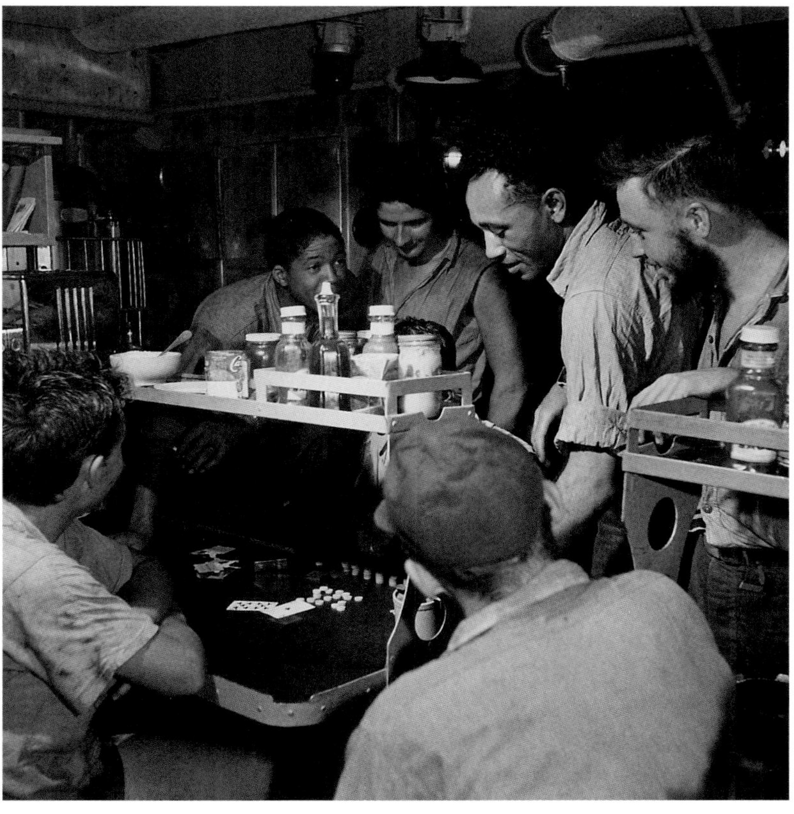

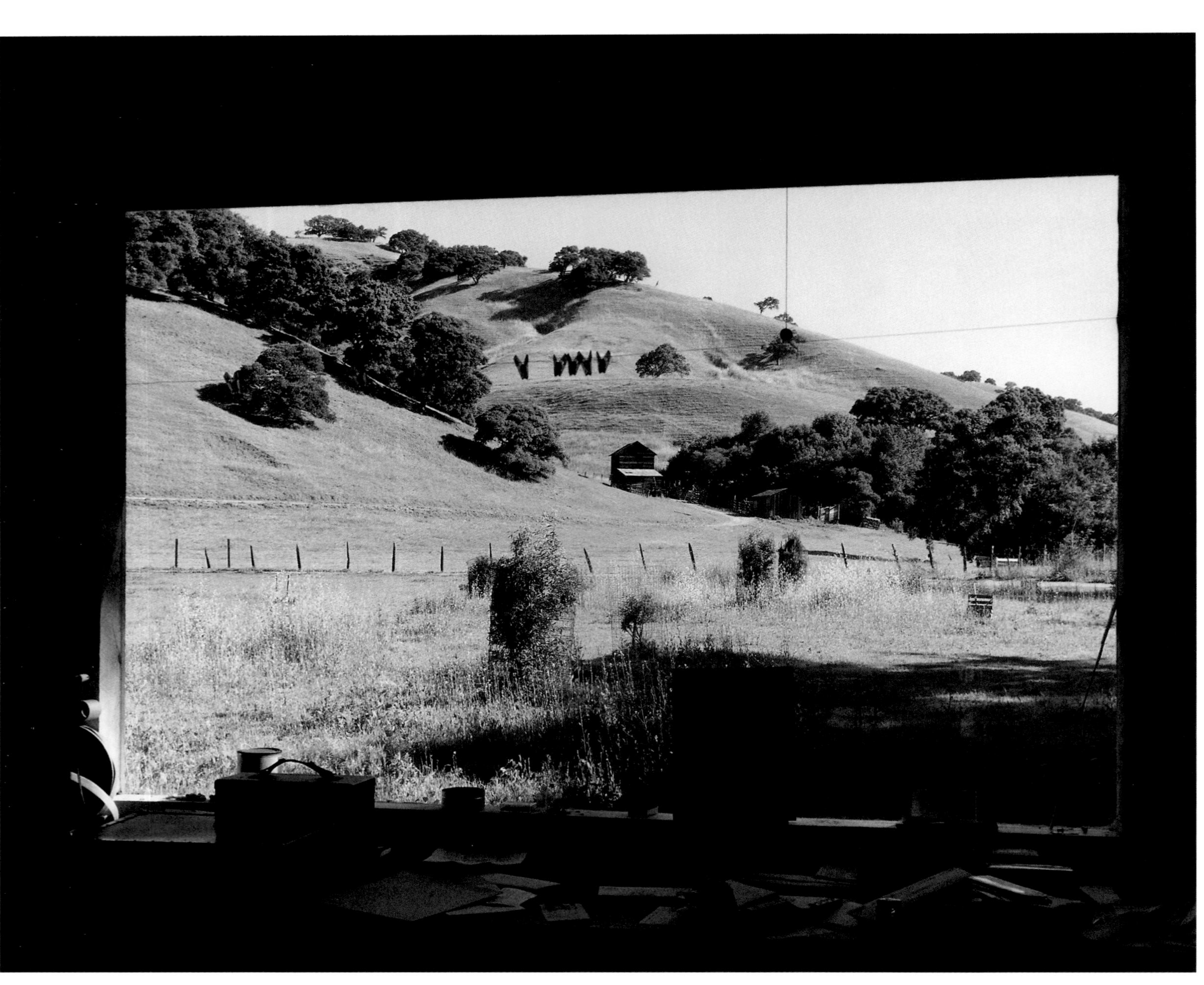

30   *View from My Studio*. Bear Creek. California. late 1950s

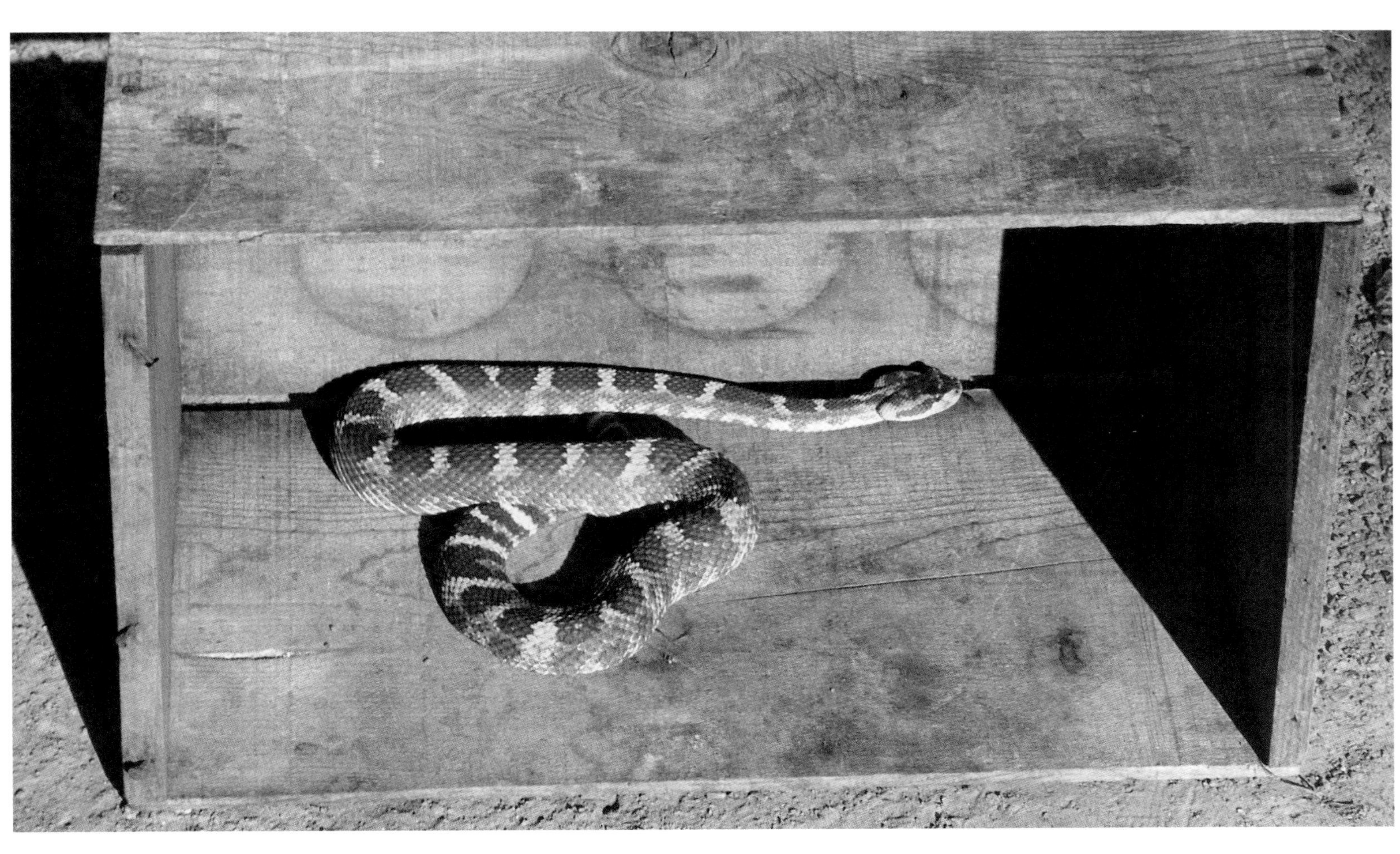

31　*Snake in a Box*. Bear Creek. California. 1953

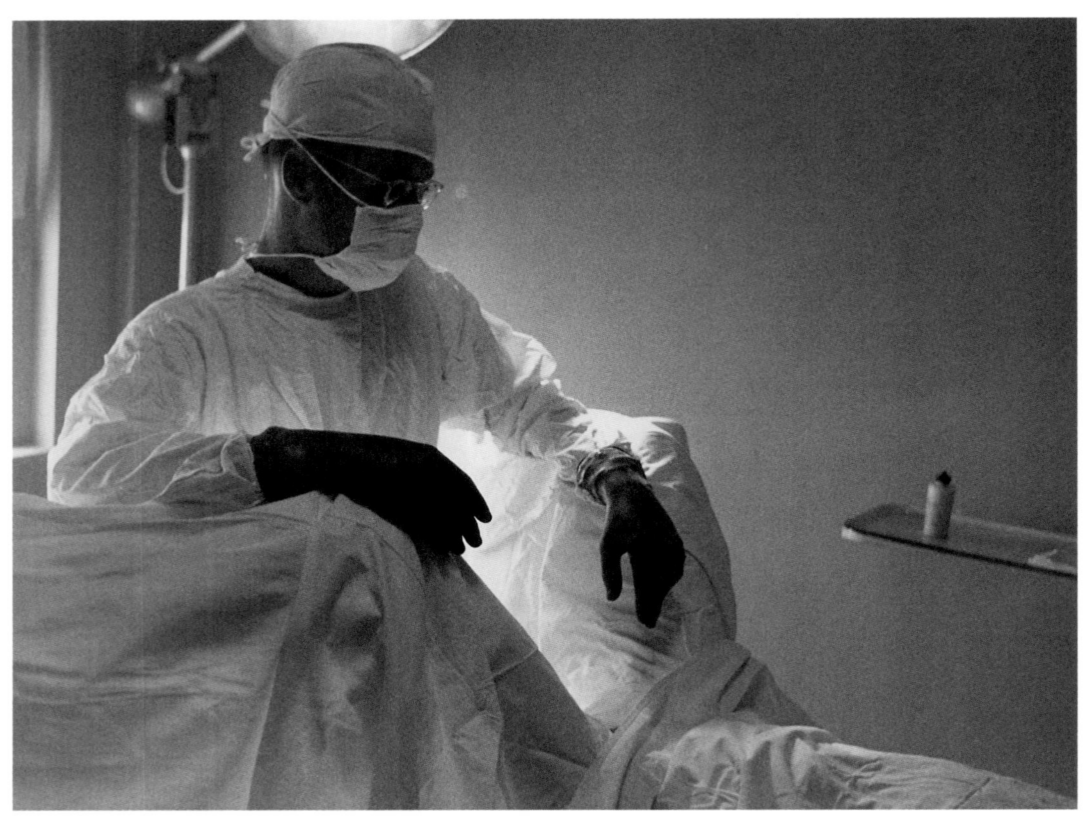

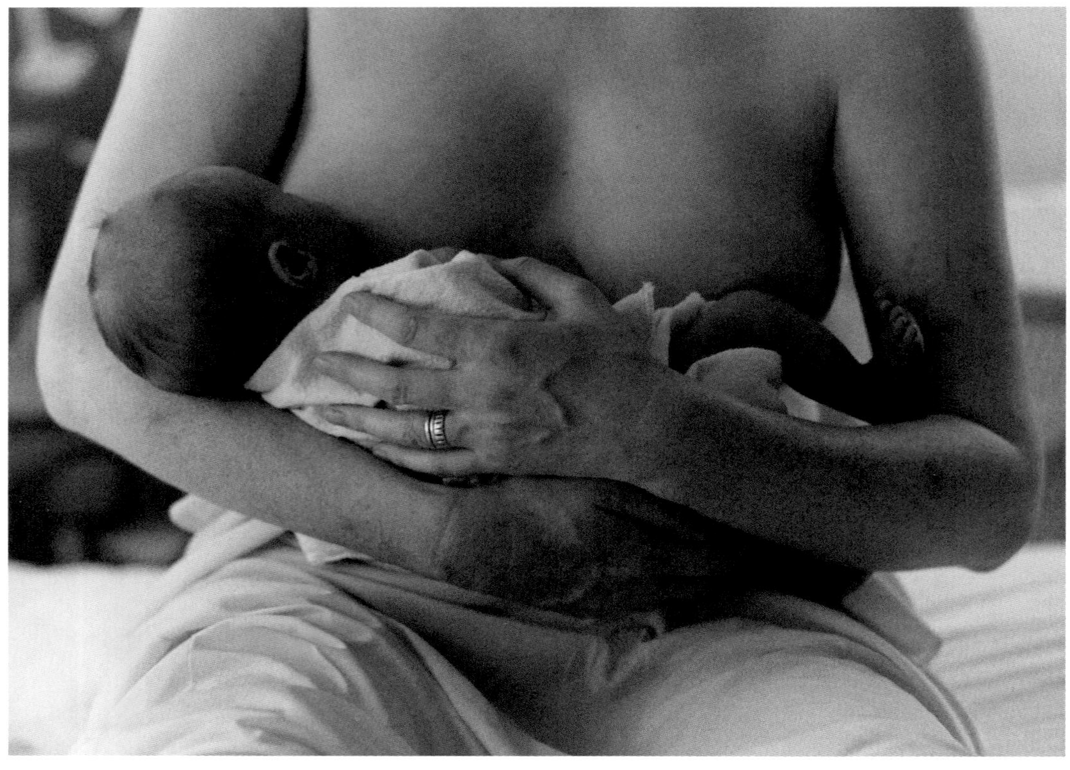

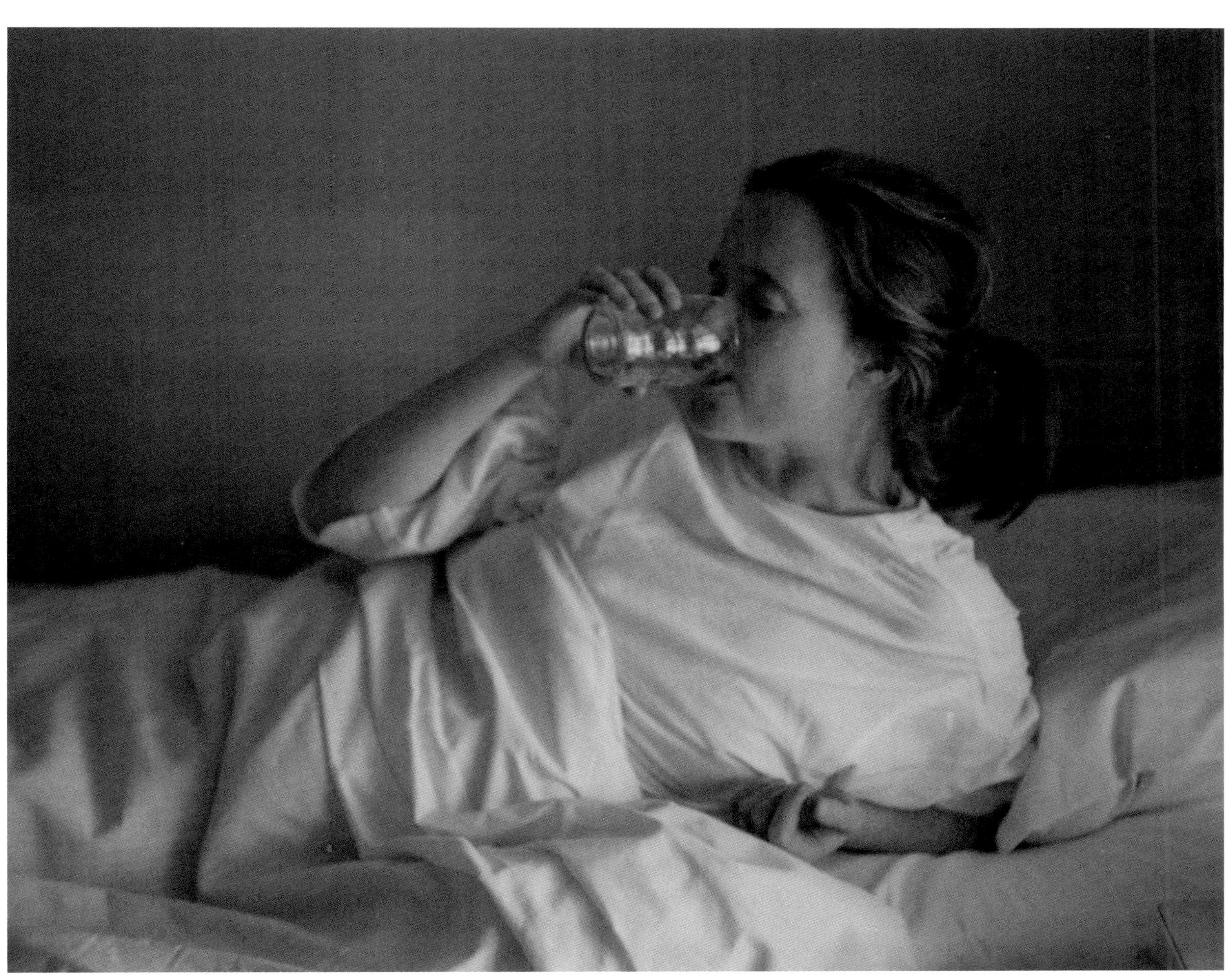

34 *Thirsty.* 1953

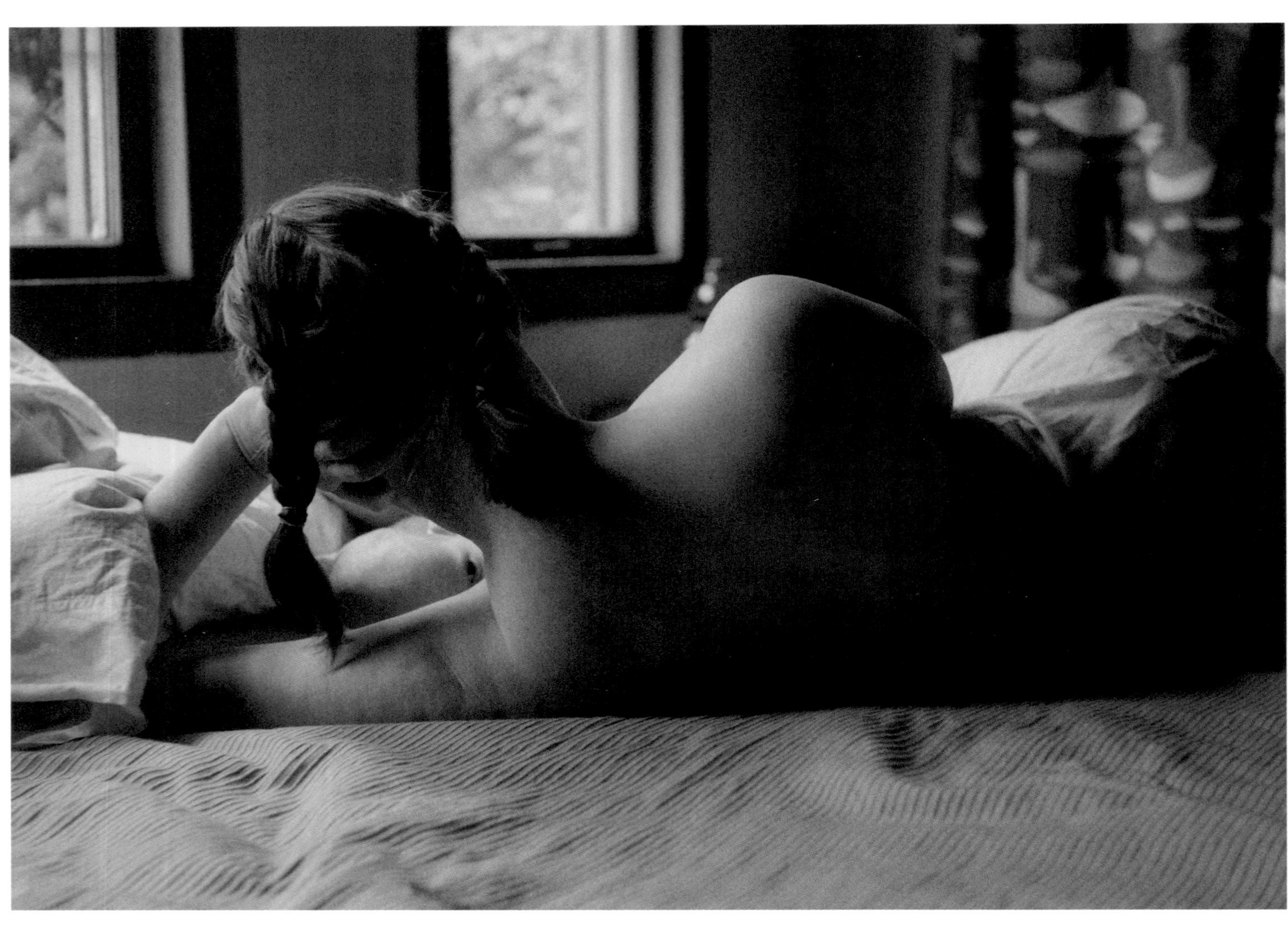

35 *The Eye.* 1953

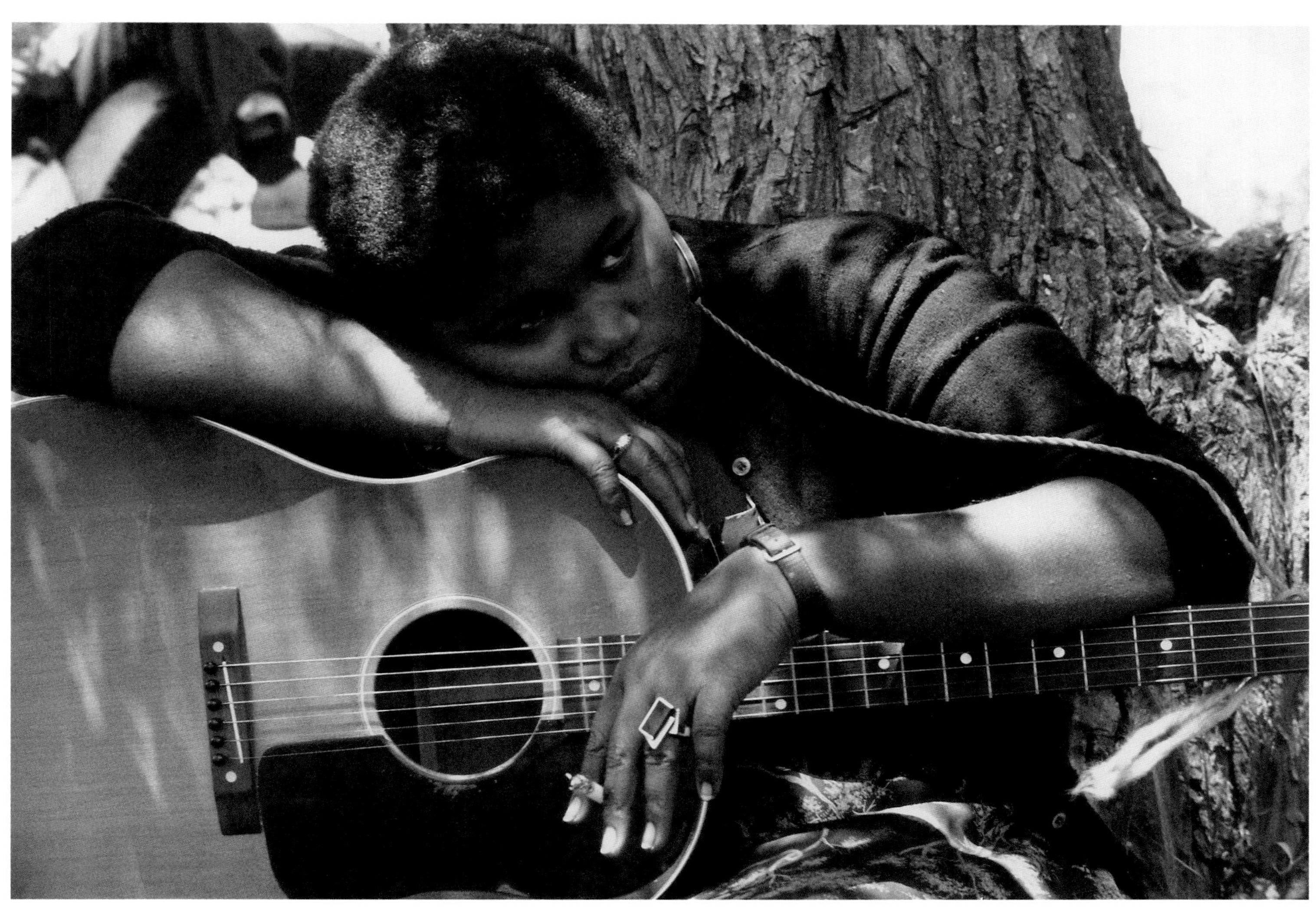

36 *Odetta*, mid-1950s

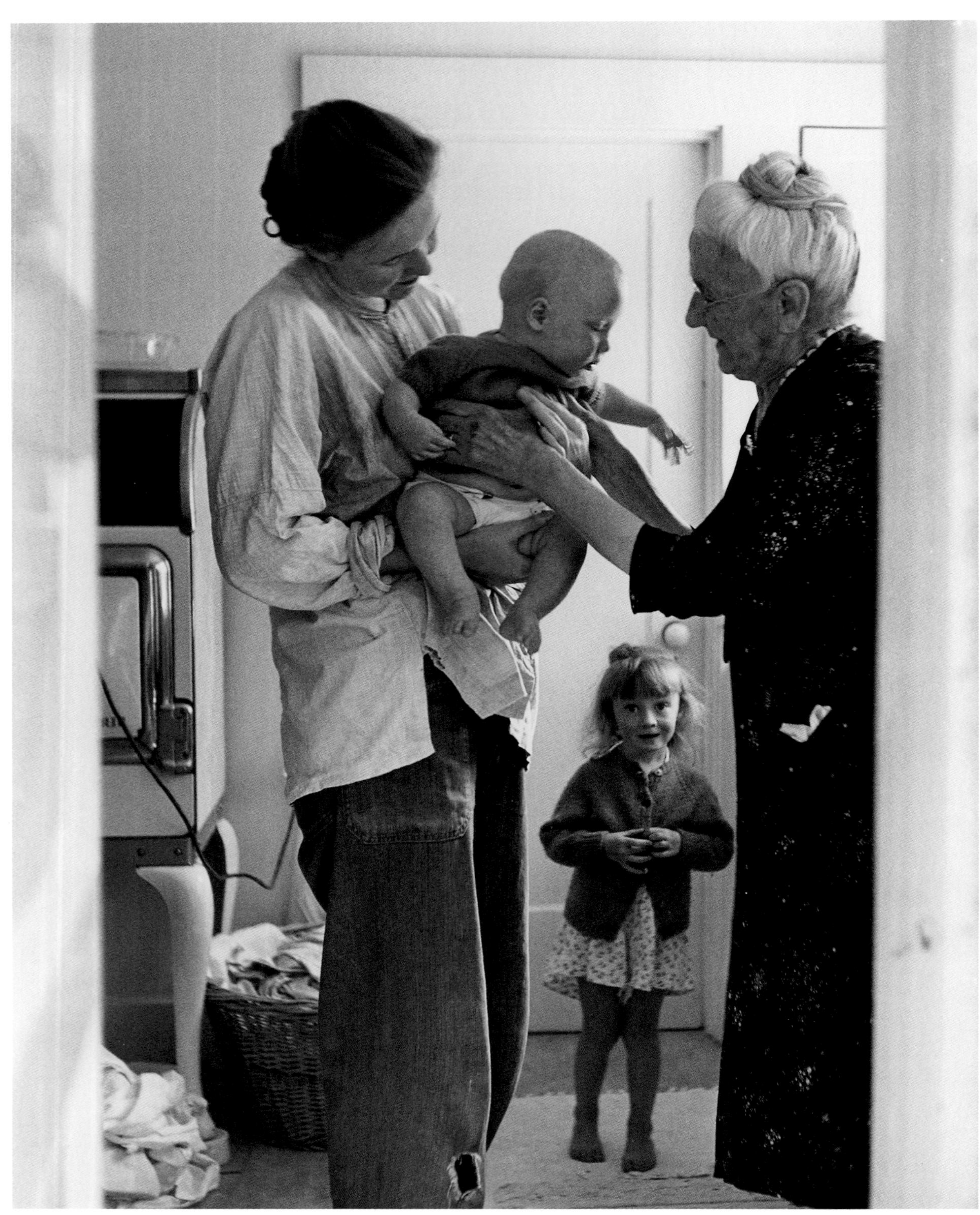

37   *Me Too.* 1948

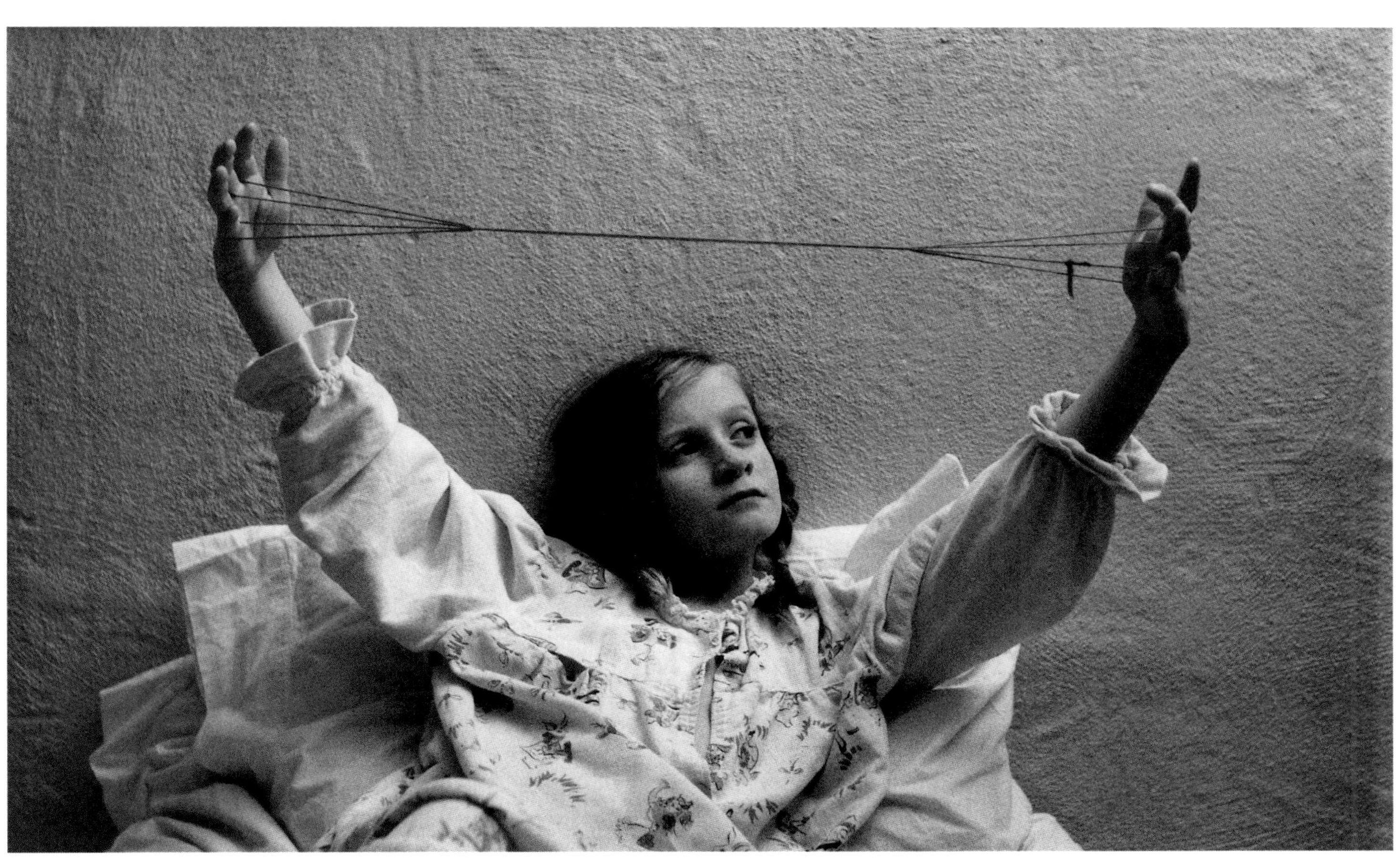

38 *Cat's Cradle. 1952*

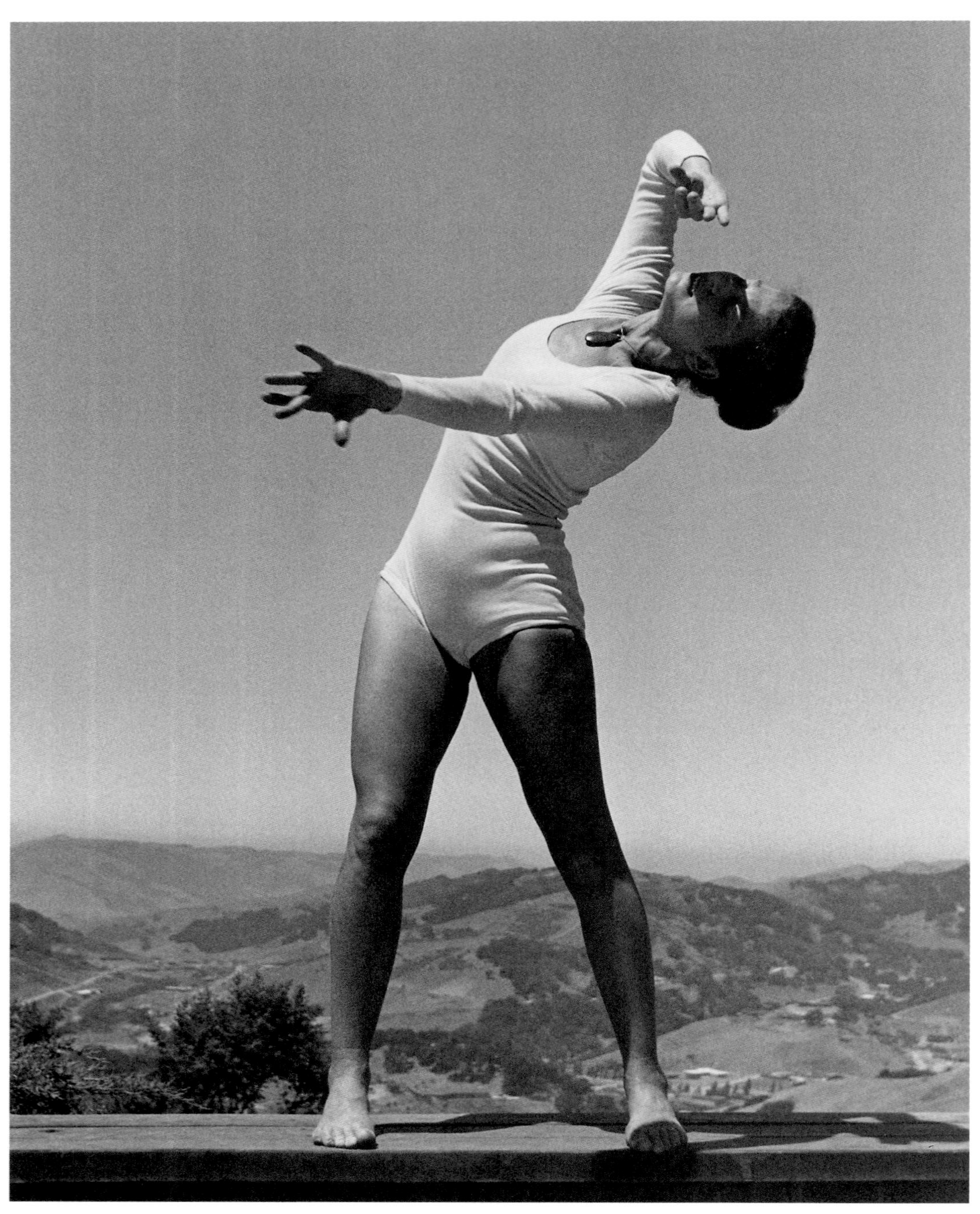

39 *Anna Halprin.* mid-1950s

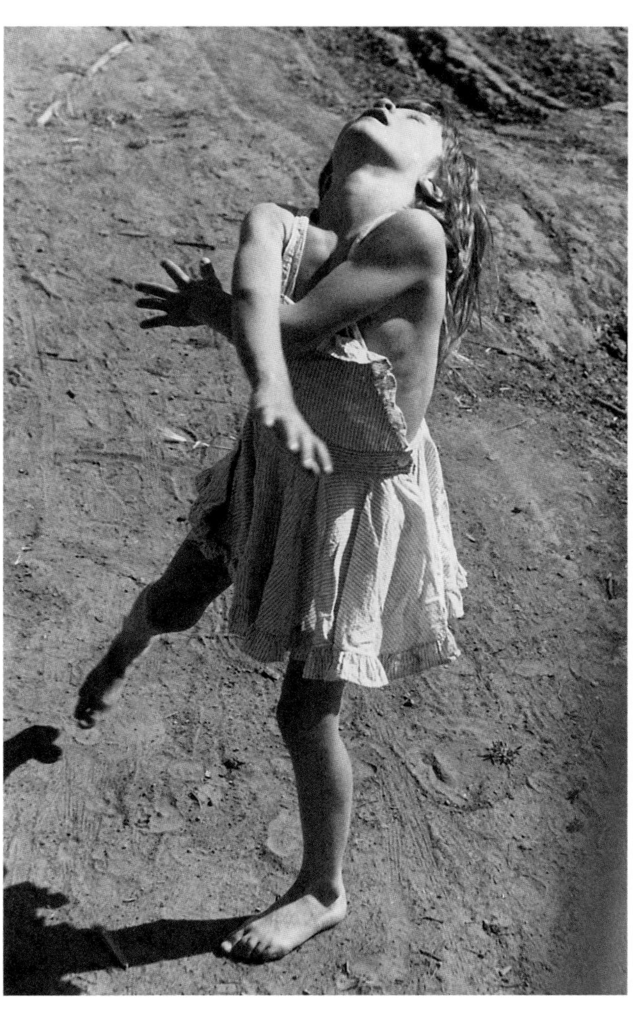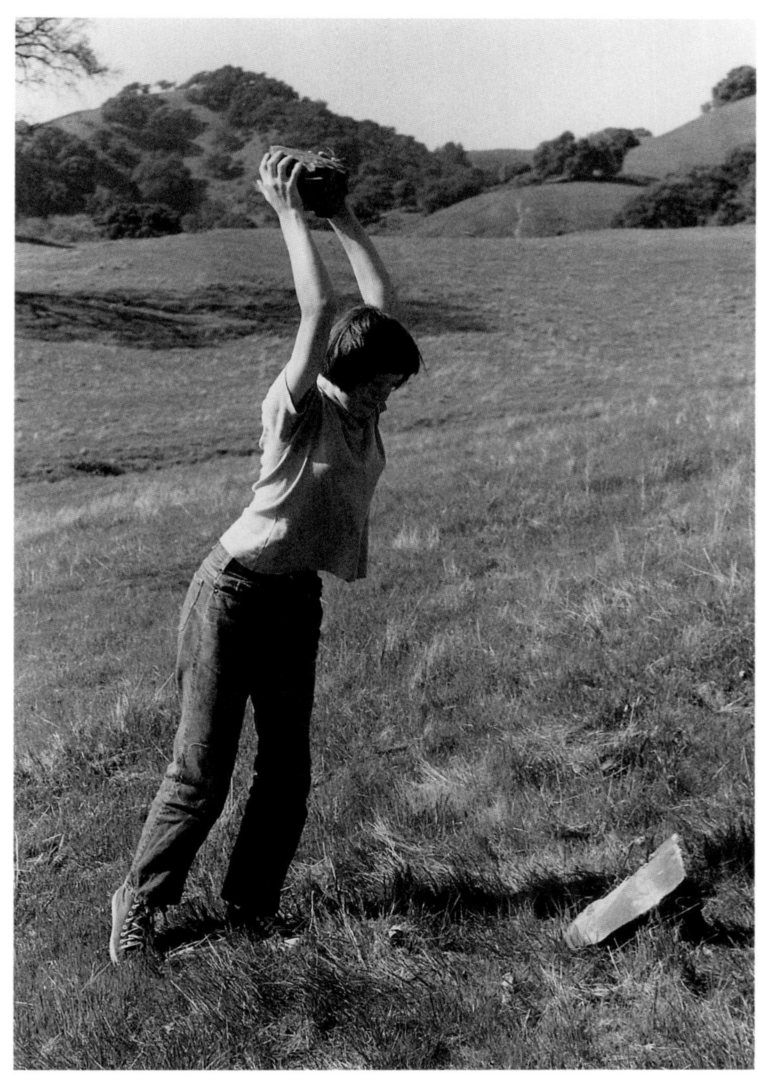

40 *Joan Dancing.* mid-1950s / **41** *Fossil Hunting.* late 1950s

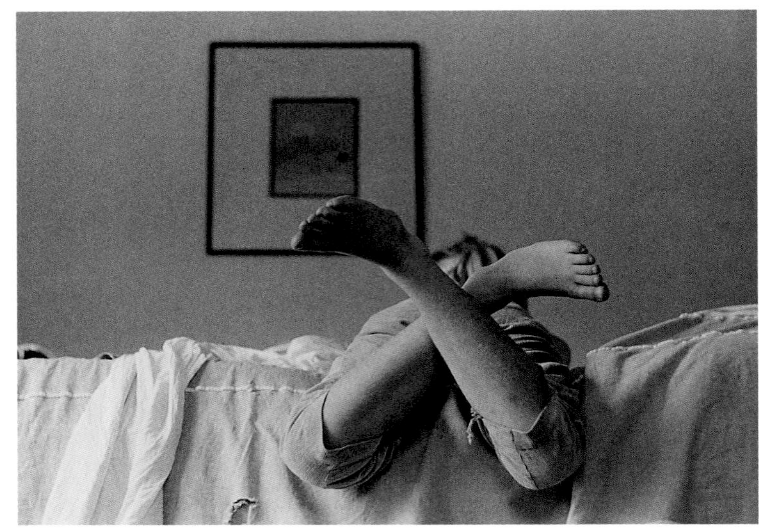

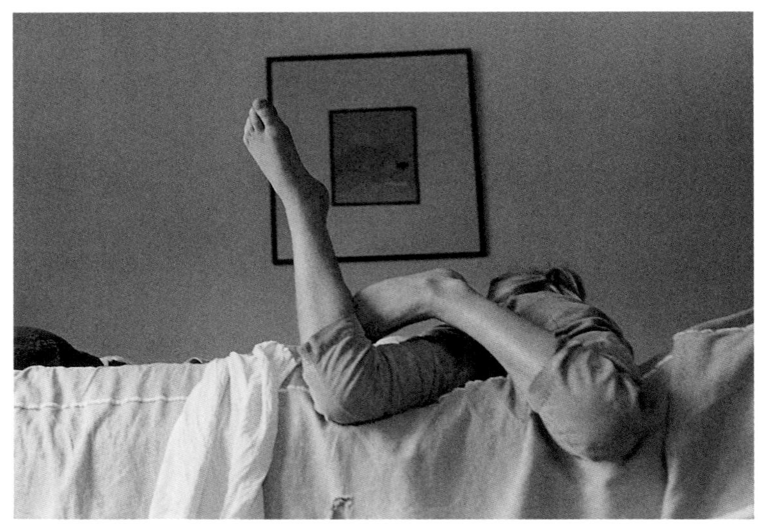

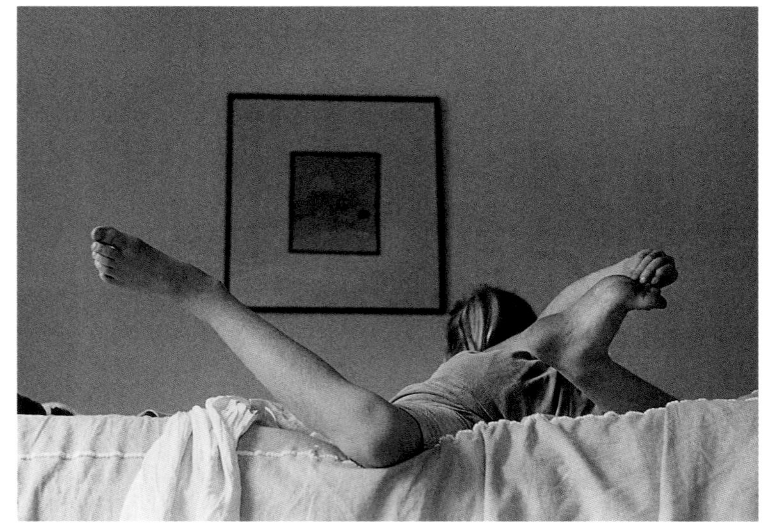

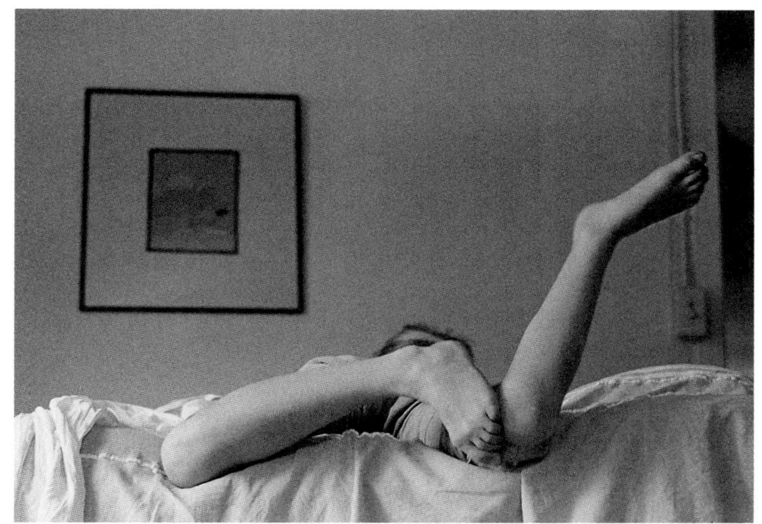

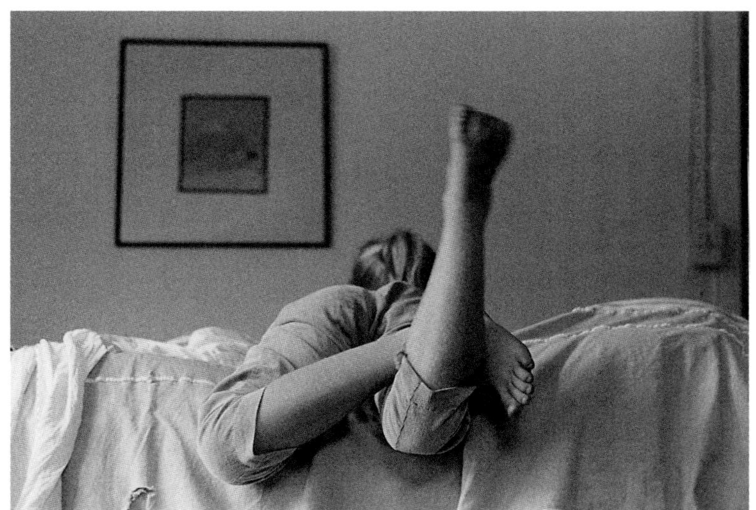

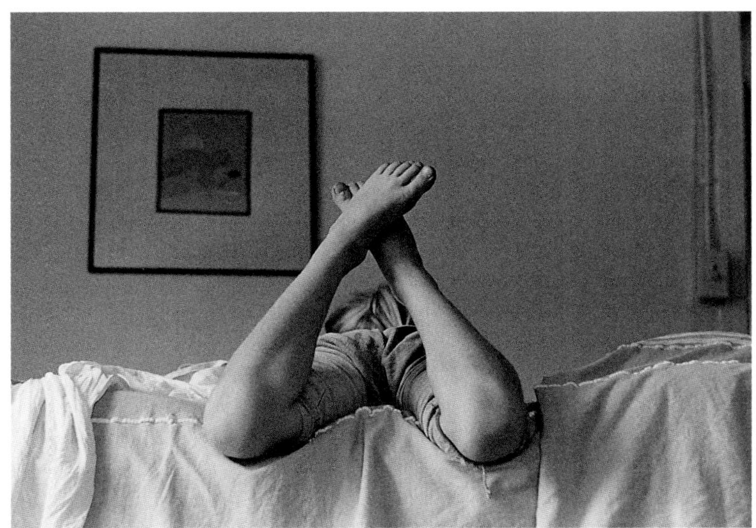

42–47 *Reading* 1–6, late 1950s

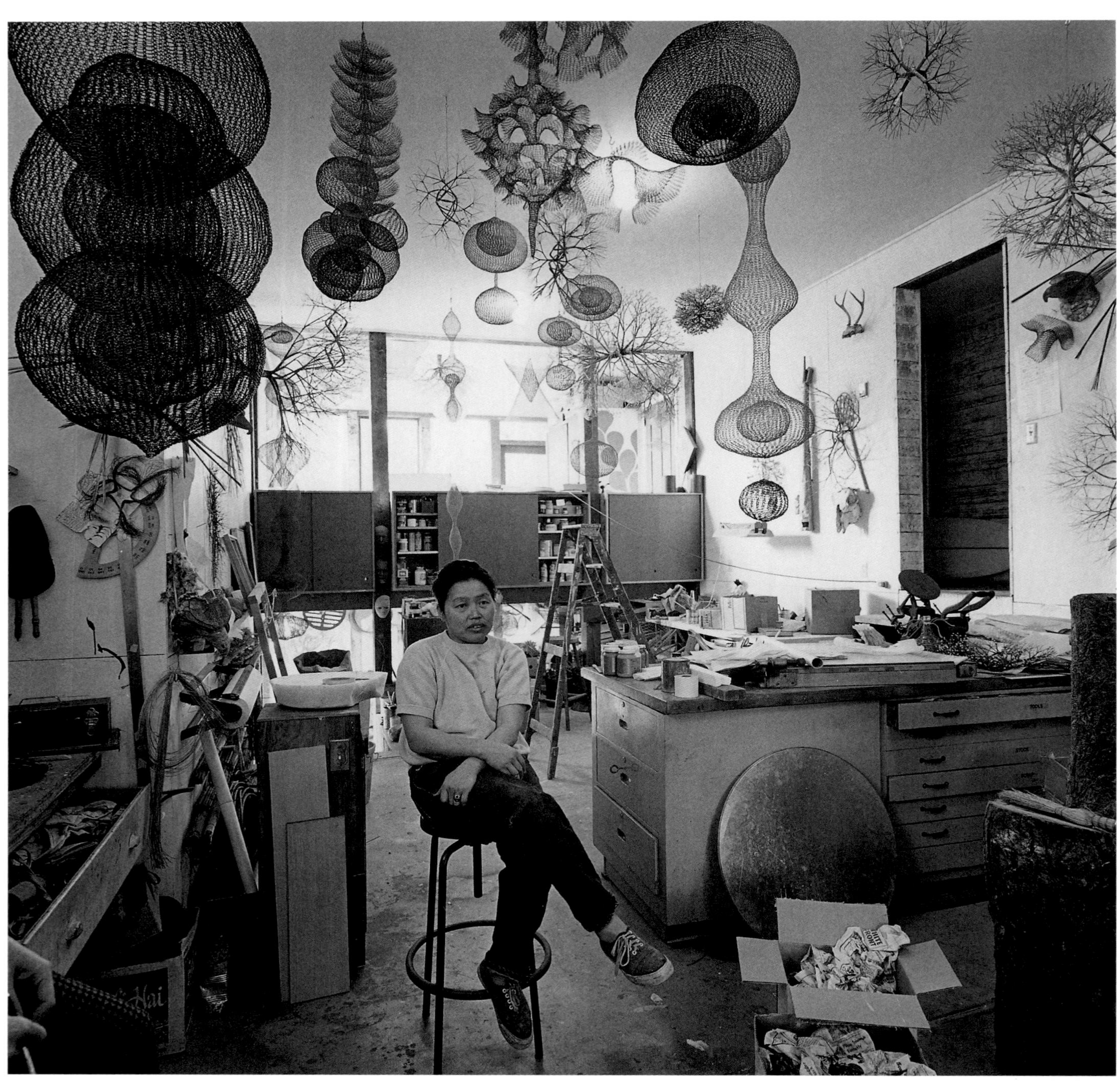

48 *Ruth Asawa in Her Studio*, San Francisco, 1969

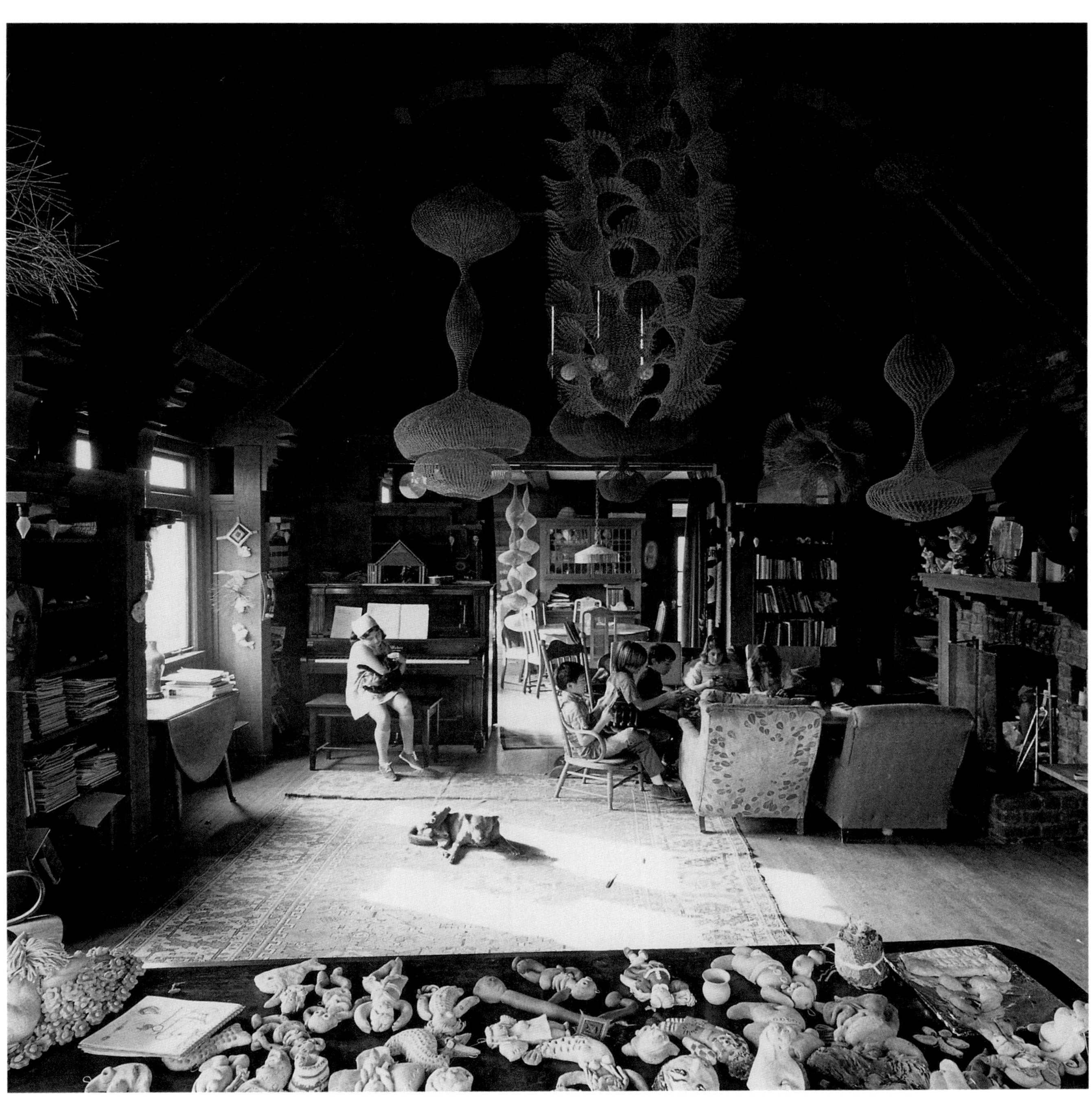

49   *Ruth Asawa's Living Room*. San Francisco. 1969

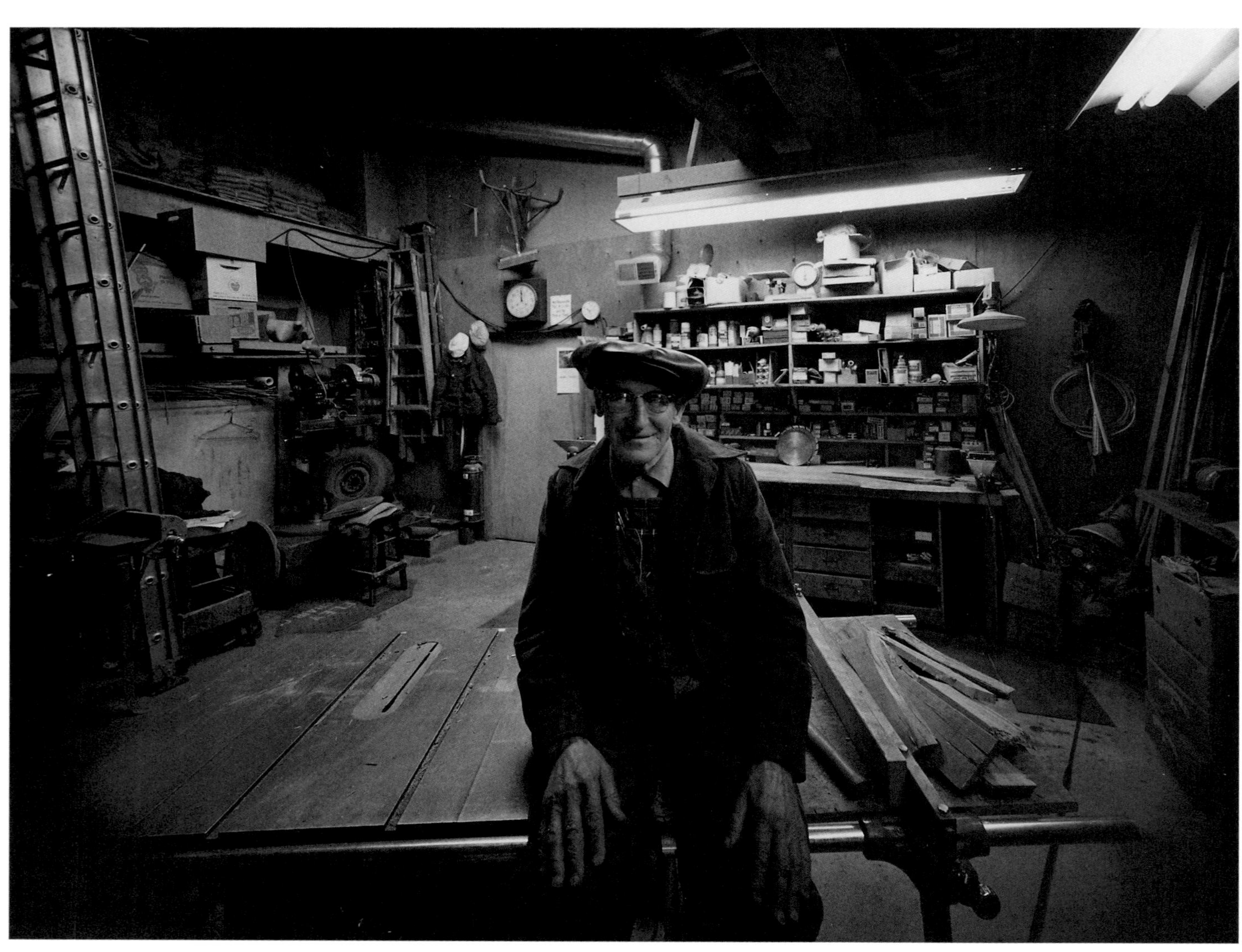

50 *Shop Carpenter*. Berkeley. California. late 1980s

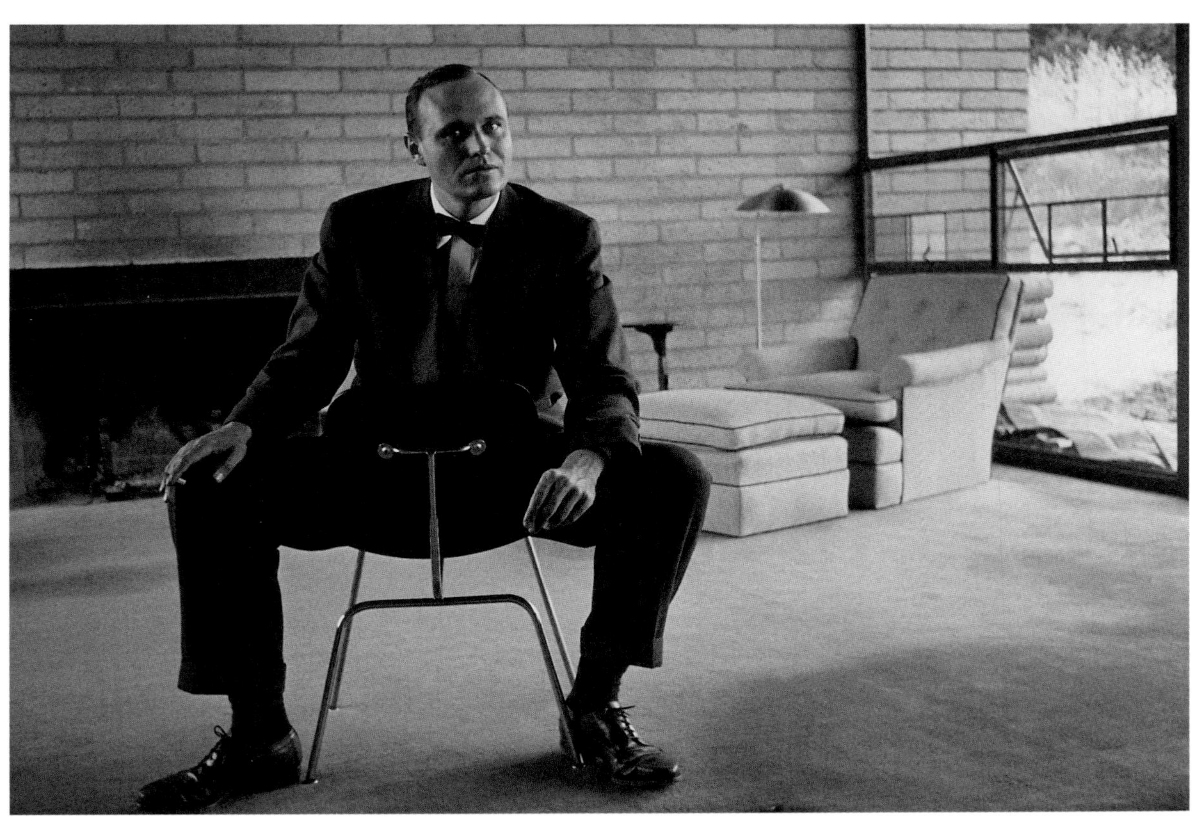

51   *John Warneke.* San Francisco, early 1960s

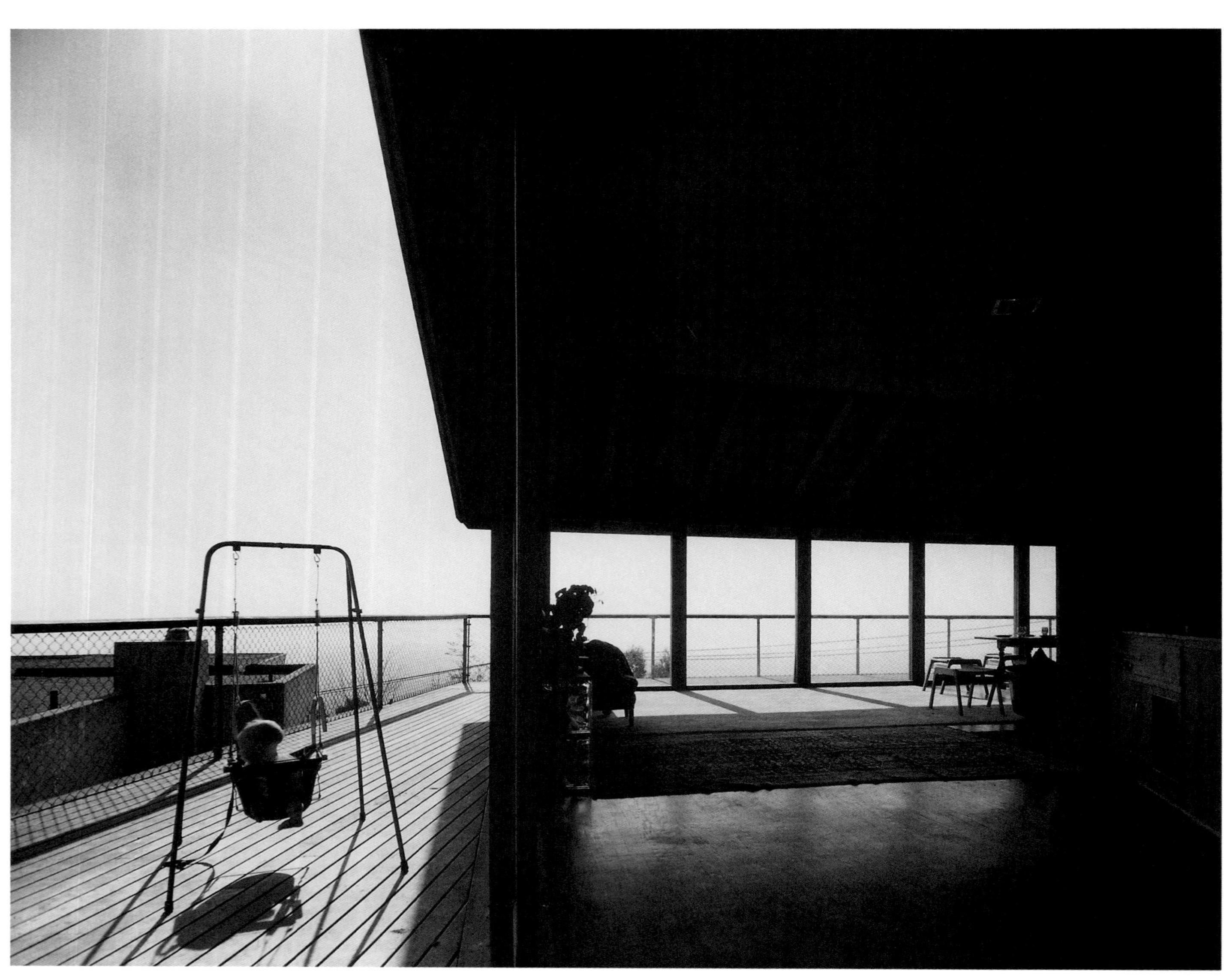

52 *Ratcliff House*, Berkeley, California, 1951

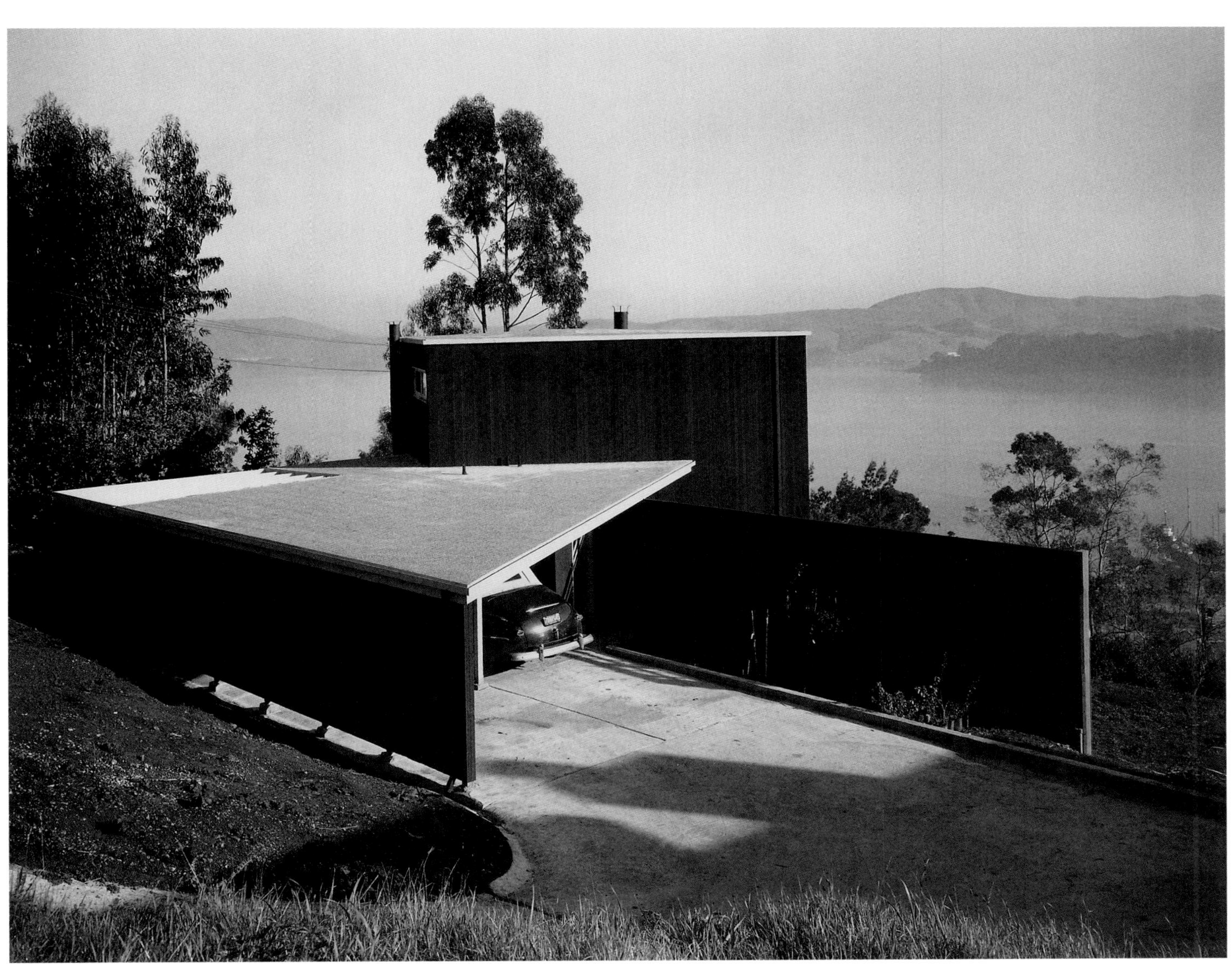

53 *Corbett House*, Tiburon, California, n.d.

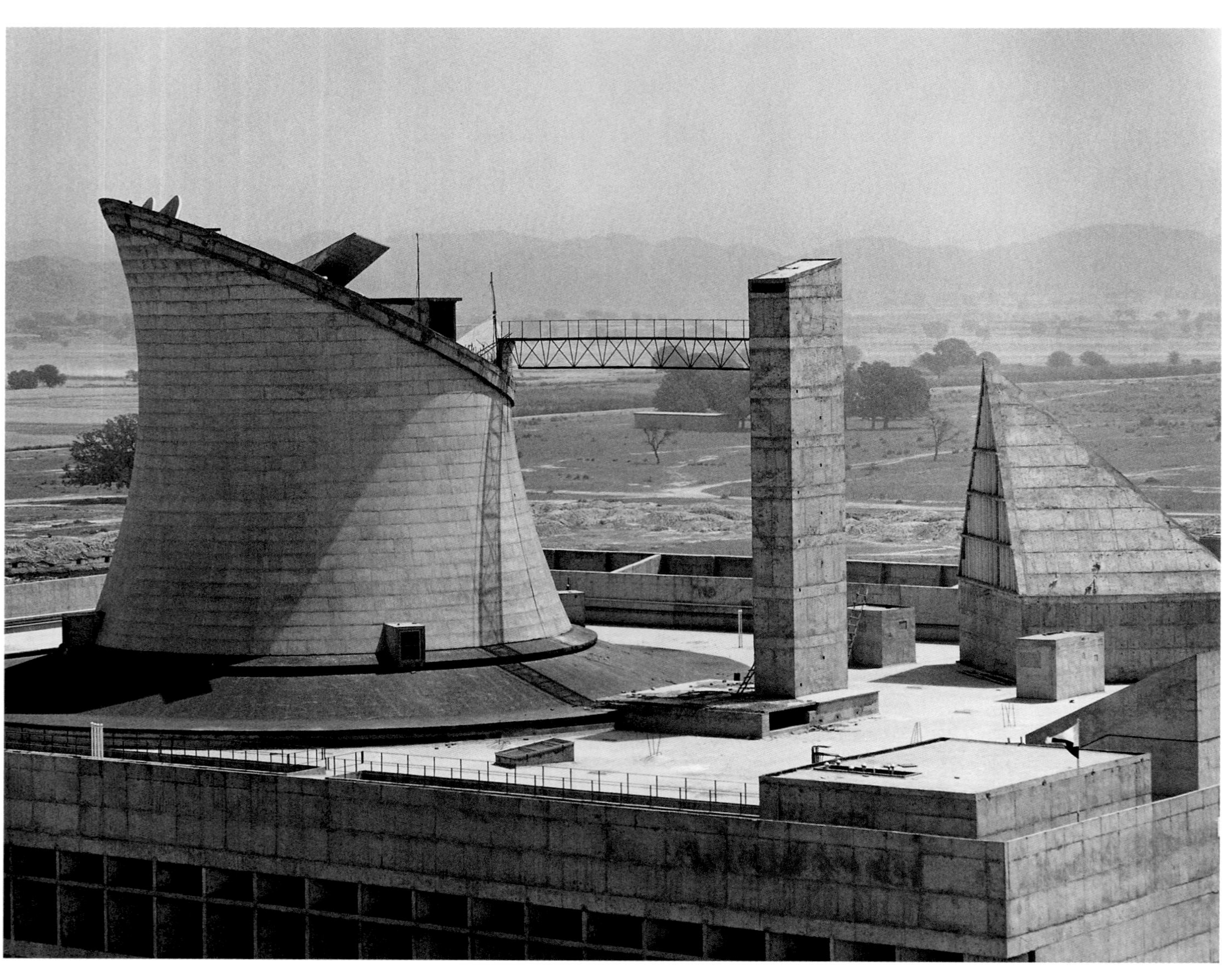

54   *The Secretariat*. Chandigarh. India. 1962

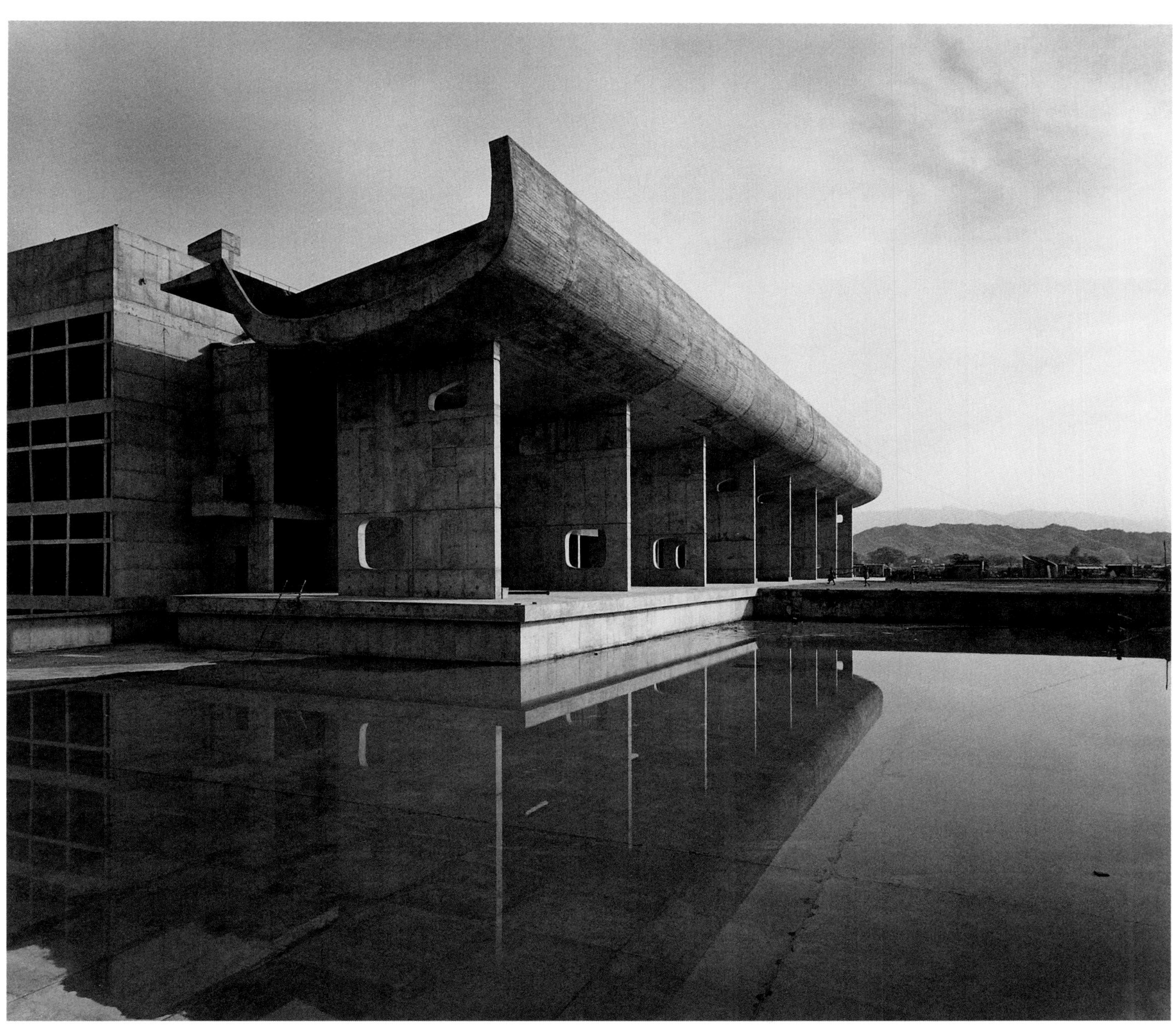

55 *Assembly Building*, Chandigarh, India, 1962

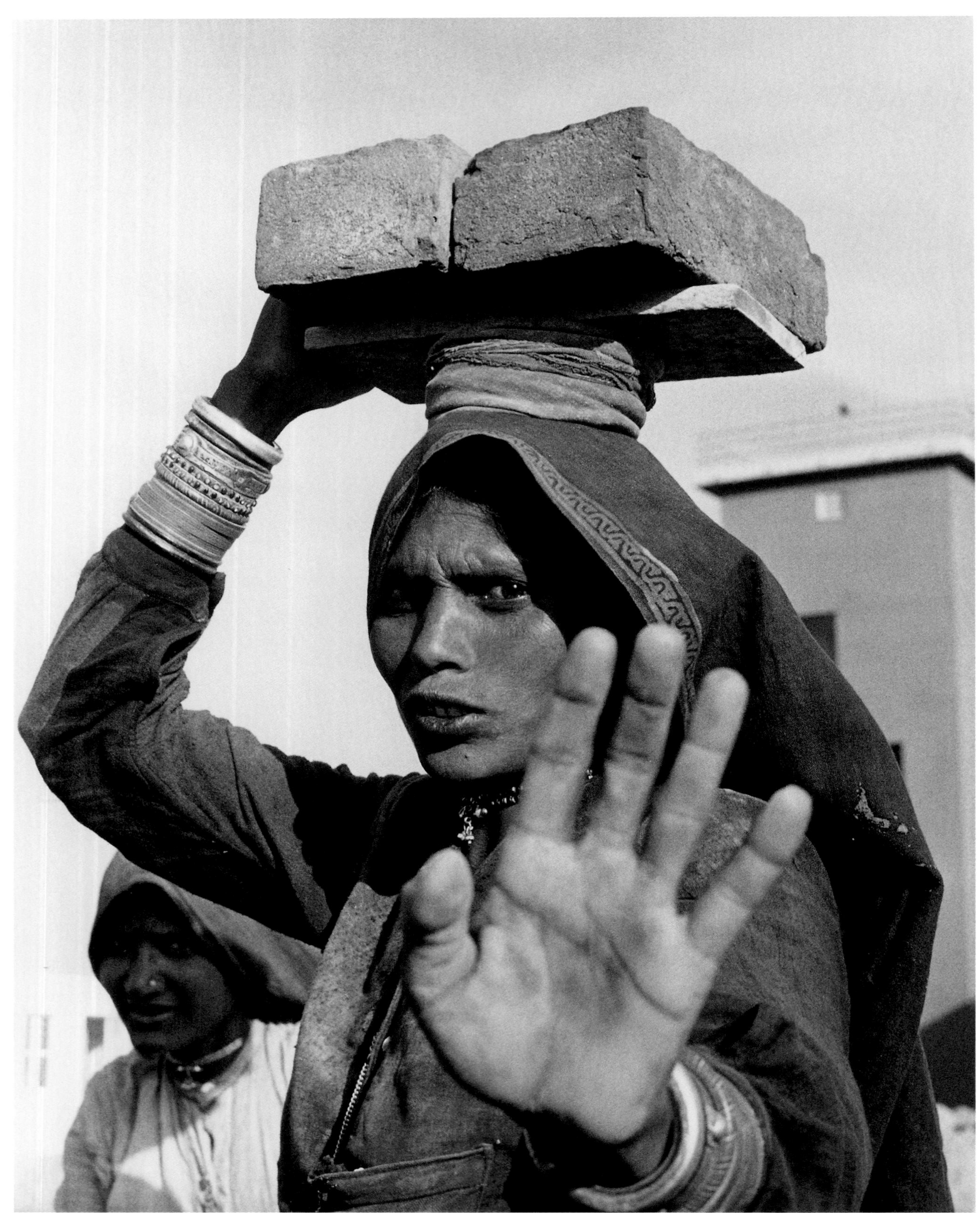

56 *Brickyard Worker. New Delhi. 1962*

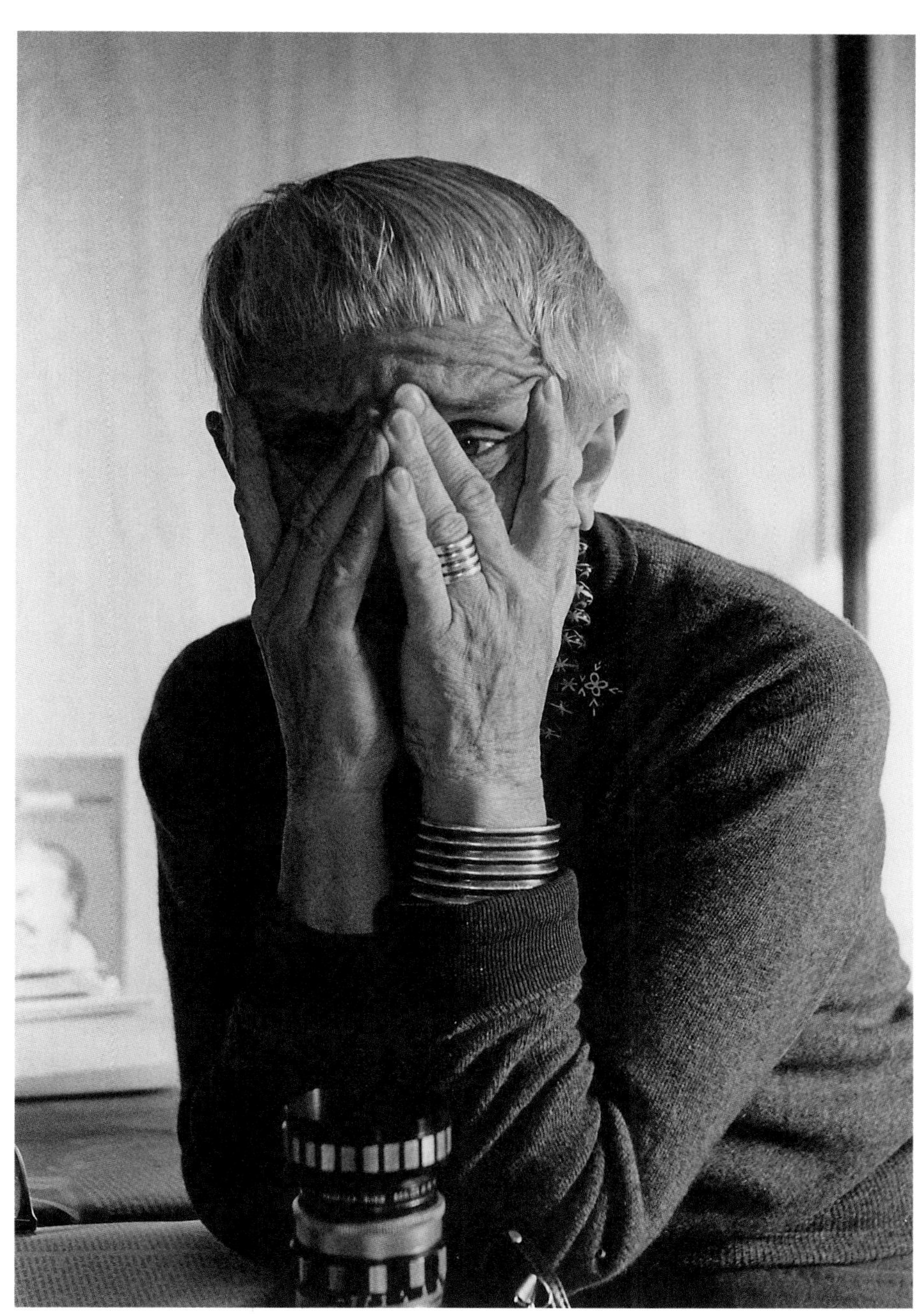

57   *Dorothea Lange.* early 1960s

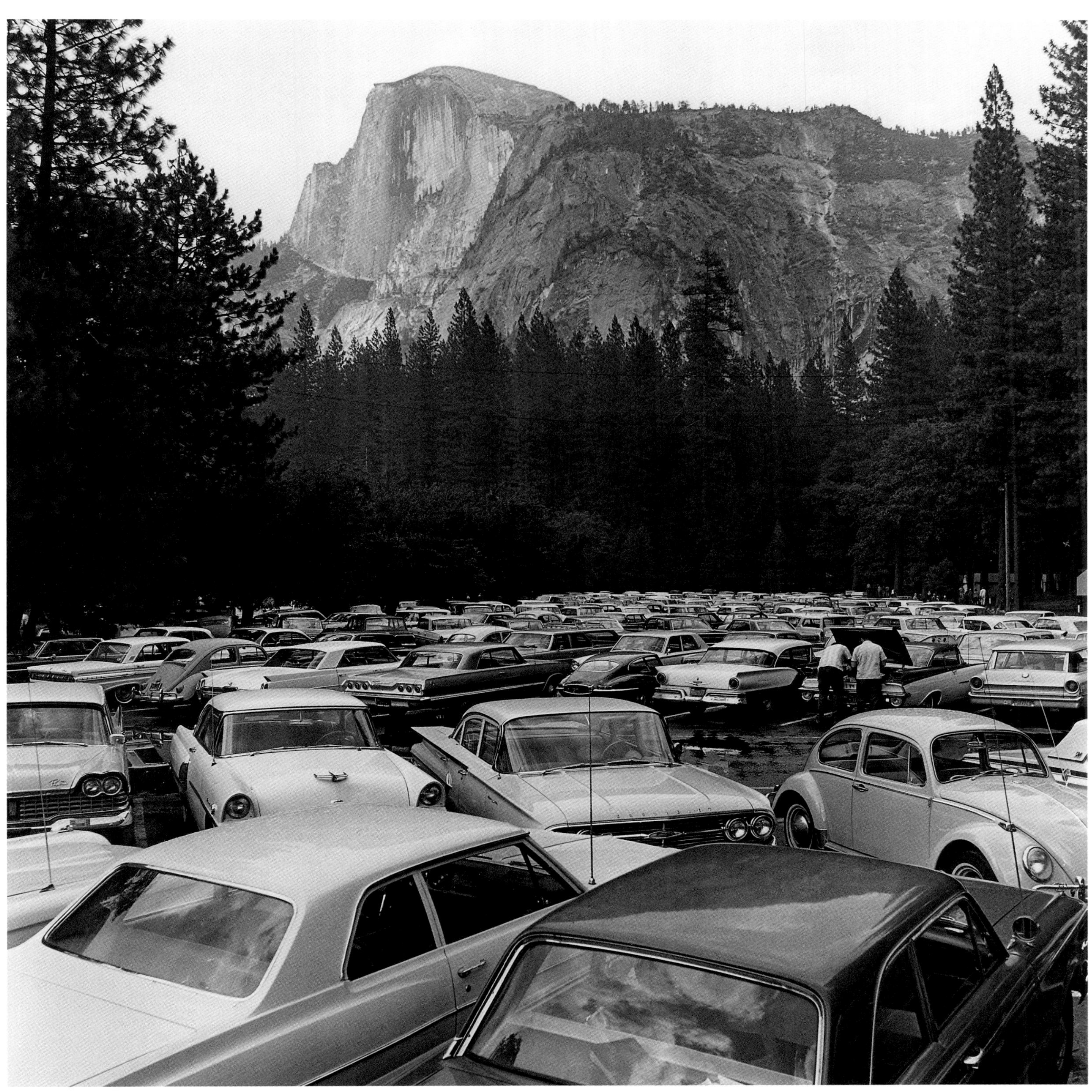

58 *Pave It and Paint It Green*, Yosemite National Park, mid-1960s

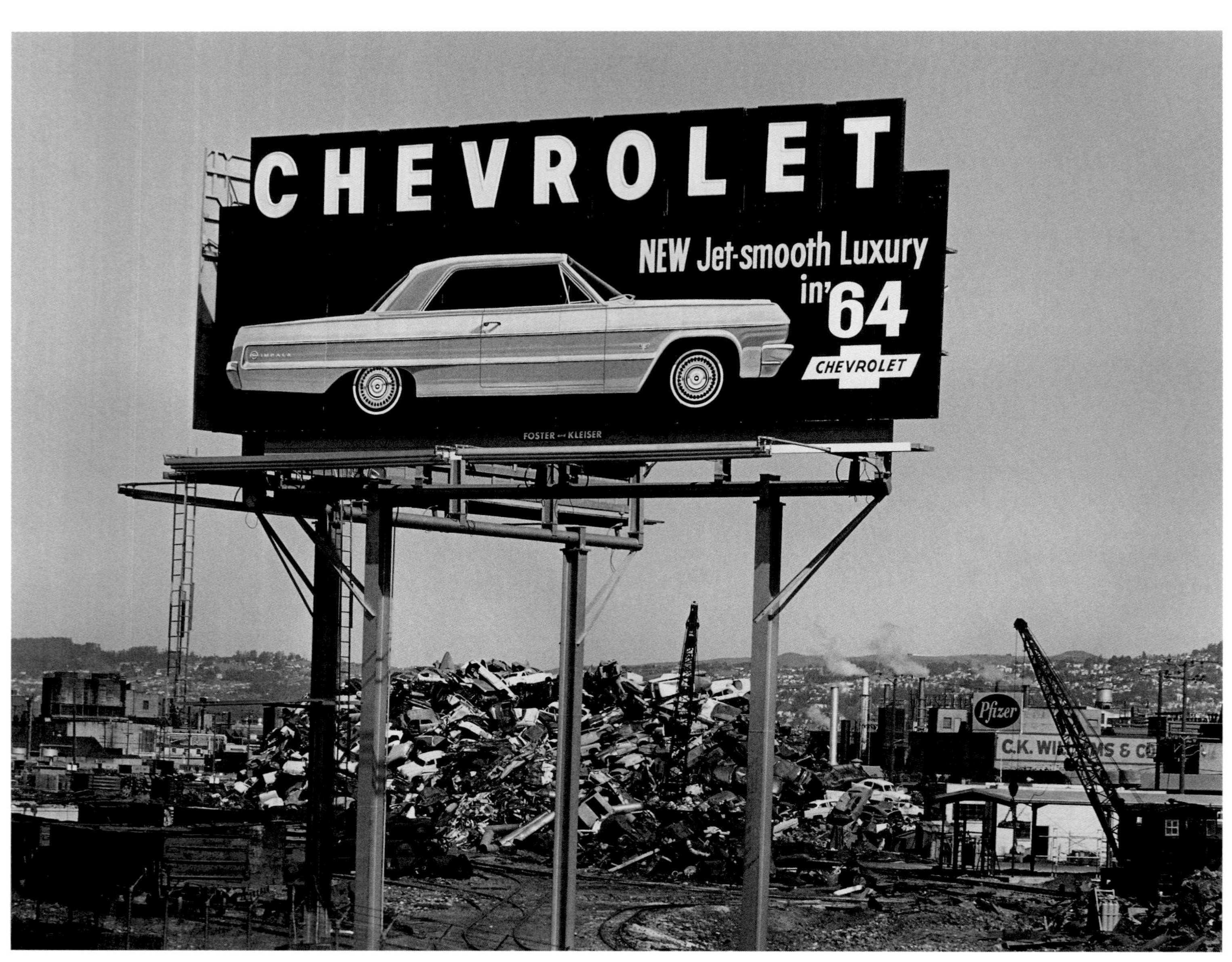

59 *New Chevy.* Emeryville. California. 1964

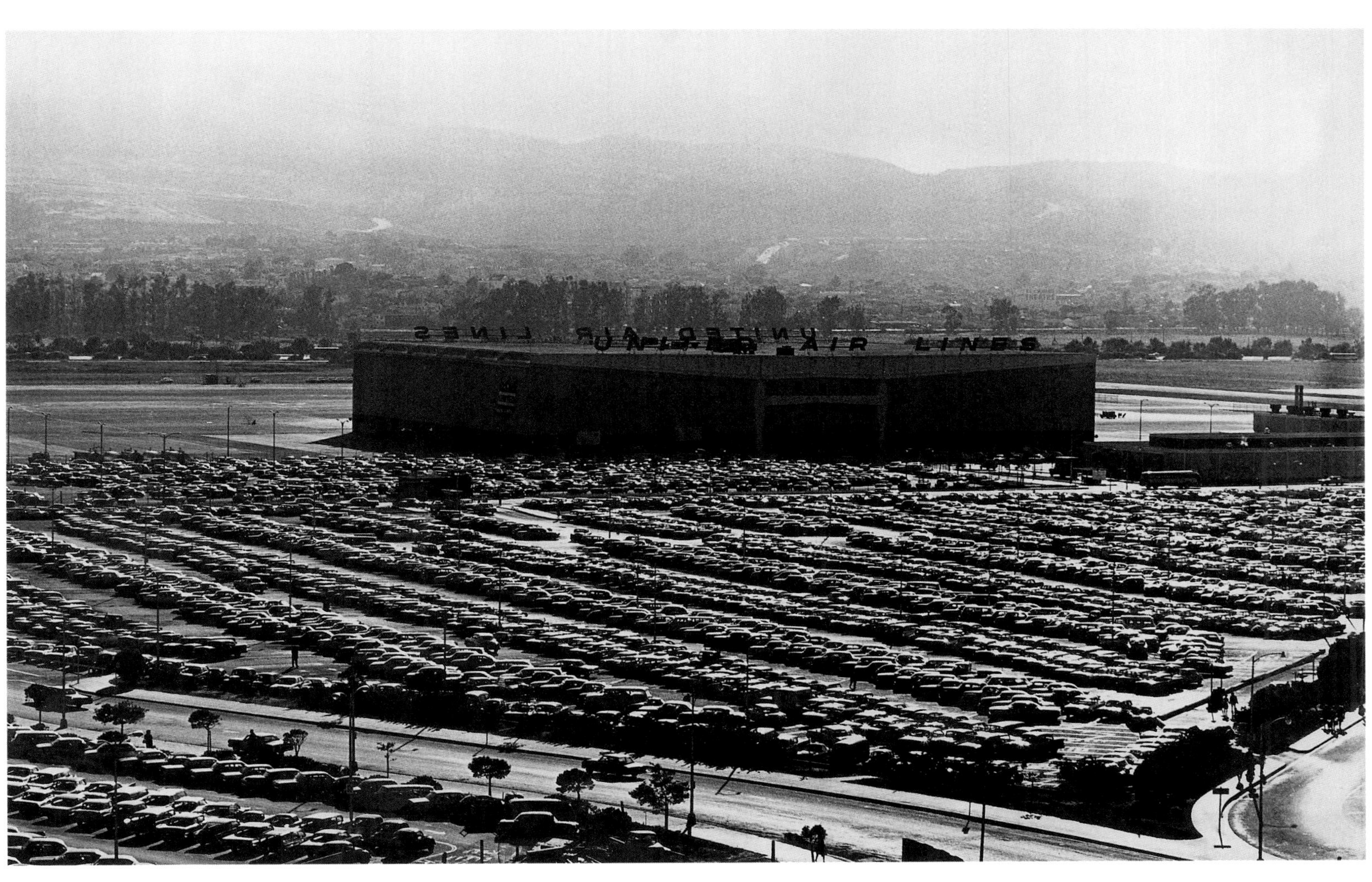

60   *Airport Parking.* San Francisco. 1965

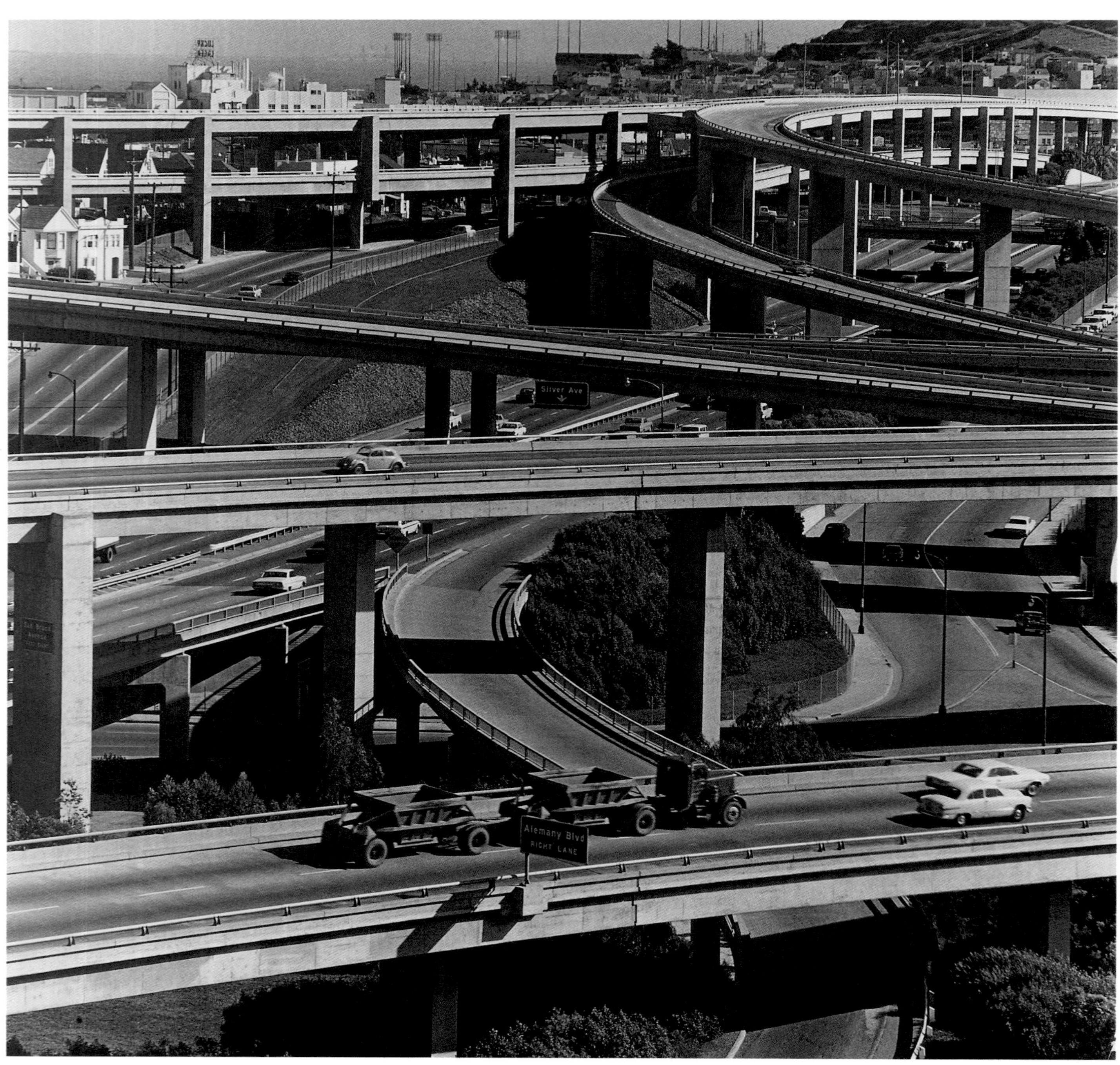

61 *Freeway*, San Francisco, late 1960s

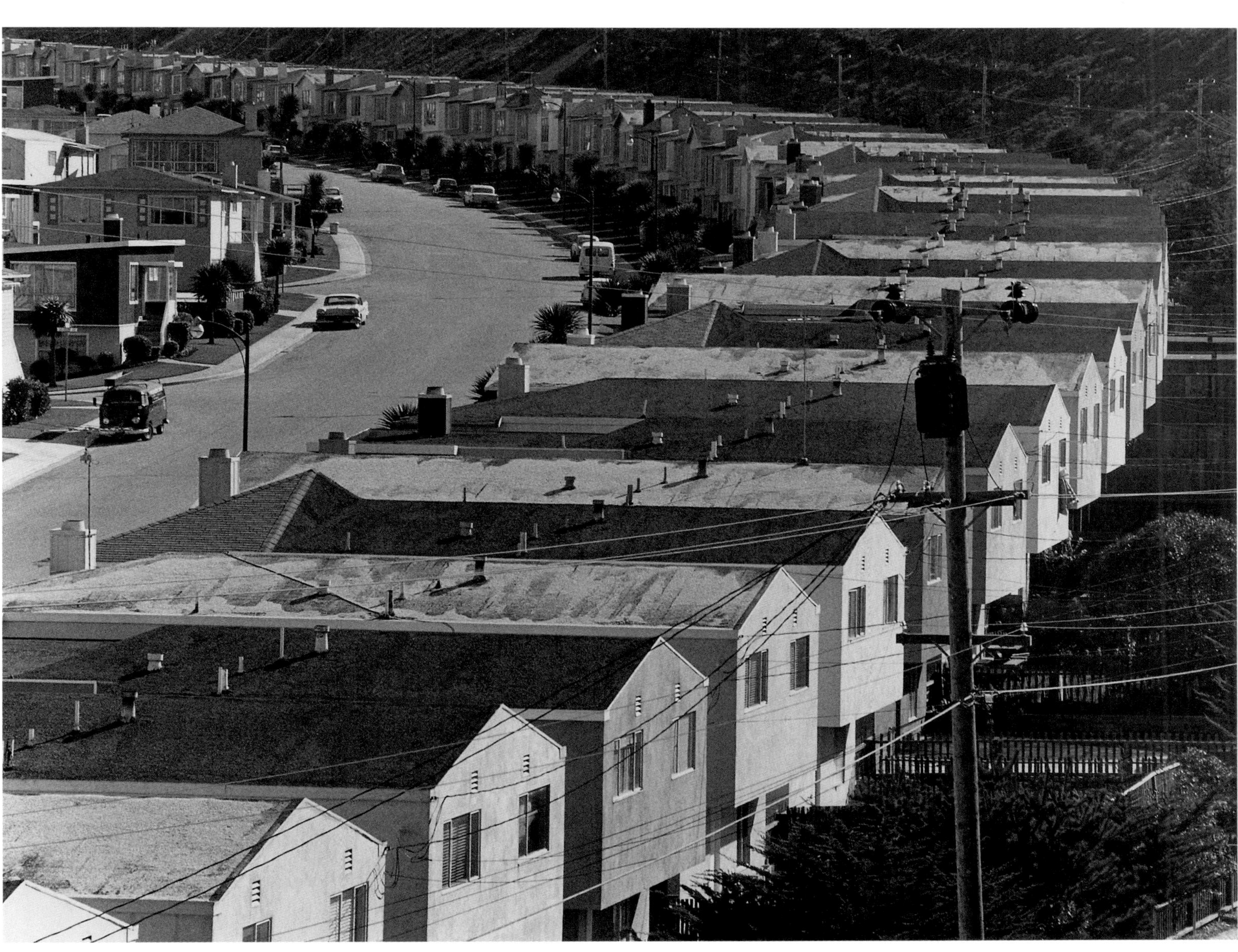

 Housing. Daly City, California, late 1960s

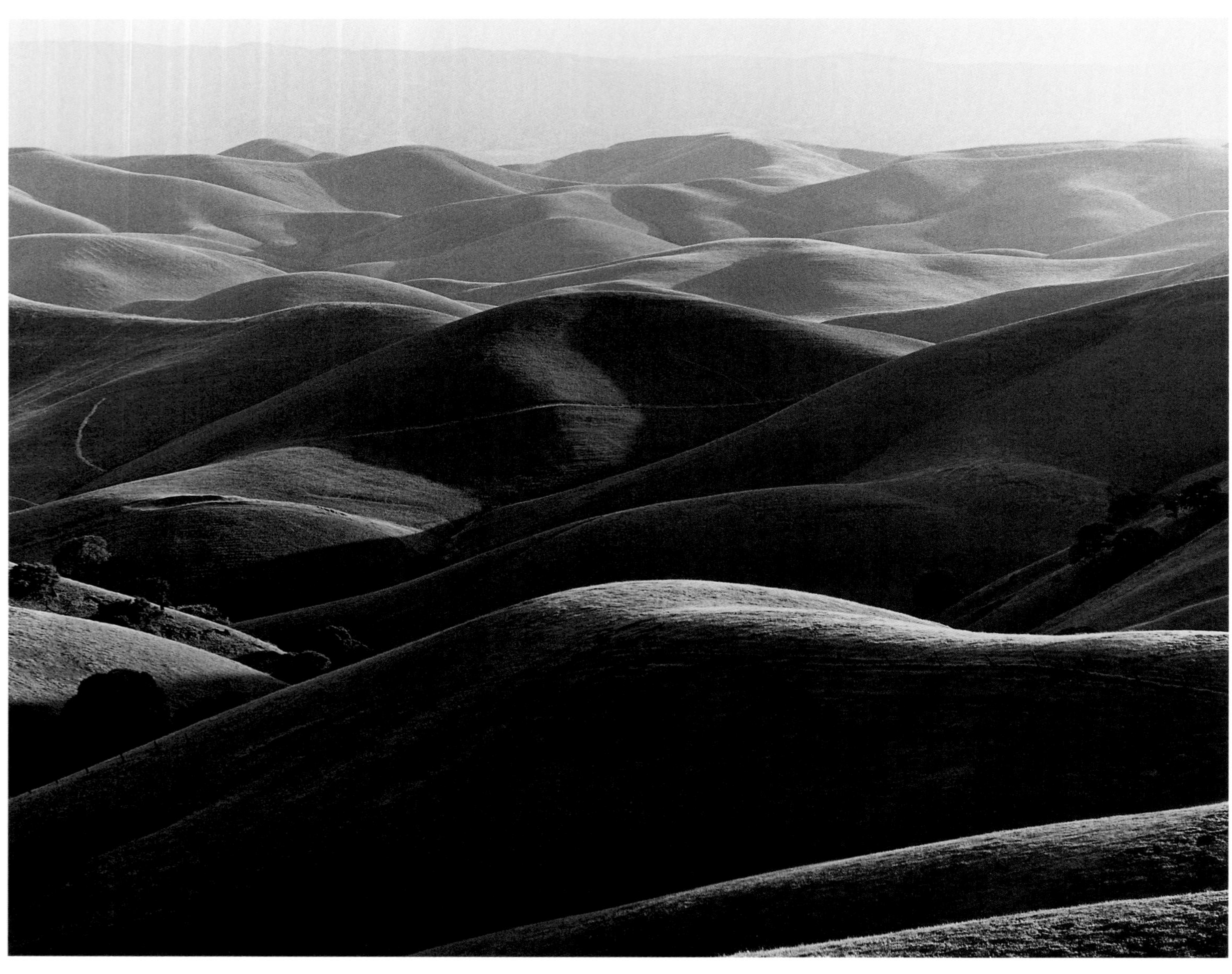

63 *Rolling Hills*. Danville. California. 1958

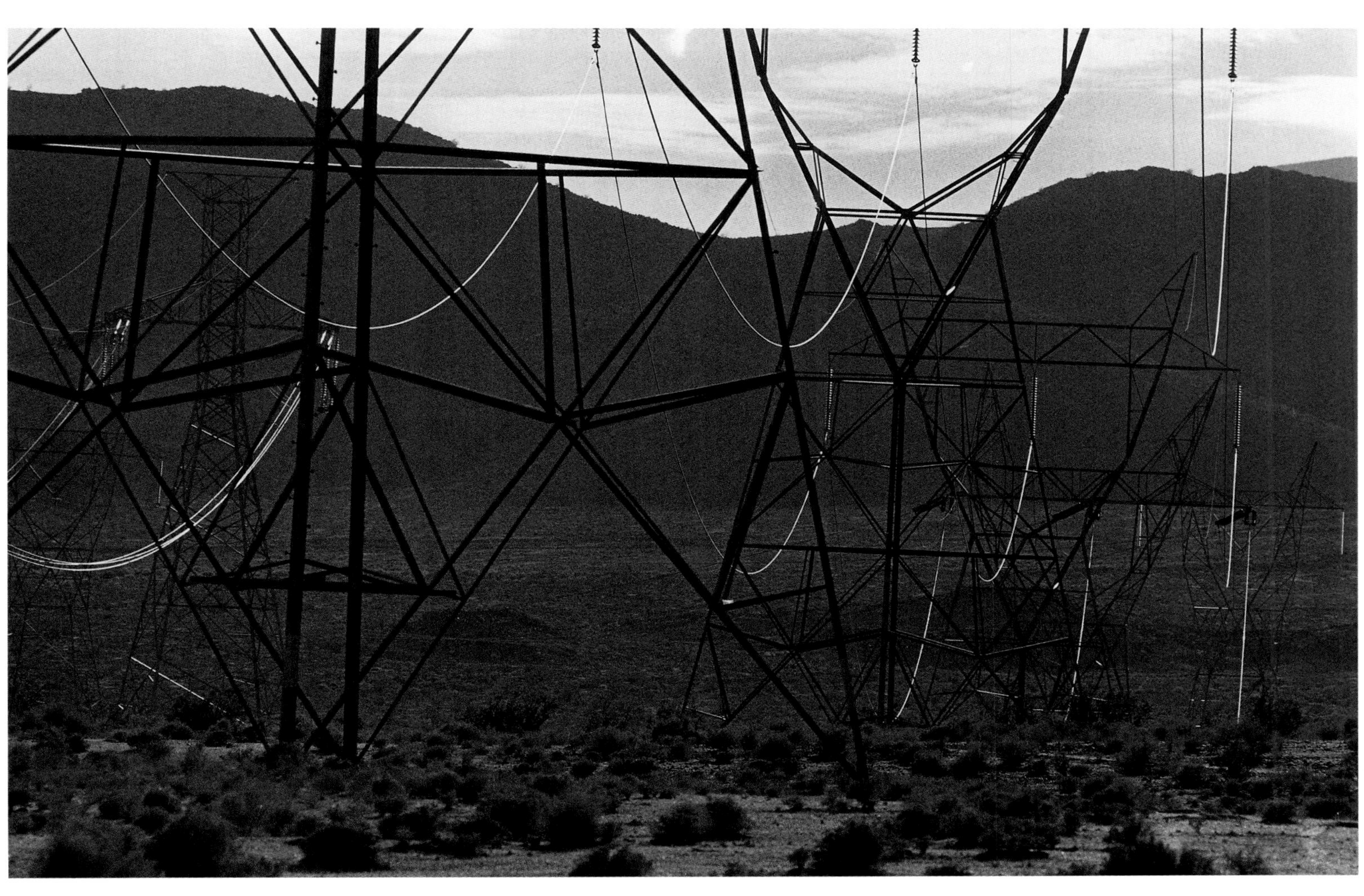

64 *Power Grid*, Southern California, early 1970s

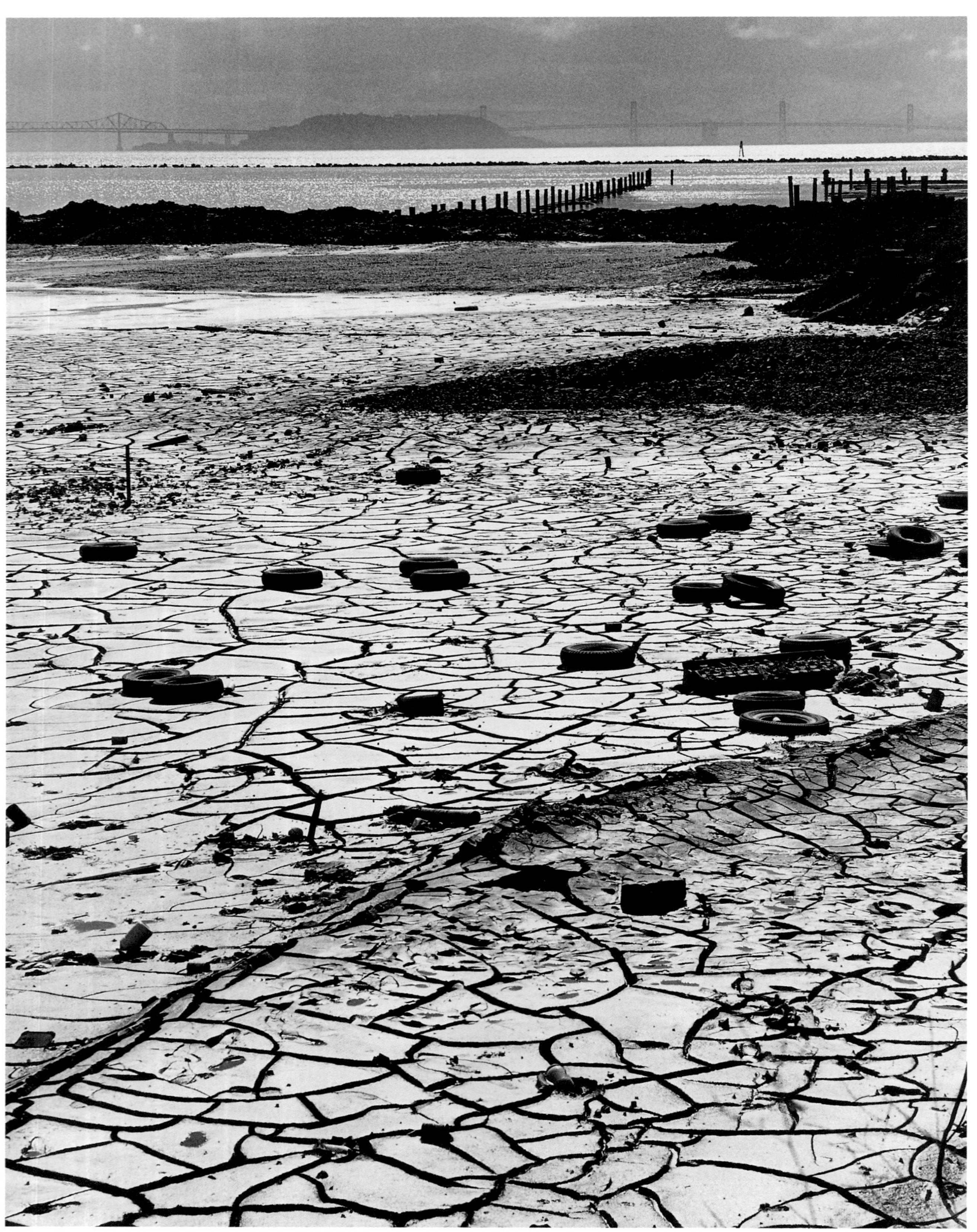

65 *Modern Midden*. Albany. California. 1965

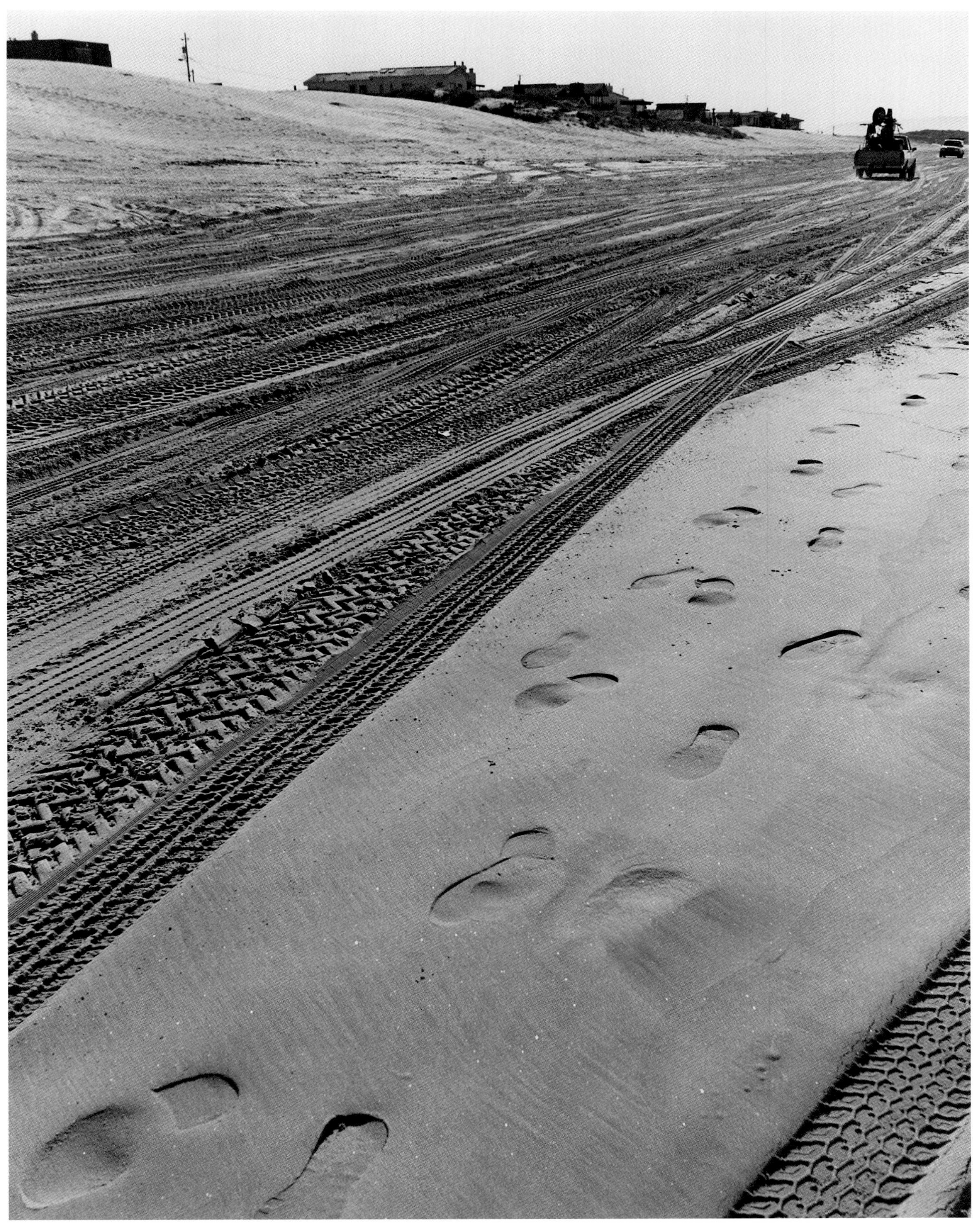

66 *Tire Marks*, Pismo Beach, California, late 1960s

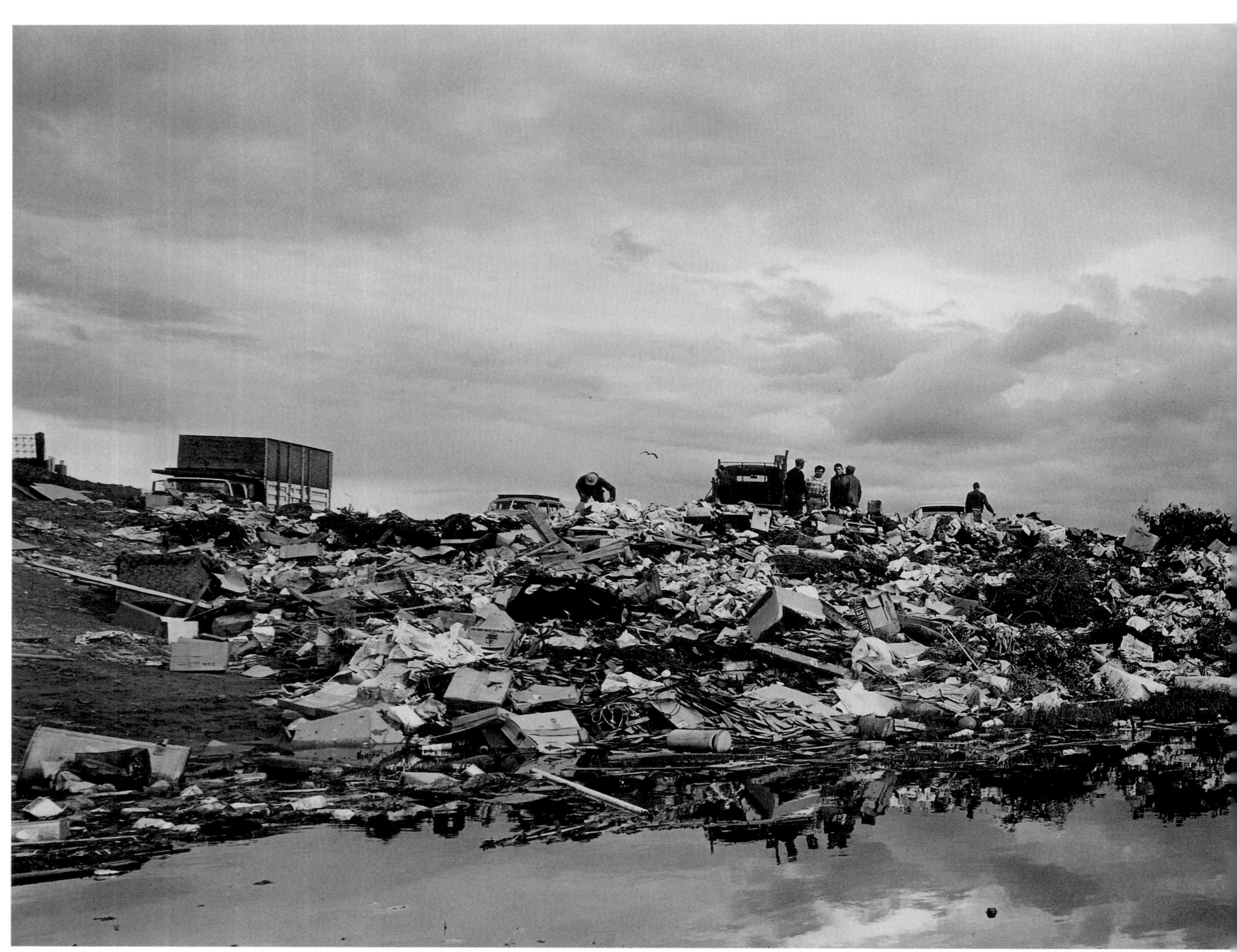

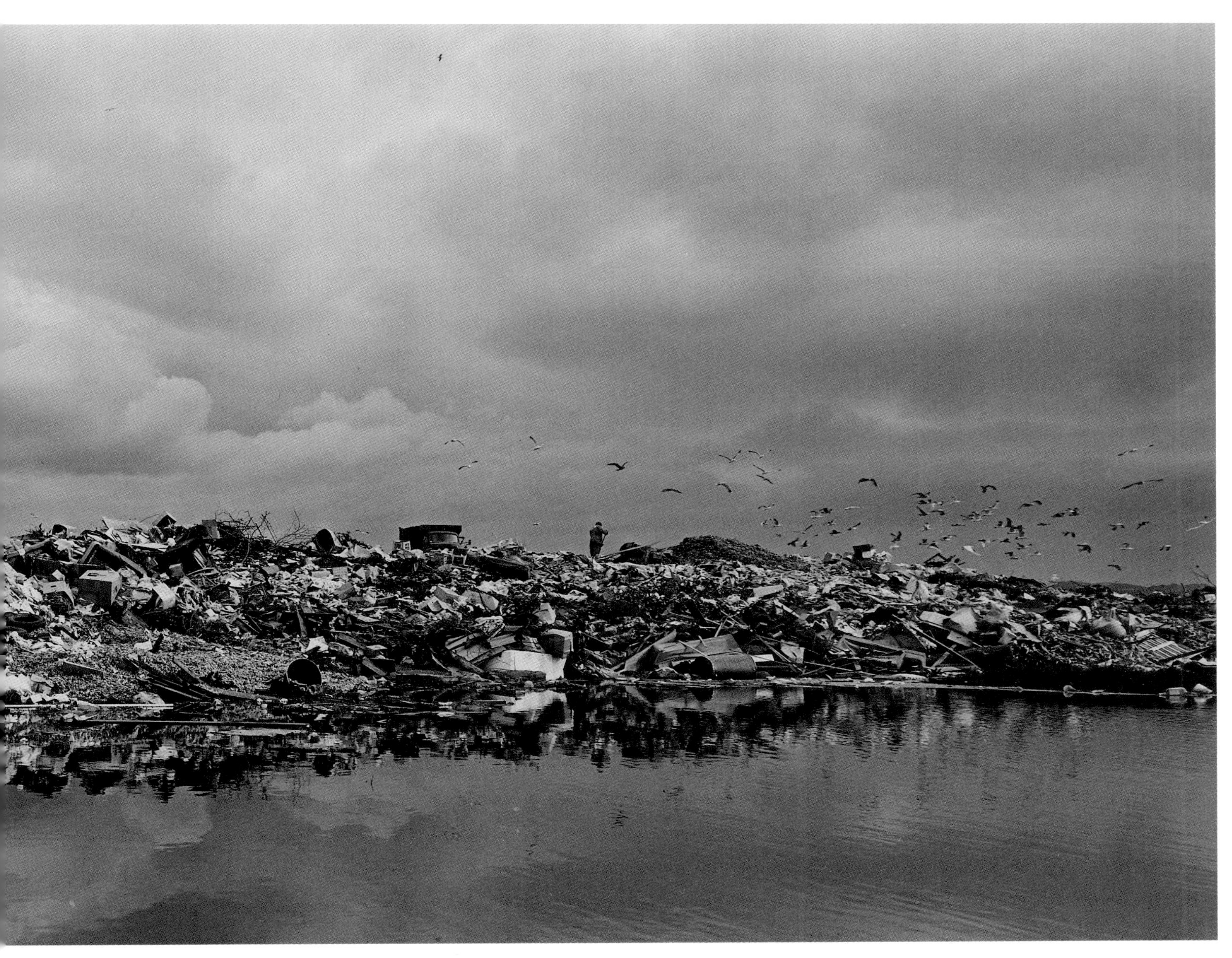

67   *Bayfill*. San Leandro. California. 1960

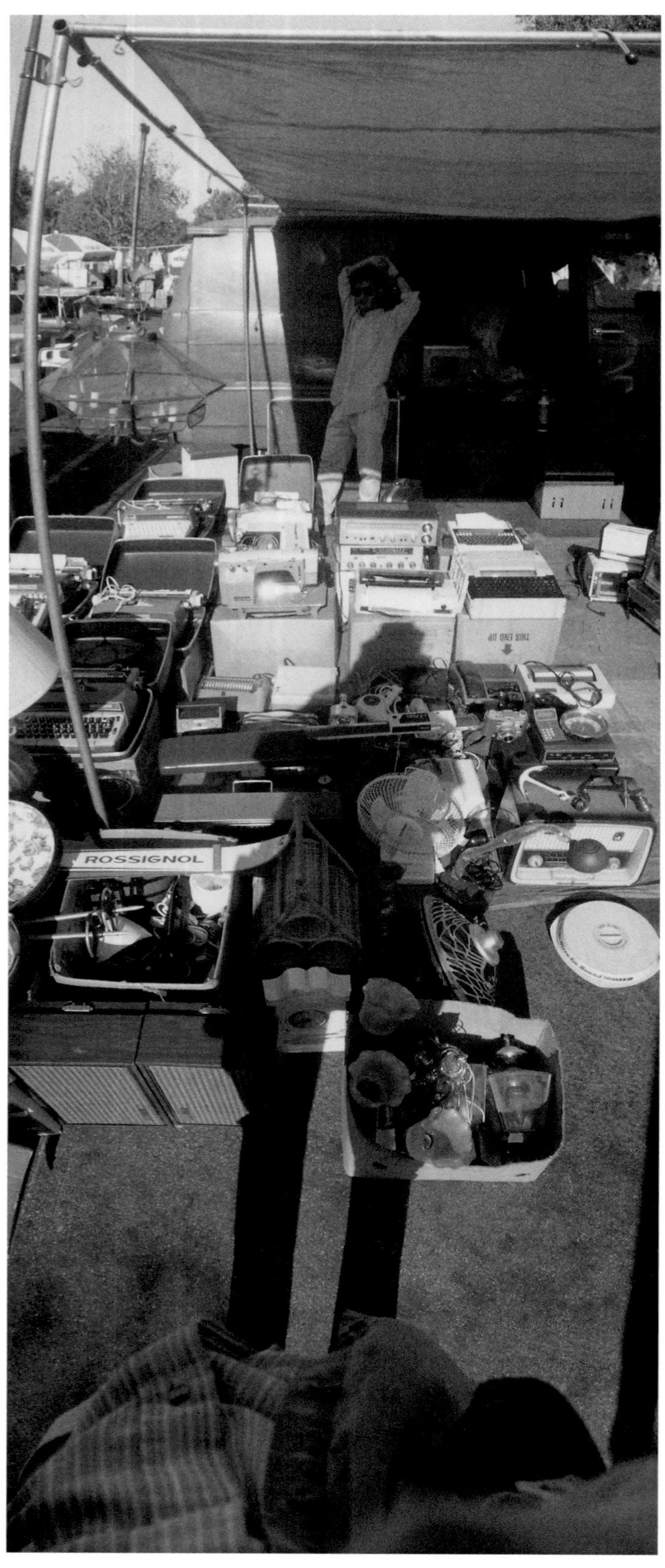
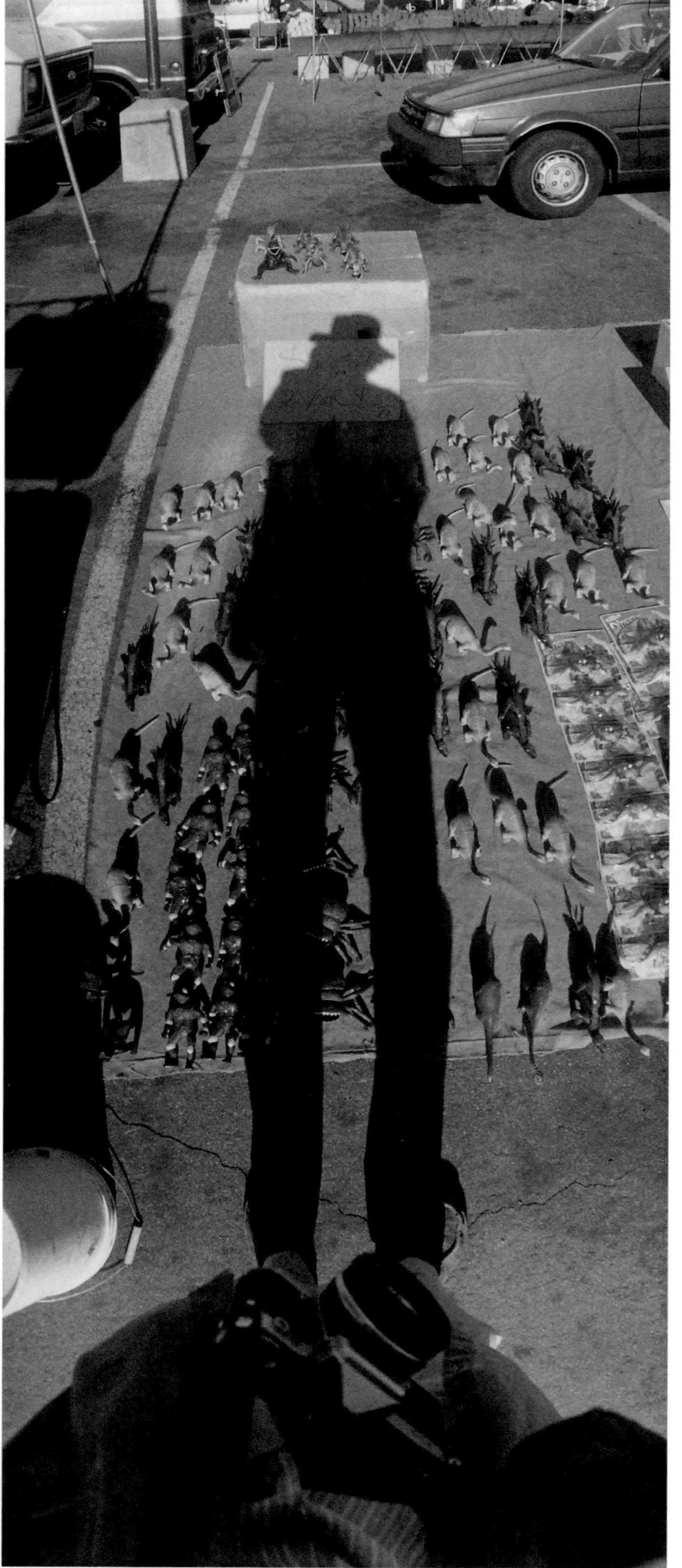

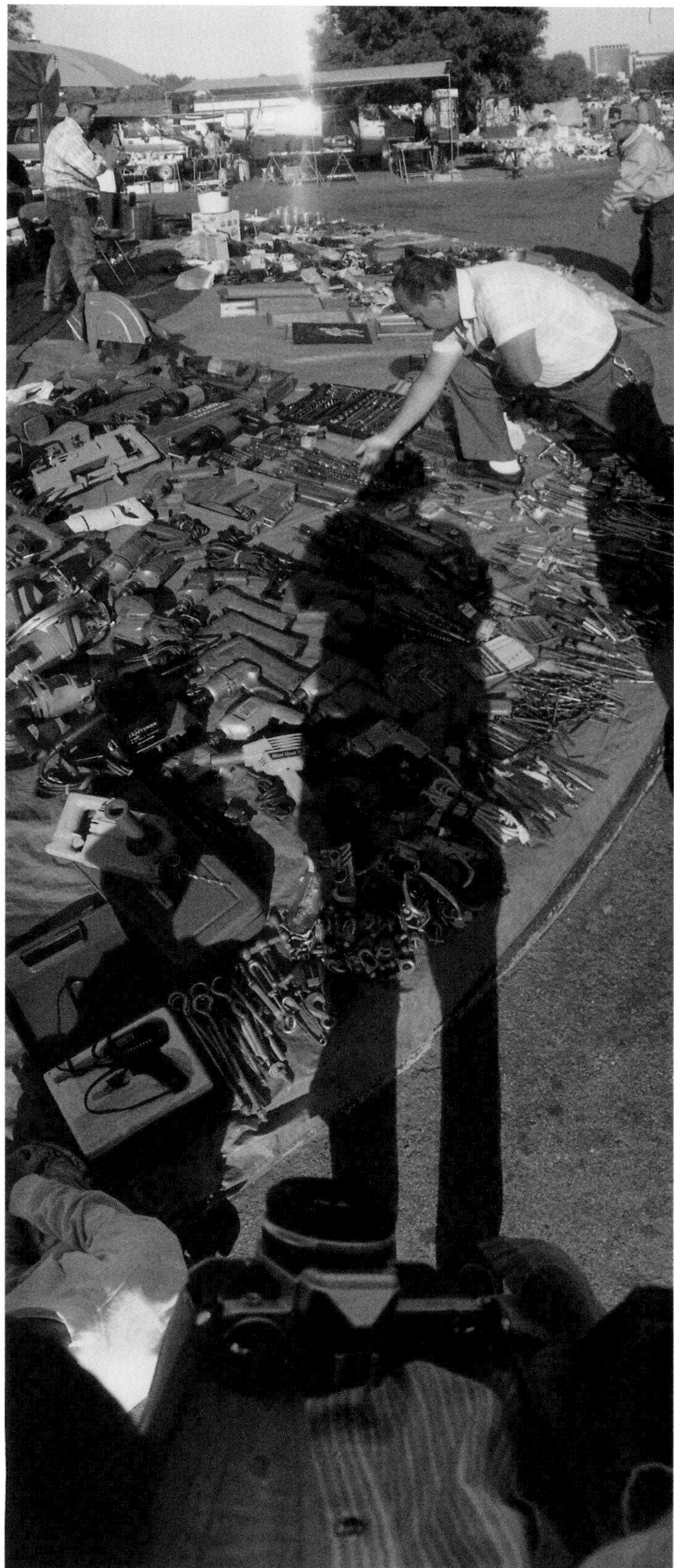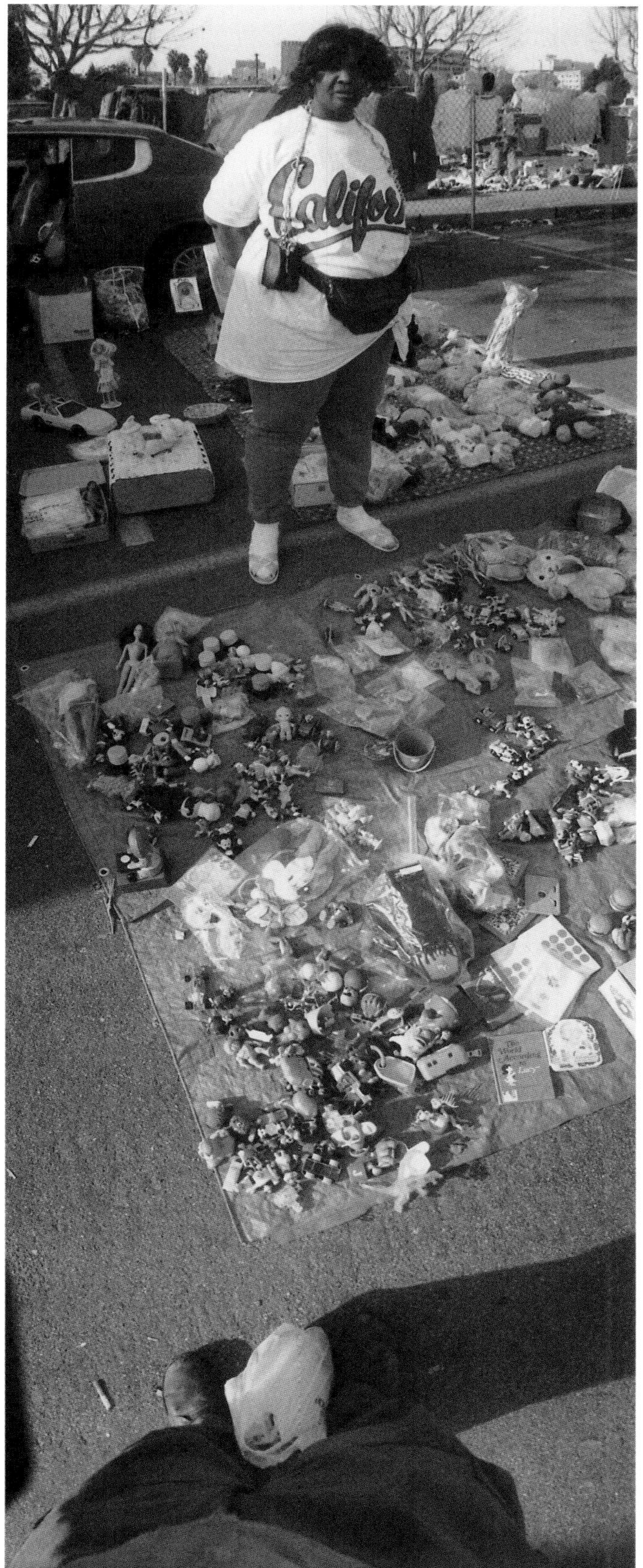

68-71 *Shadow as Substance* 1-4. Oakland, California, late 1990s

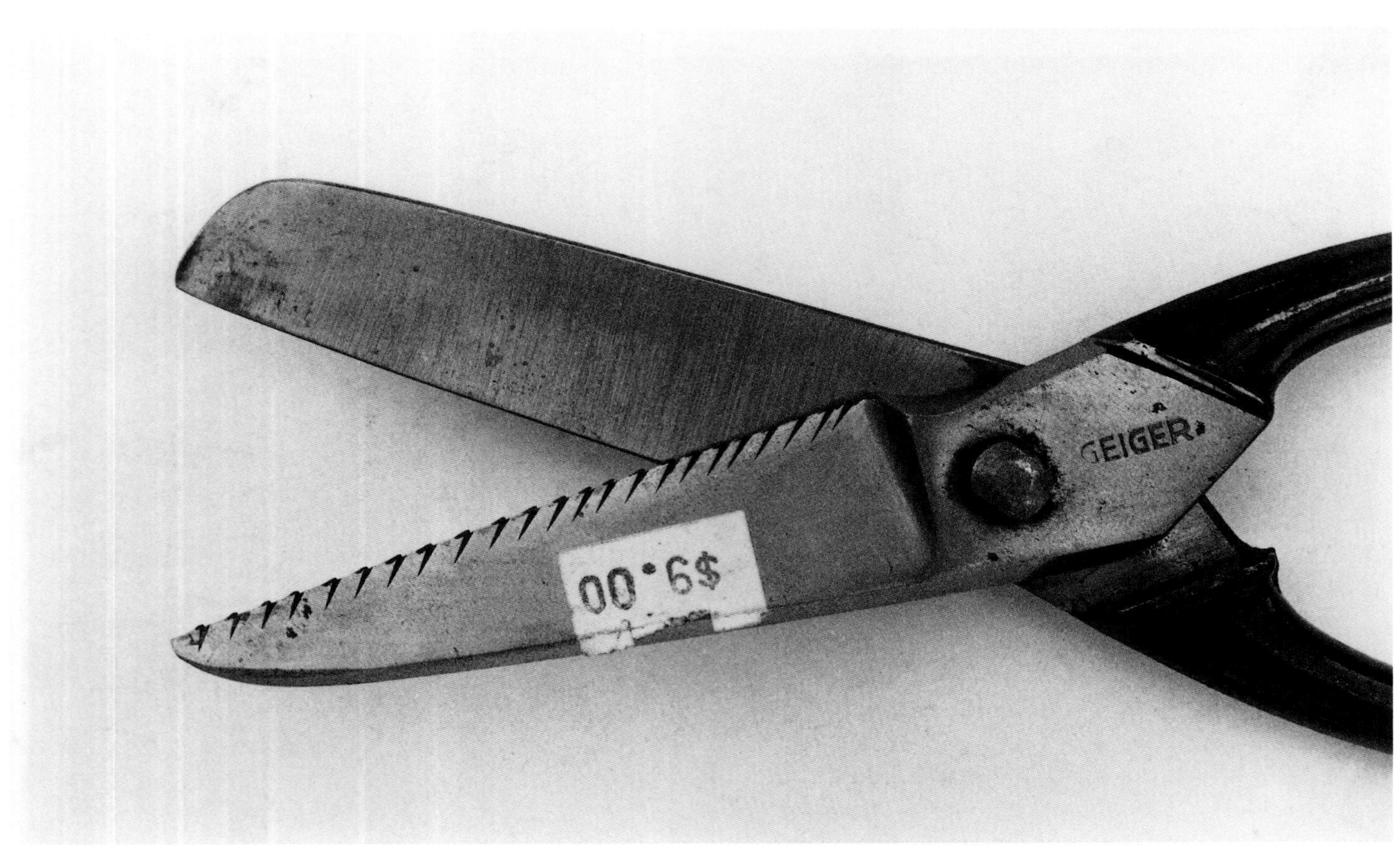

72   *Poultry Shears. 1997*

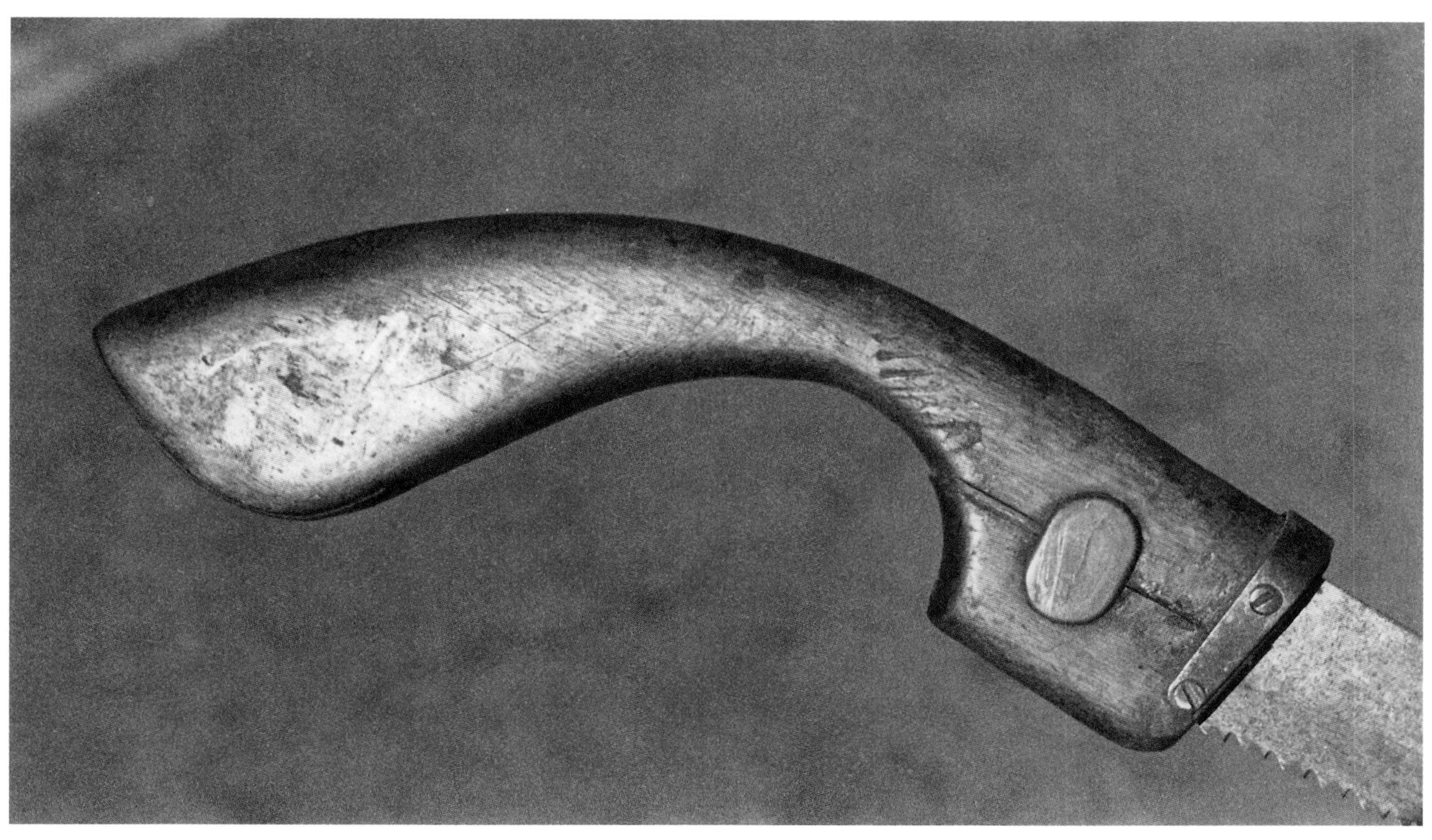

73   *Handle of a Keyhole Saw.* 1996

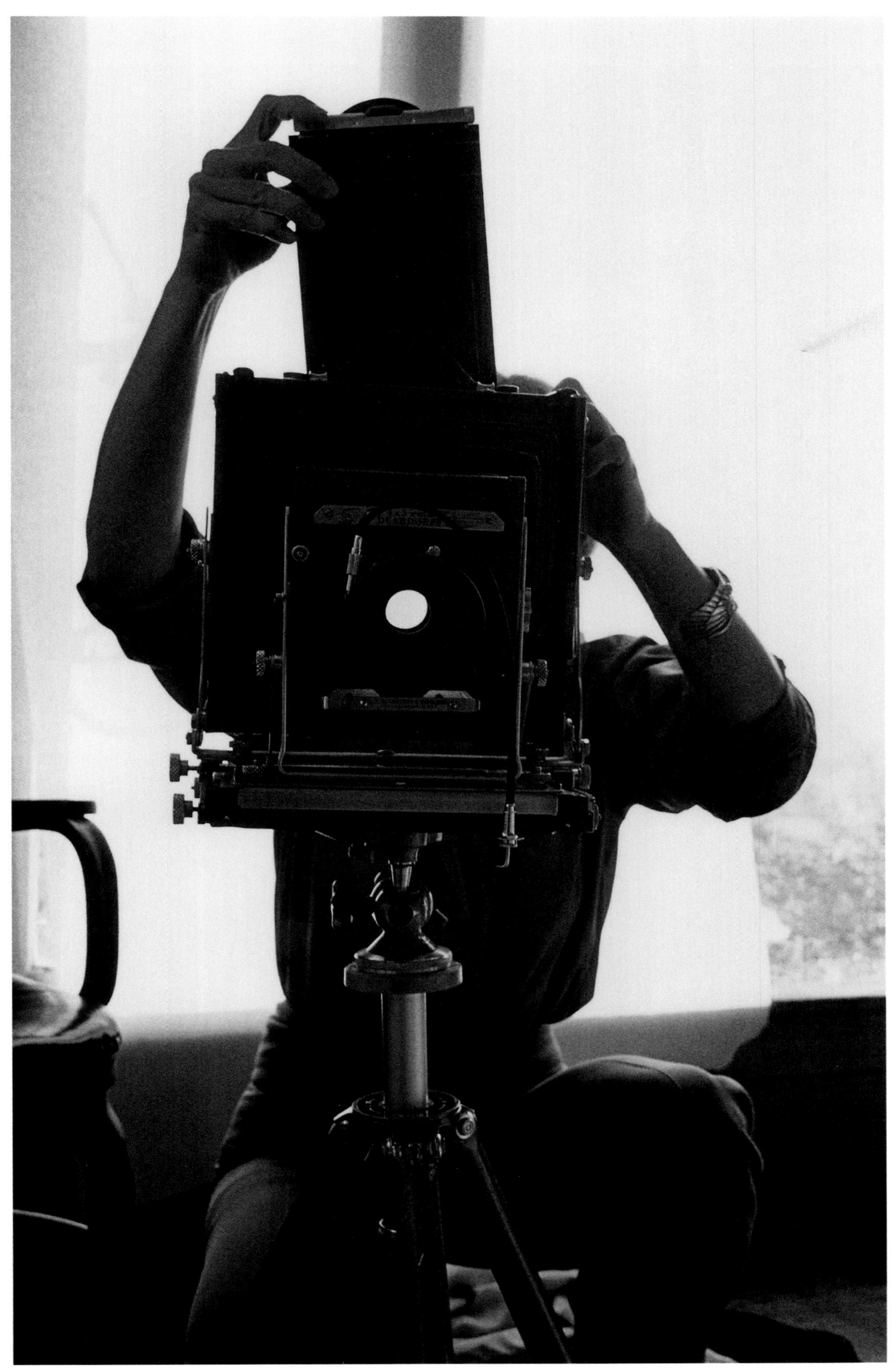

74   *Judy Dater.* 1978

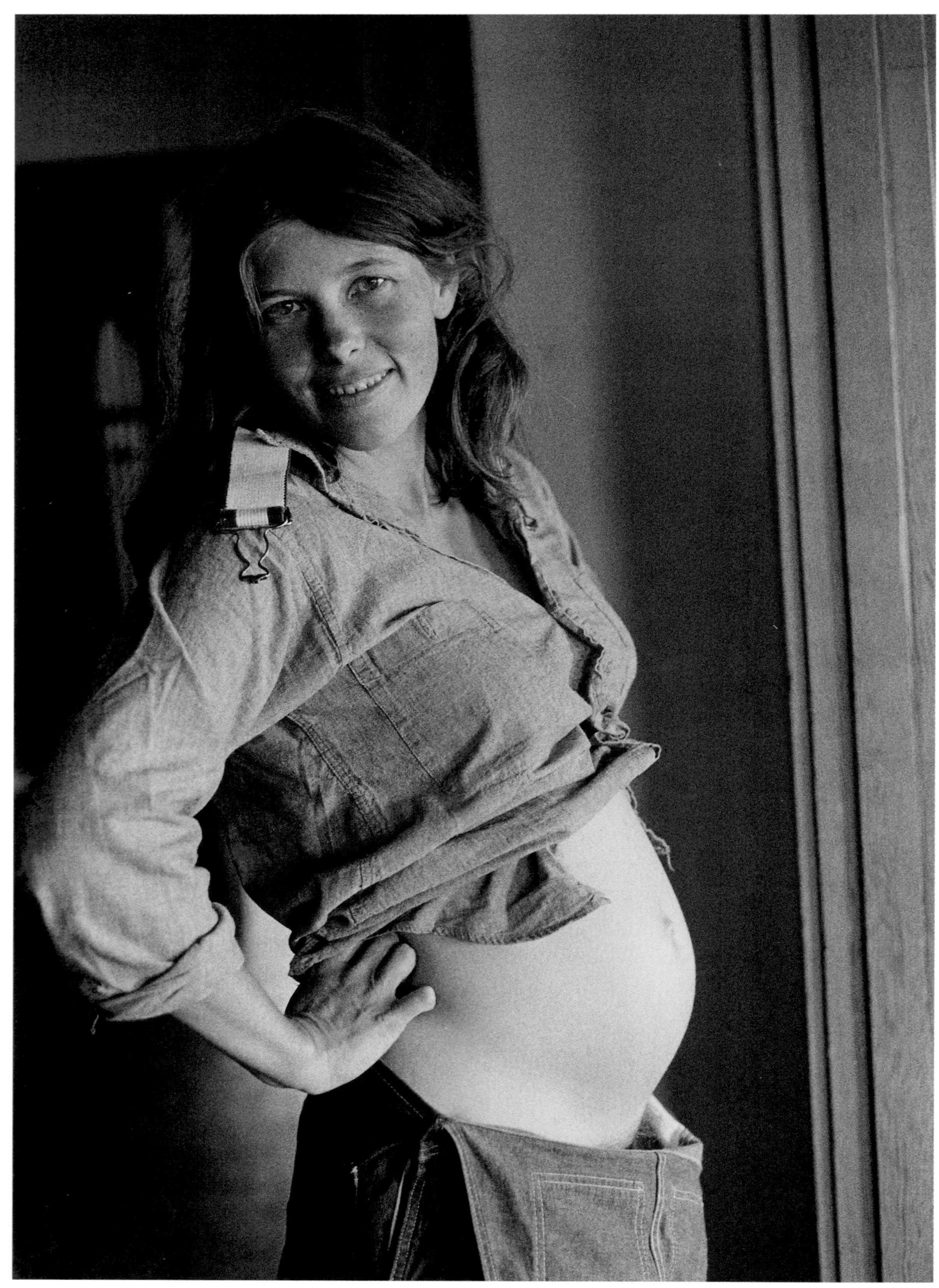

75 *Pregnant and Proud.* 1976

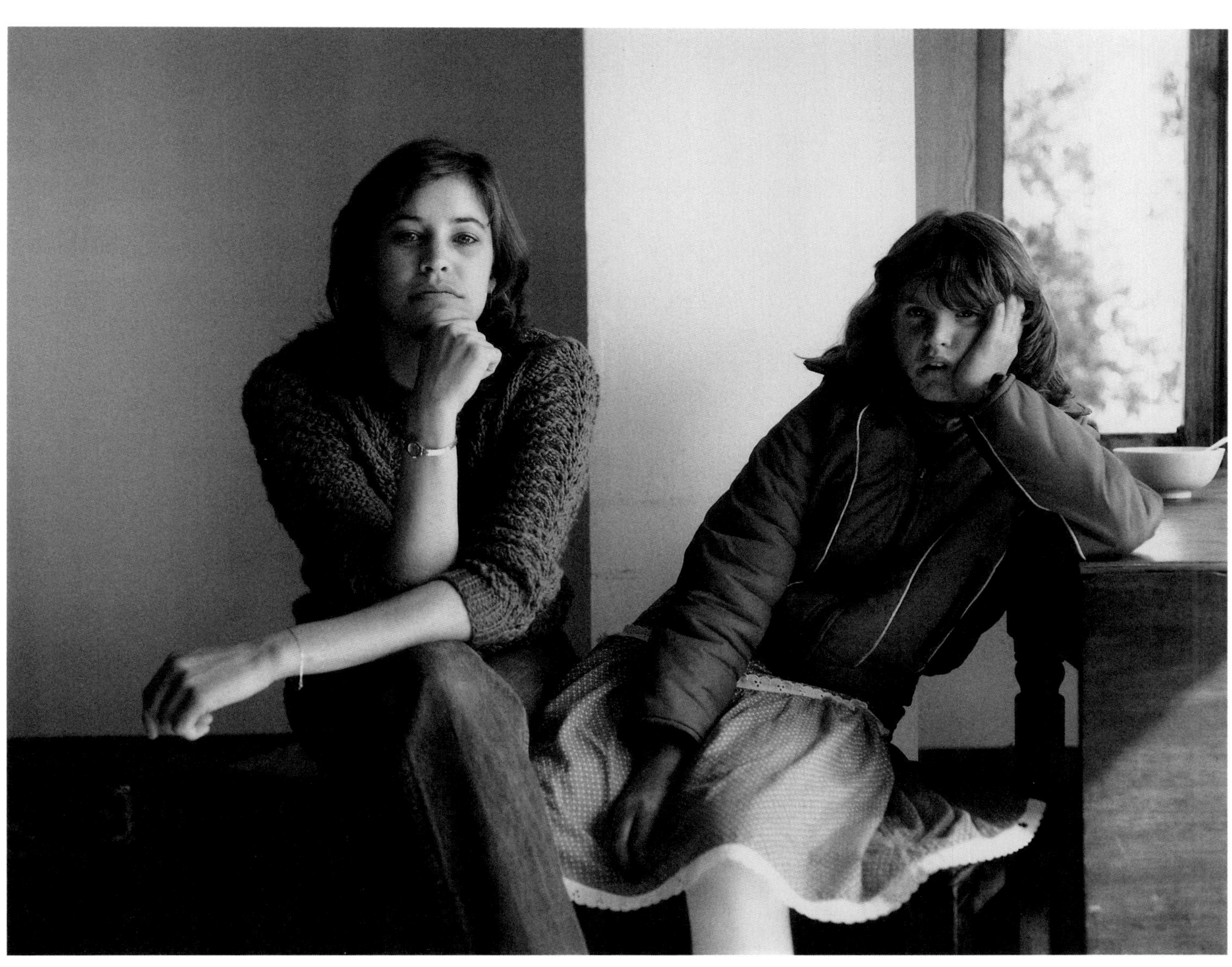

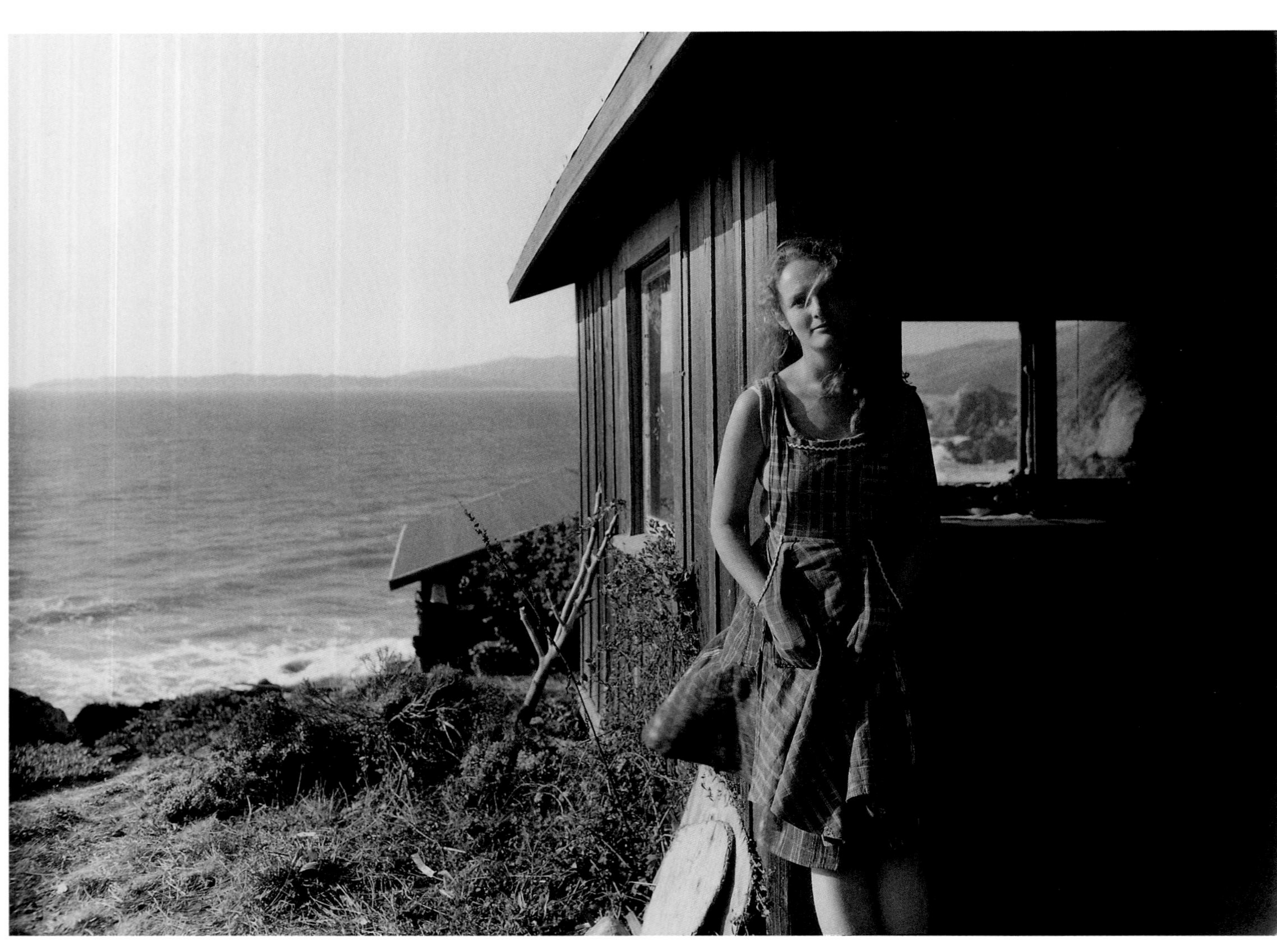

77   *Annie at Steep Ravine*, Marin County, California, 1972

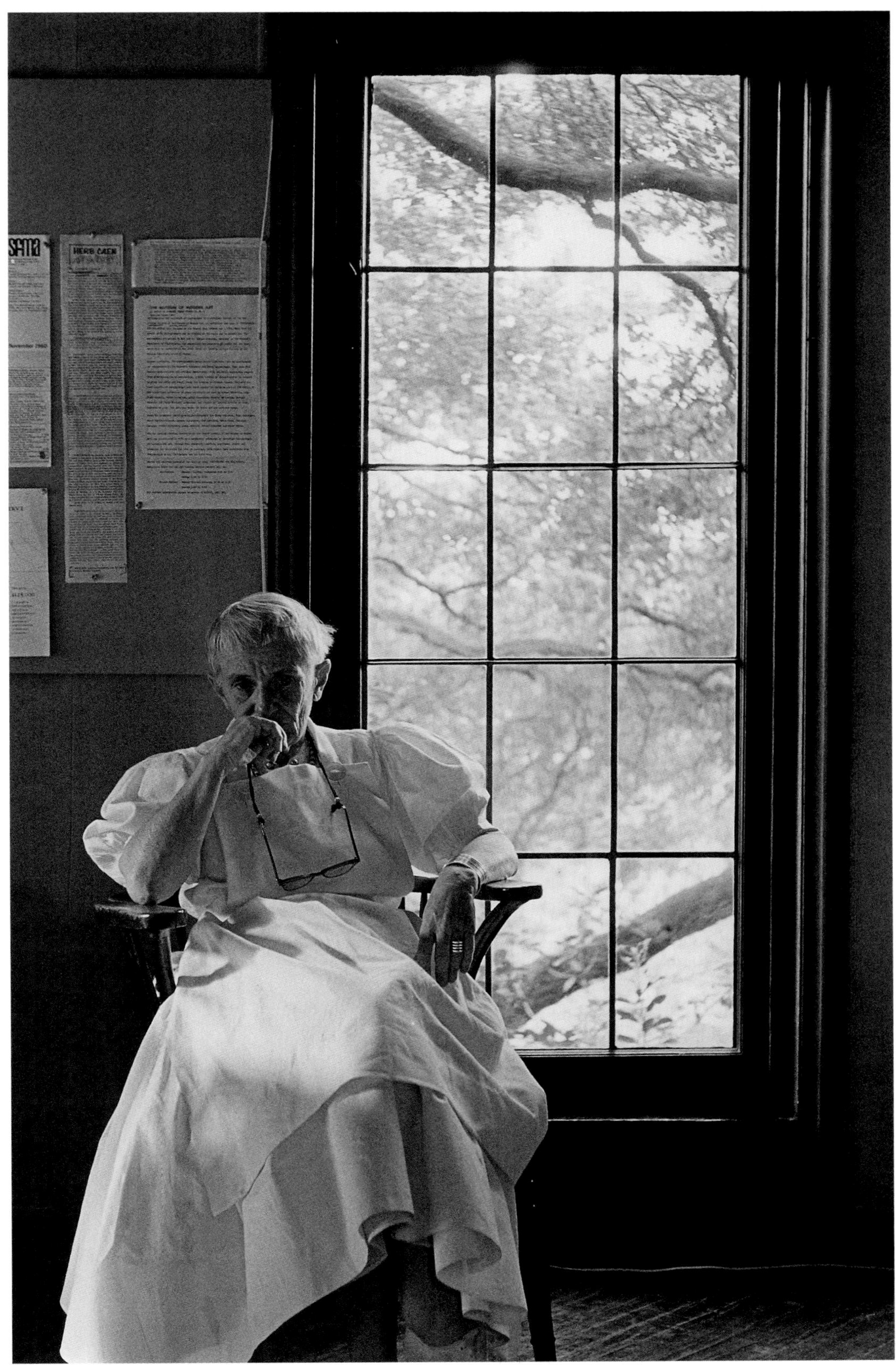

78 *Dorothea Lange,* early 1960s

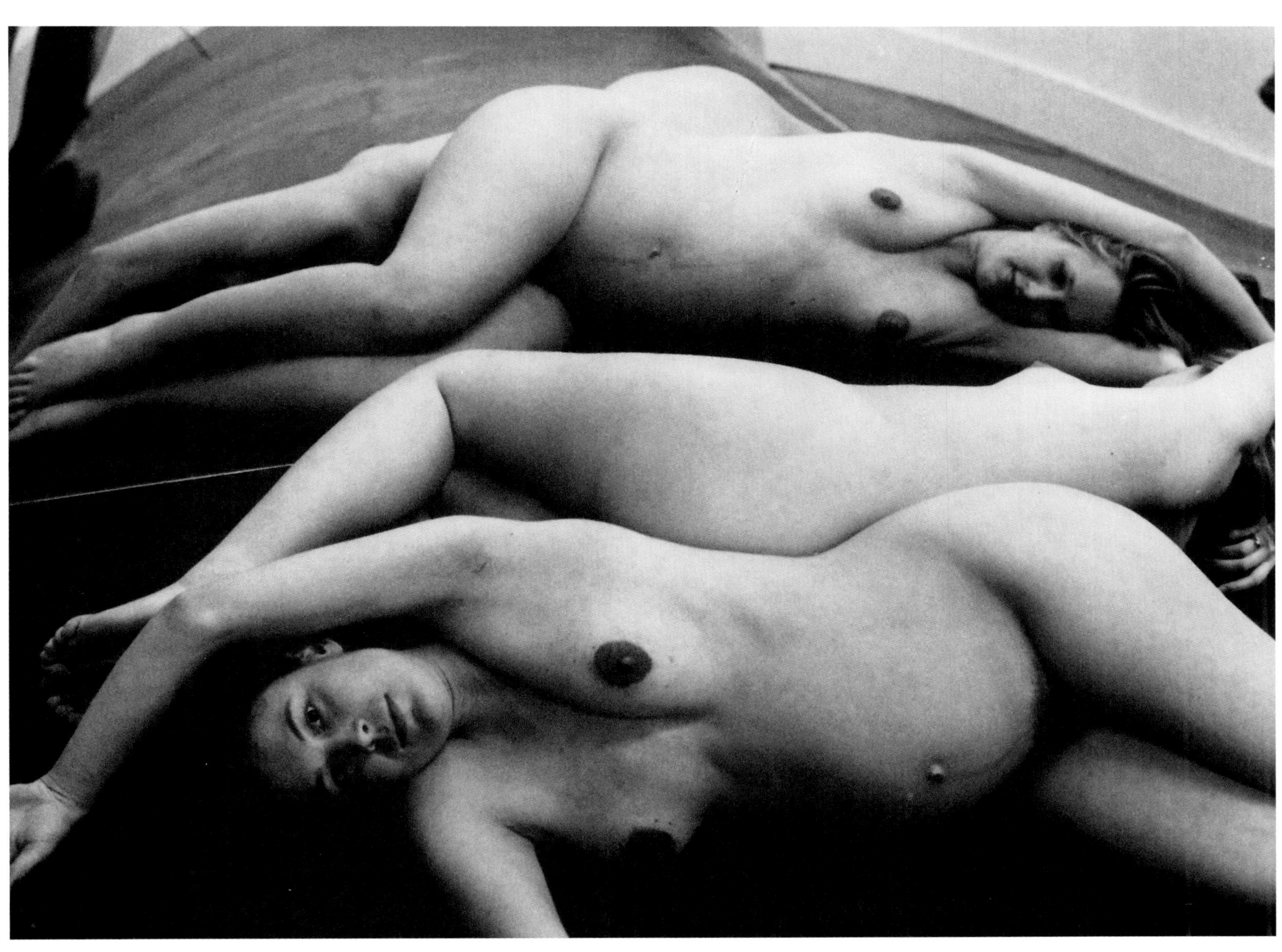

79 *Sisters.* 2000

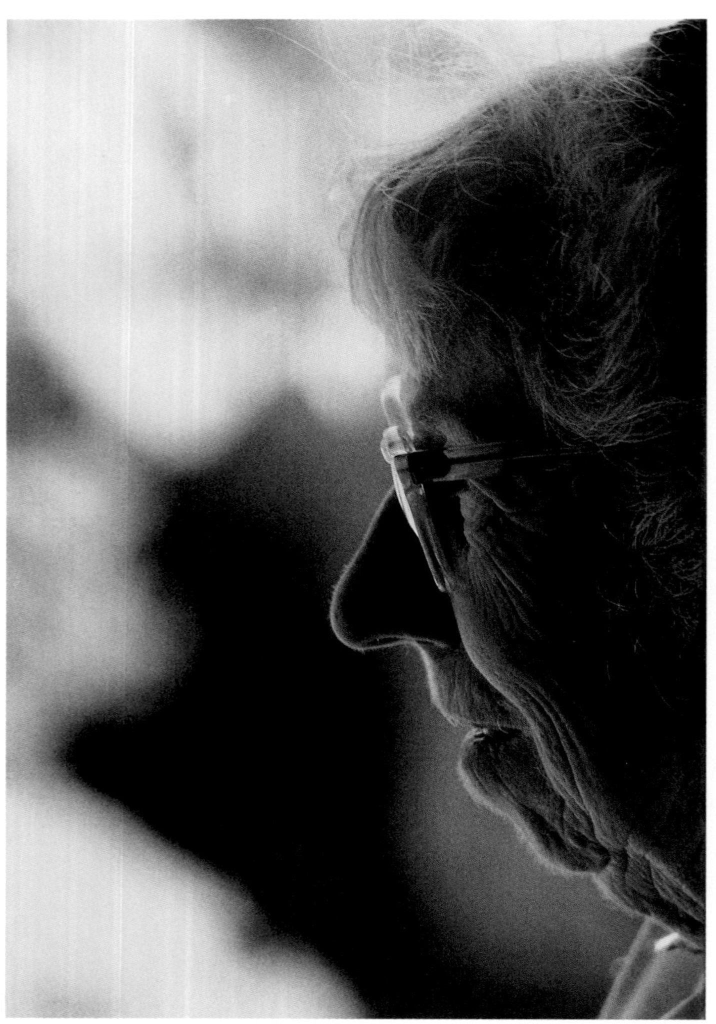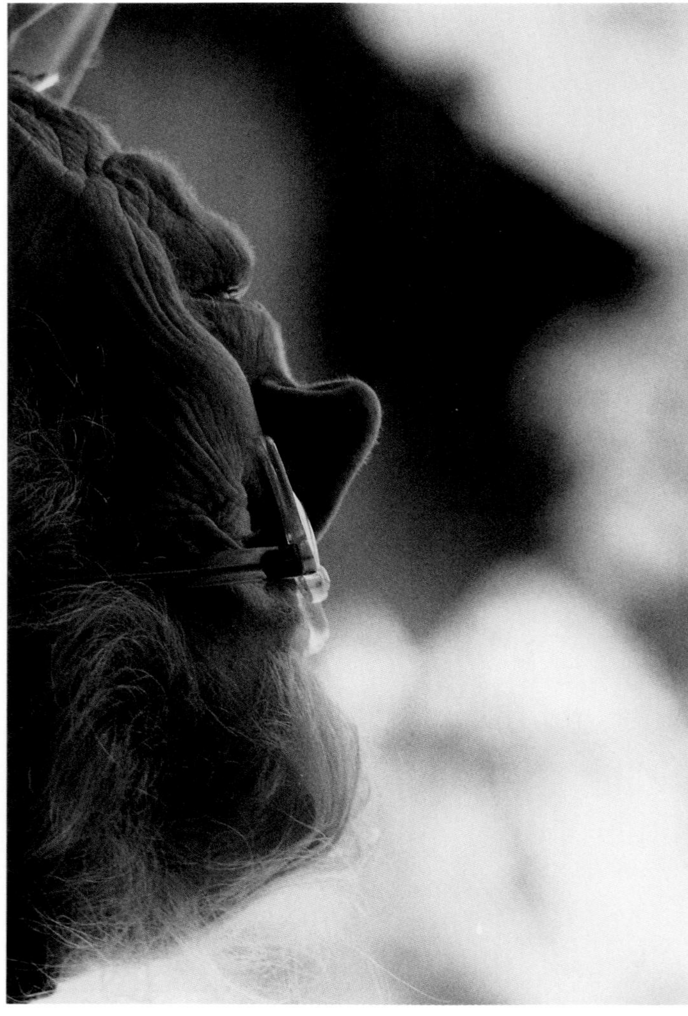

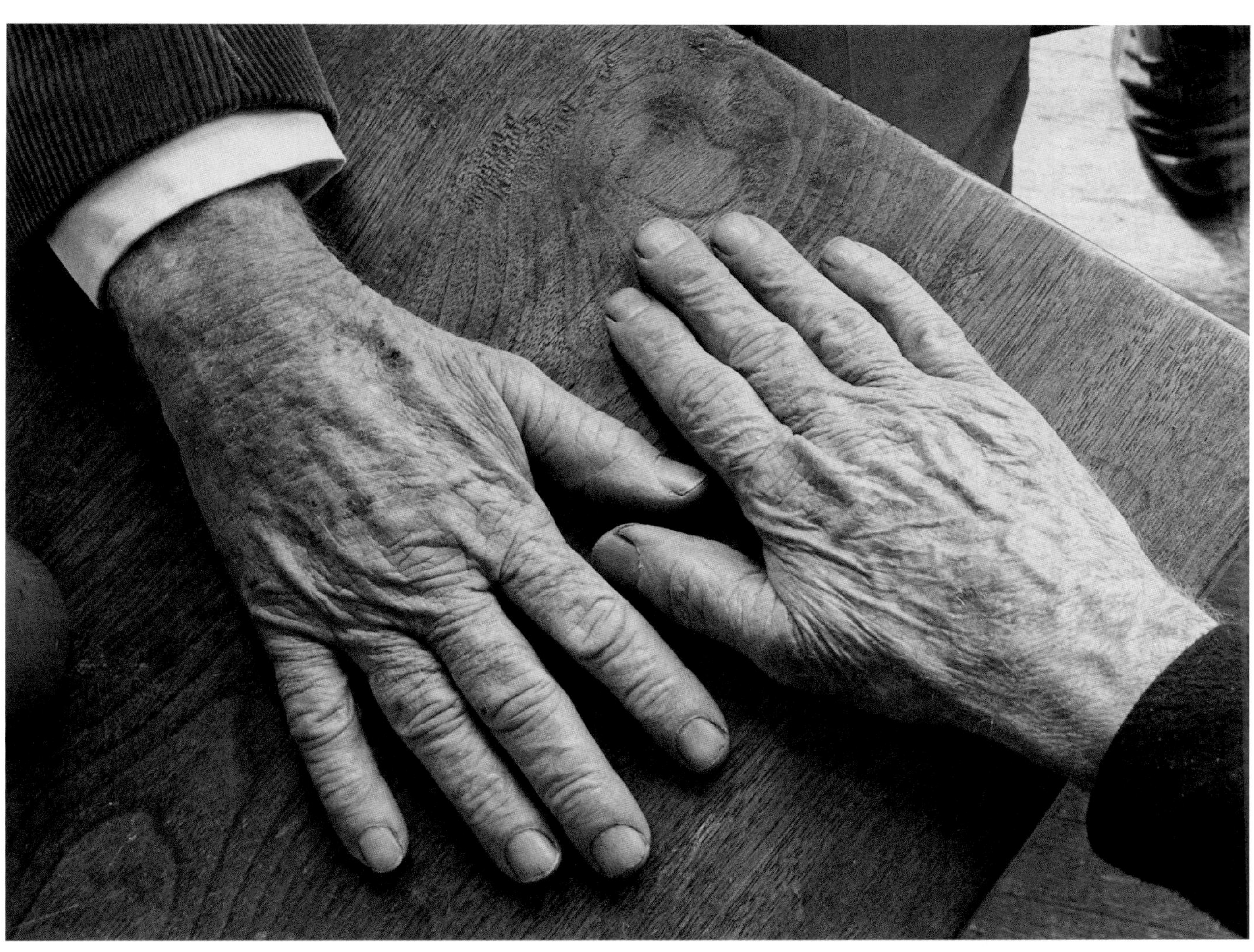

81   *Two Right Hands.* 1988

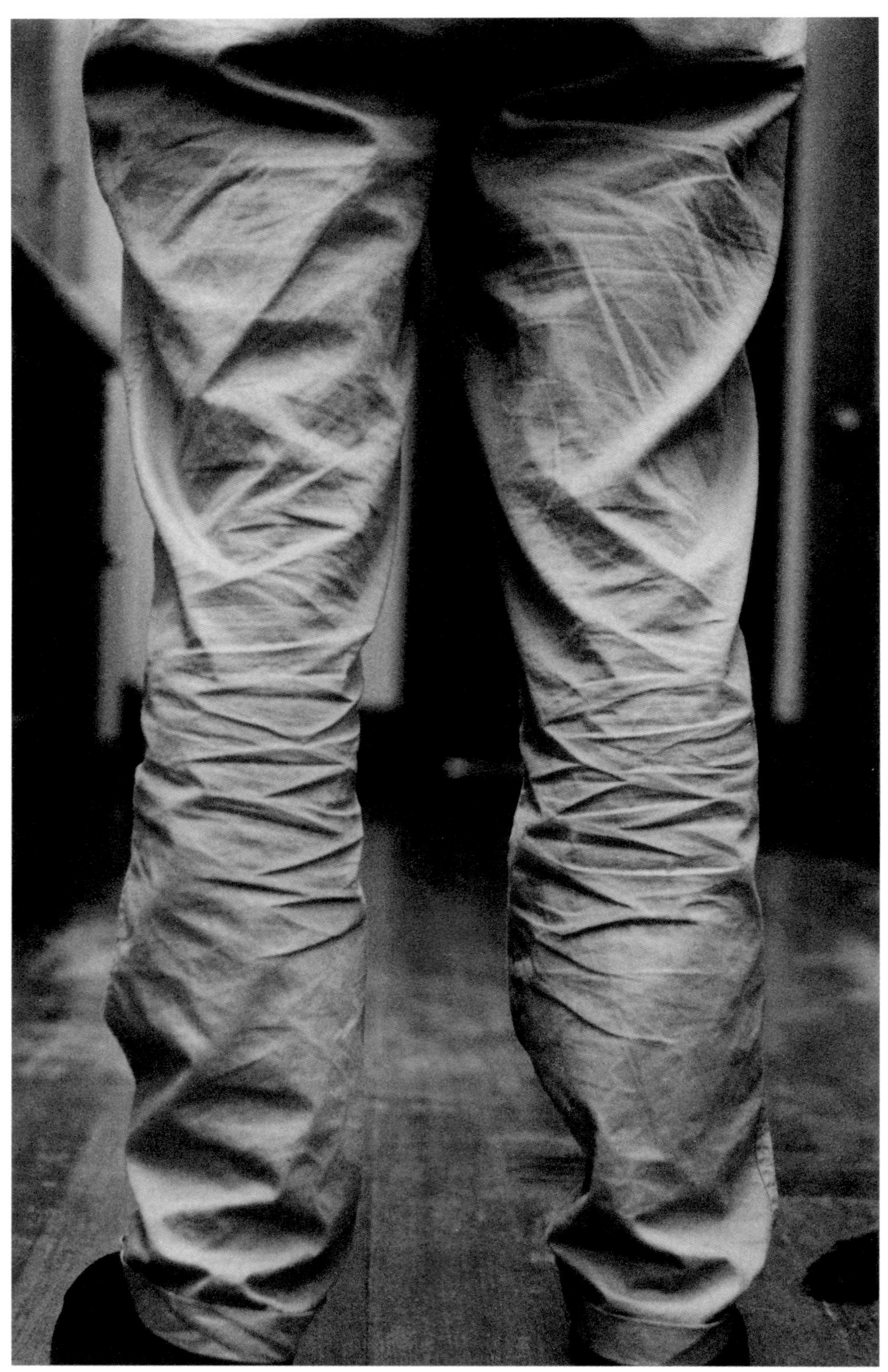

82 *Aaron's Silicon Valley Pants. 1994*

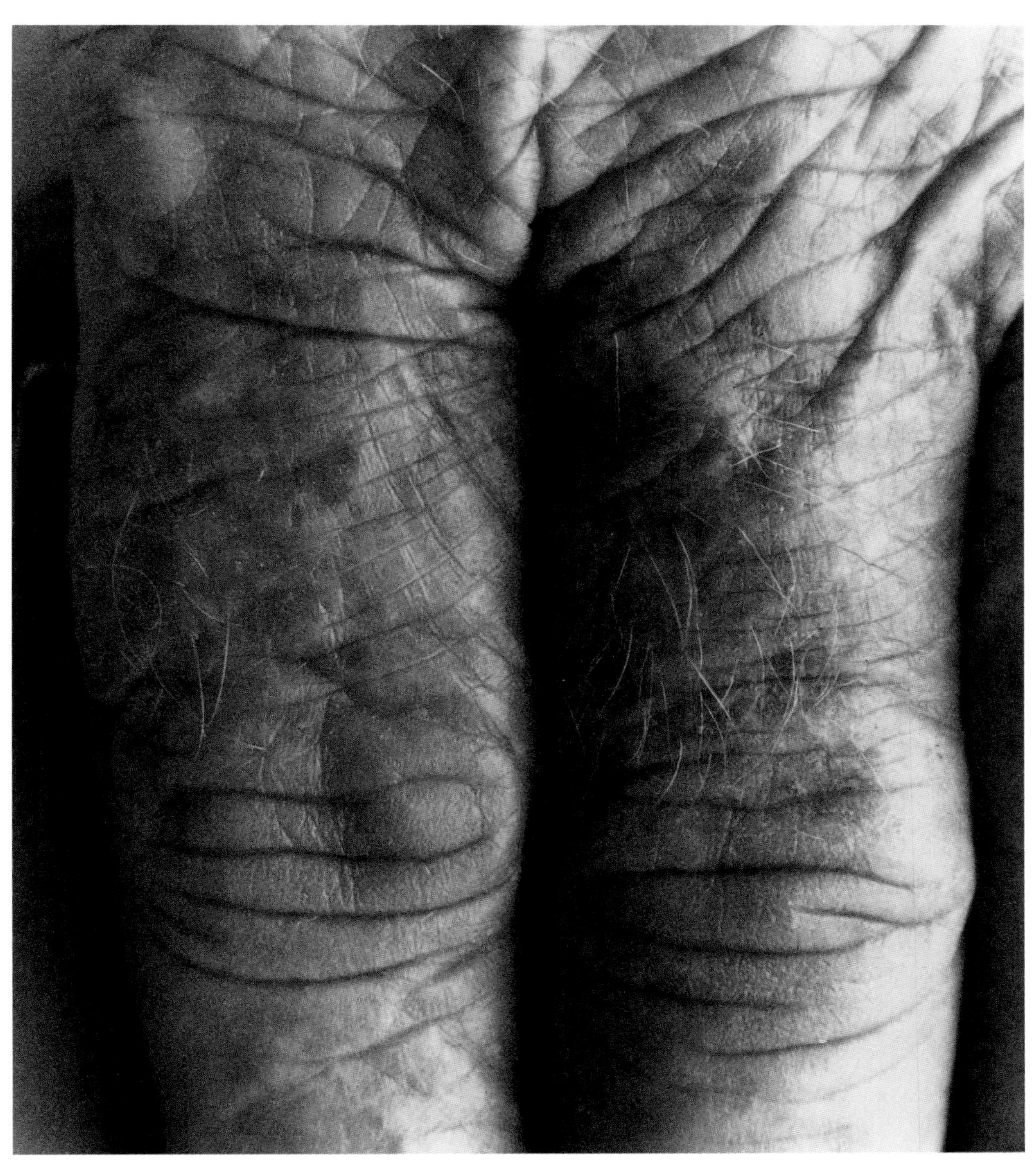

83   *My Fingers.* 1996

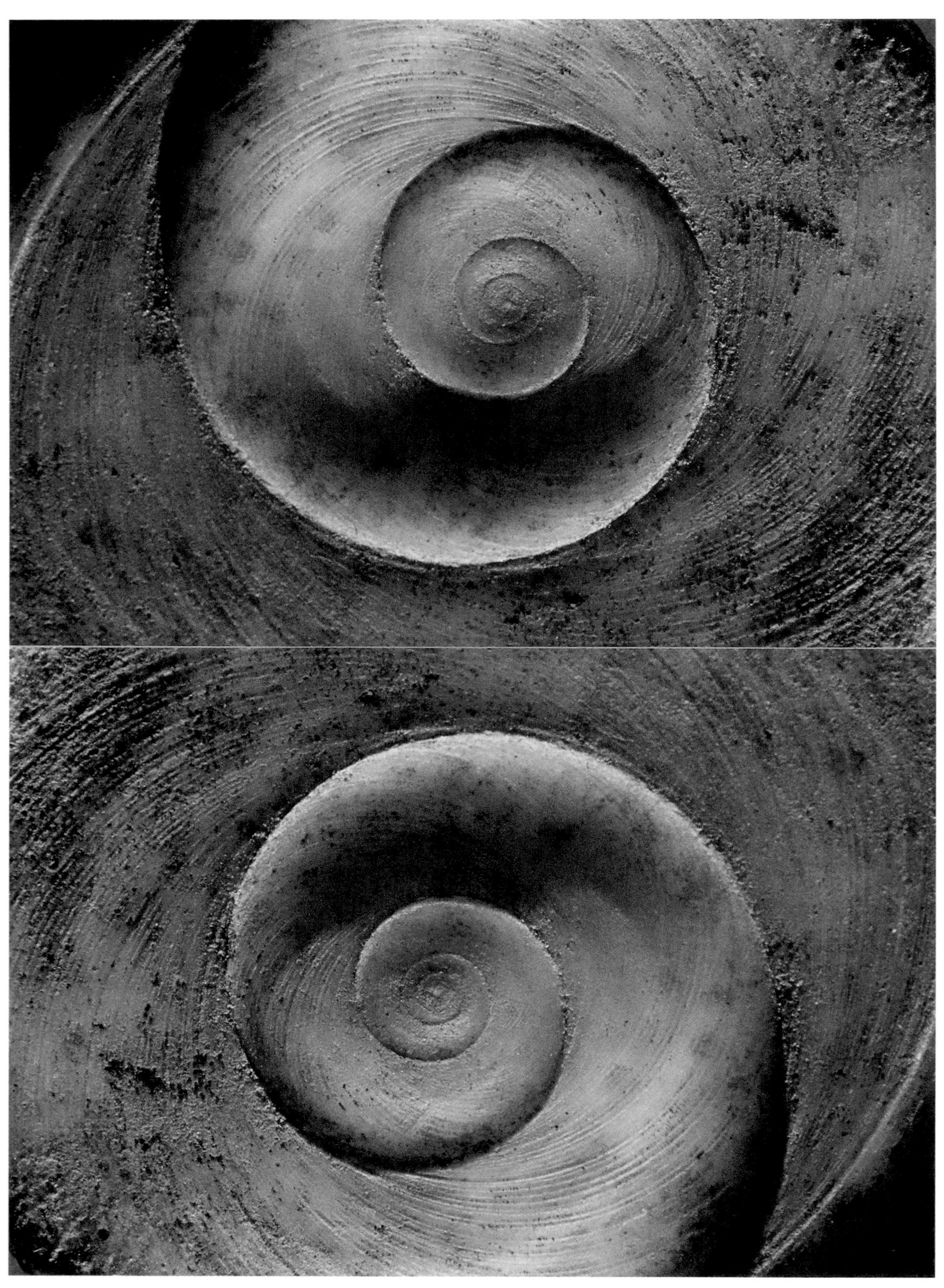

84   *Shell Shadows.* 1989

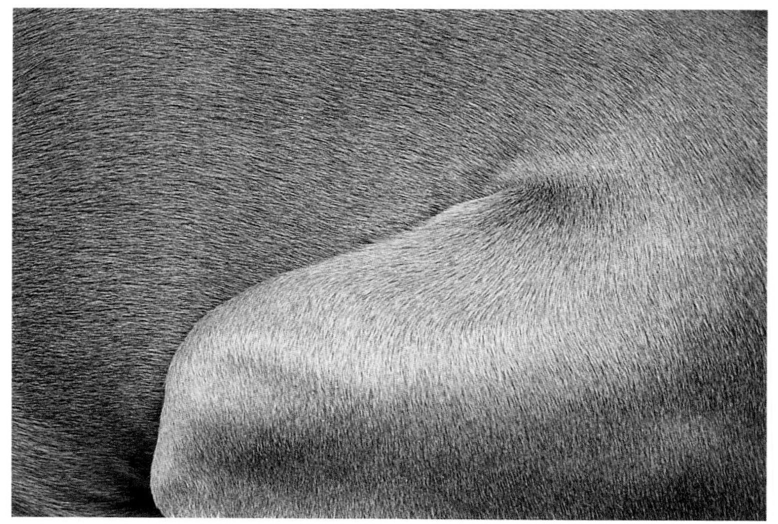

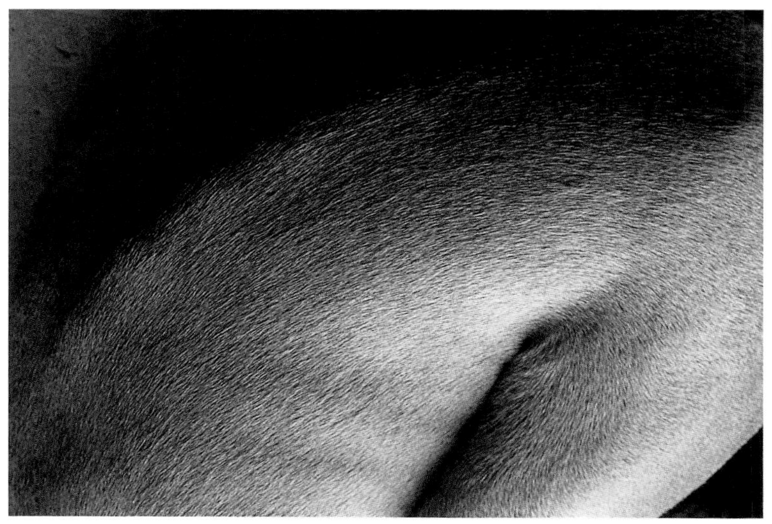

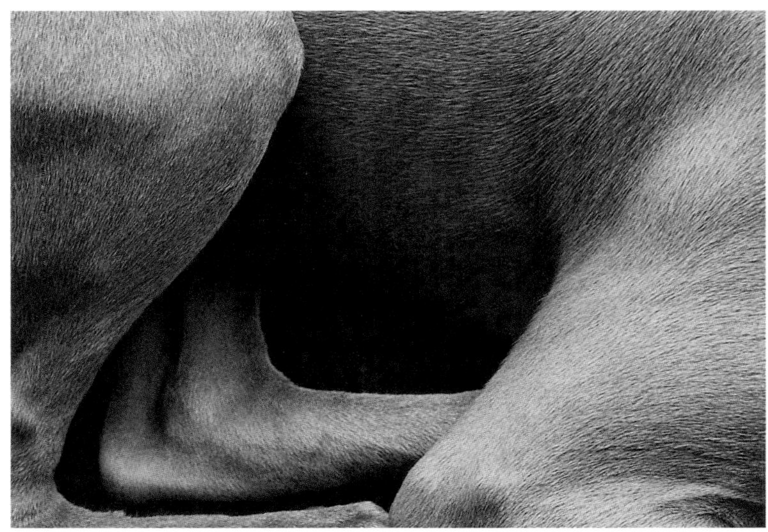

85-87 *Chester 1-3, 1982*

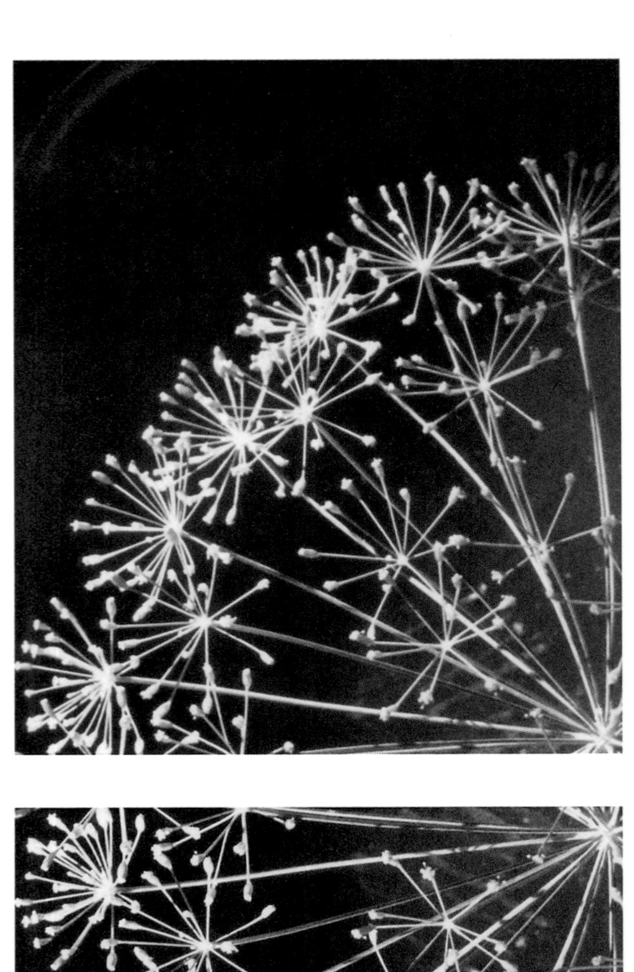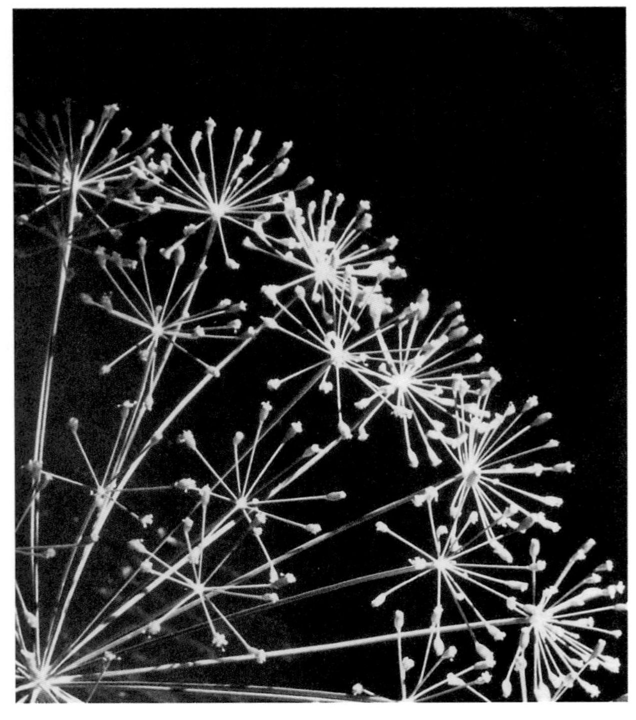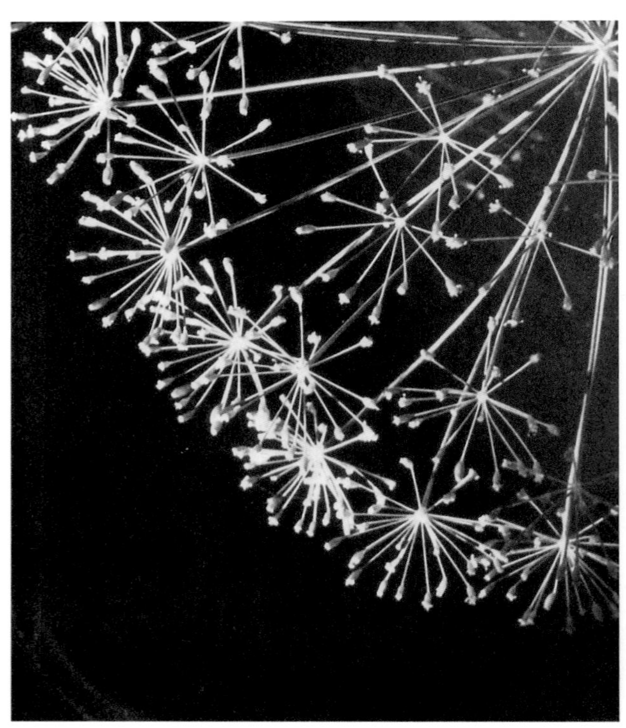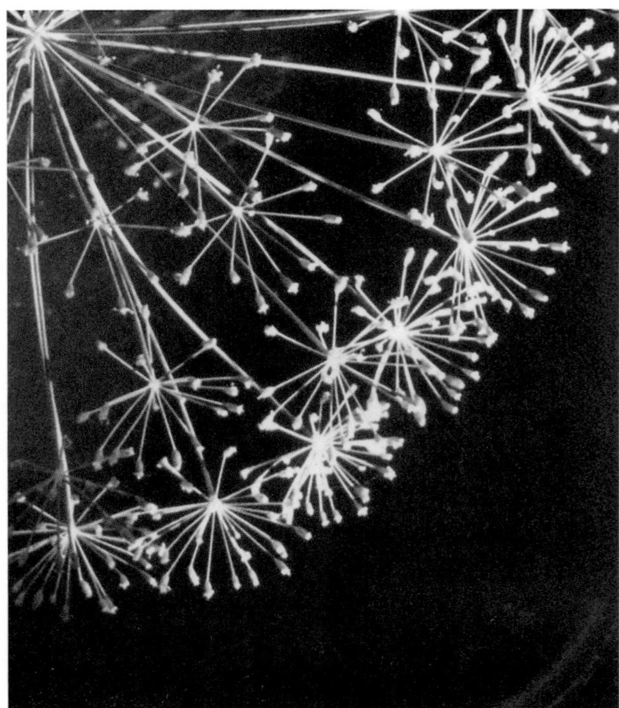

88   *Anise Quartet.* 1995

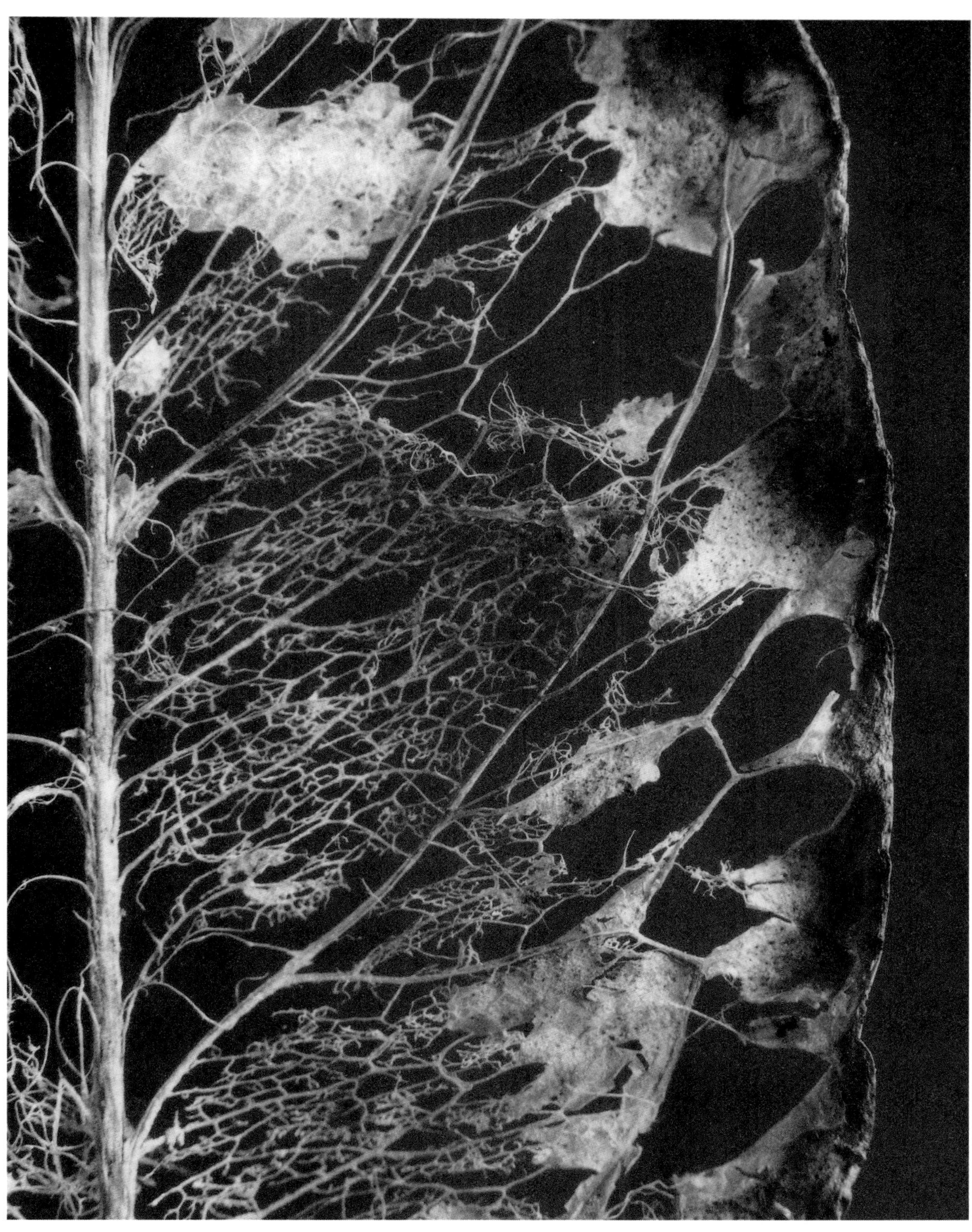

89   *Decaying Leaf.* 1995

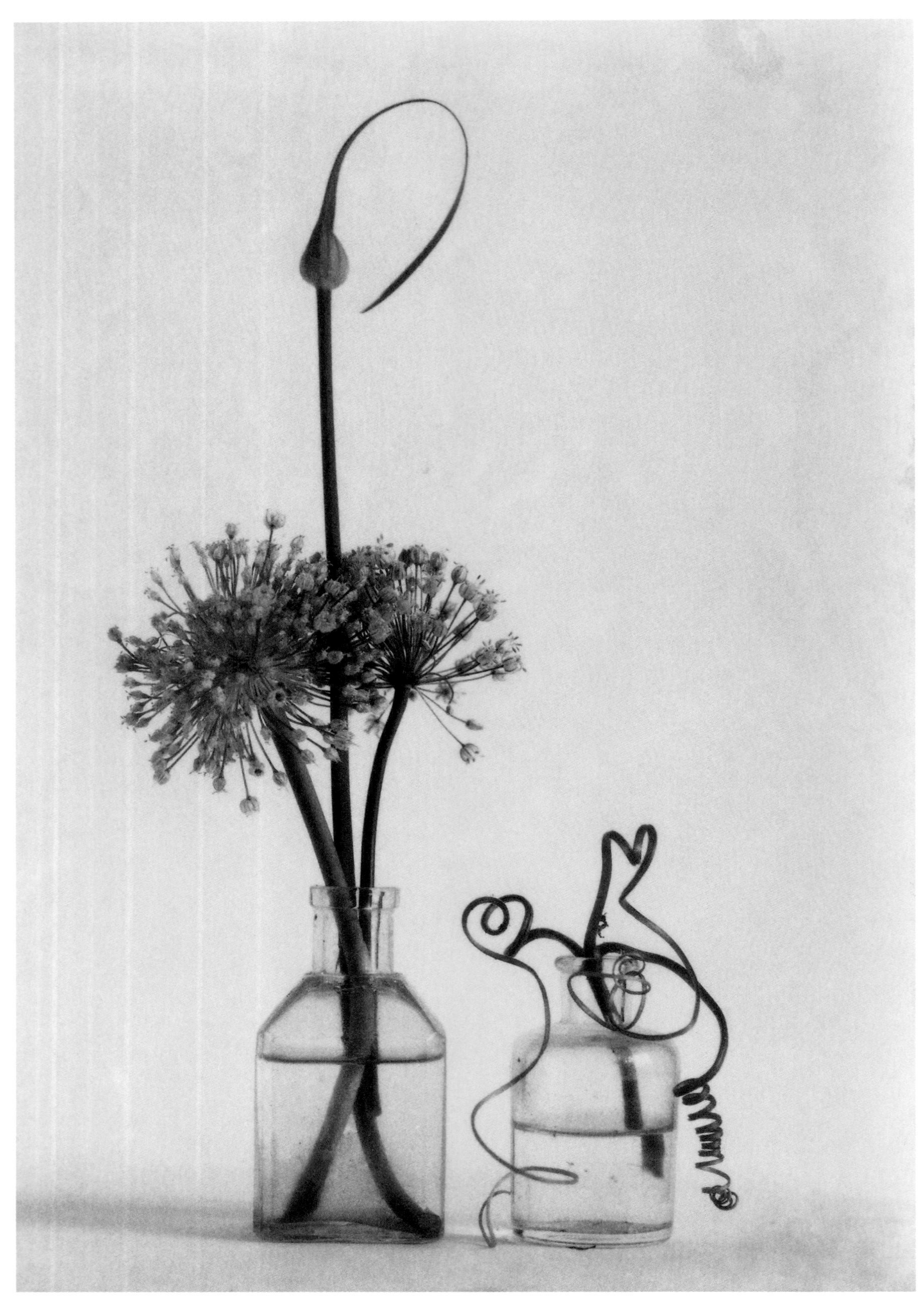

90 *Leek and Squash Tendrils.* 1995

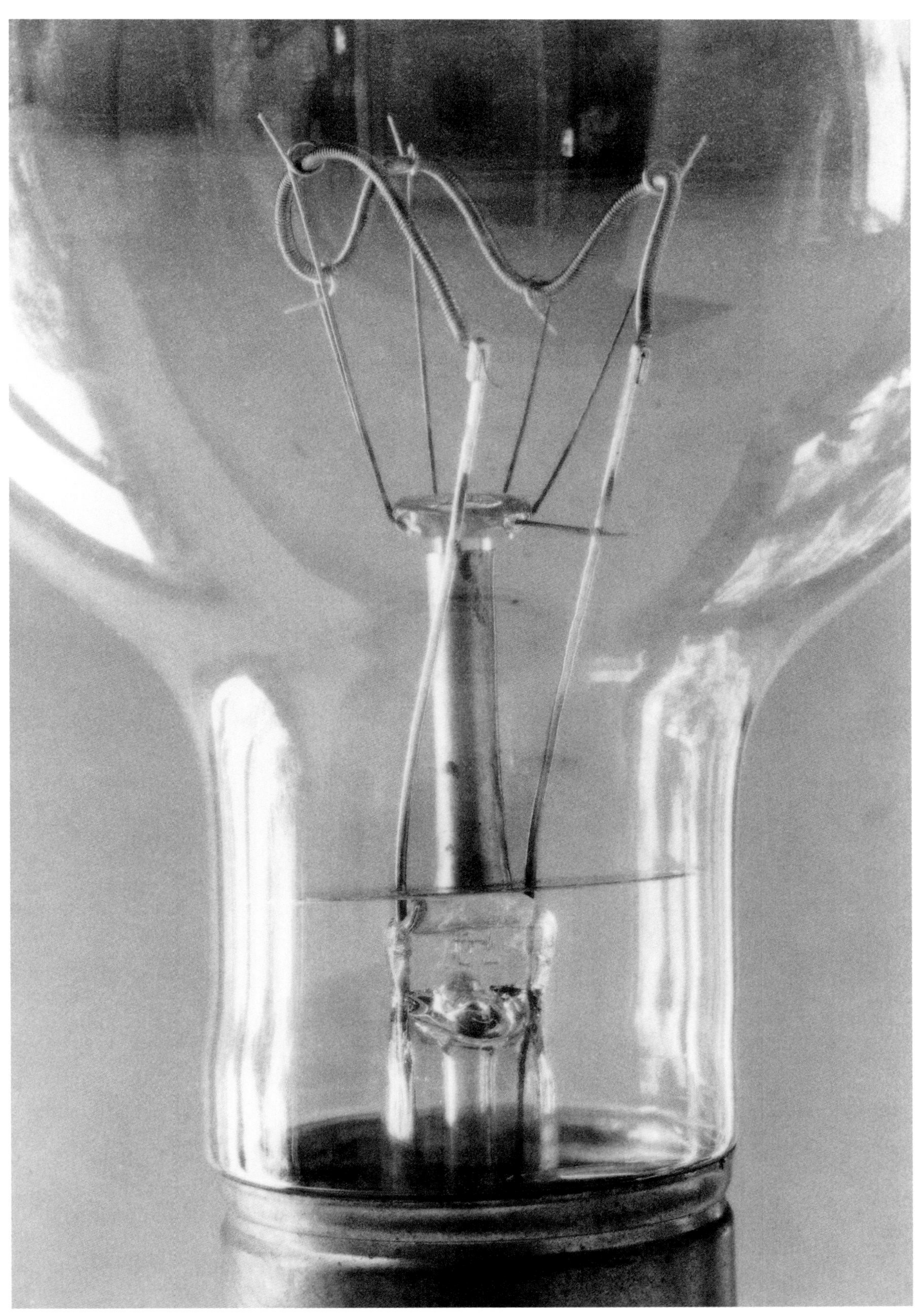

91   *Industrial Bulb.* 1995

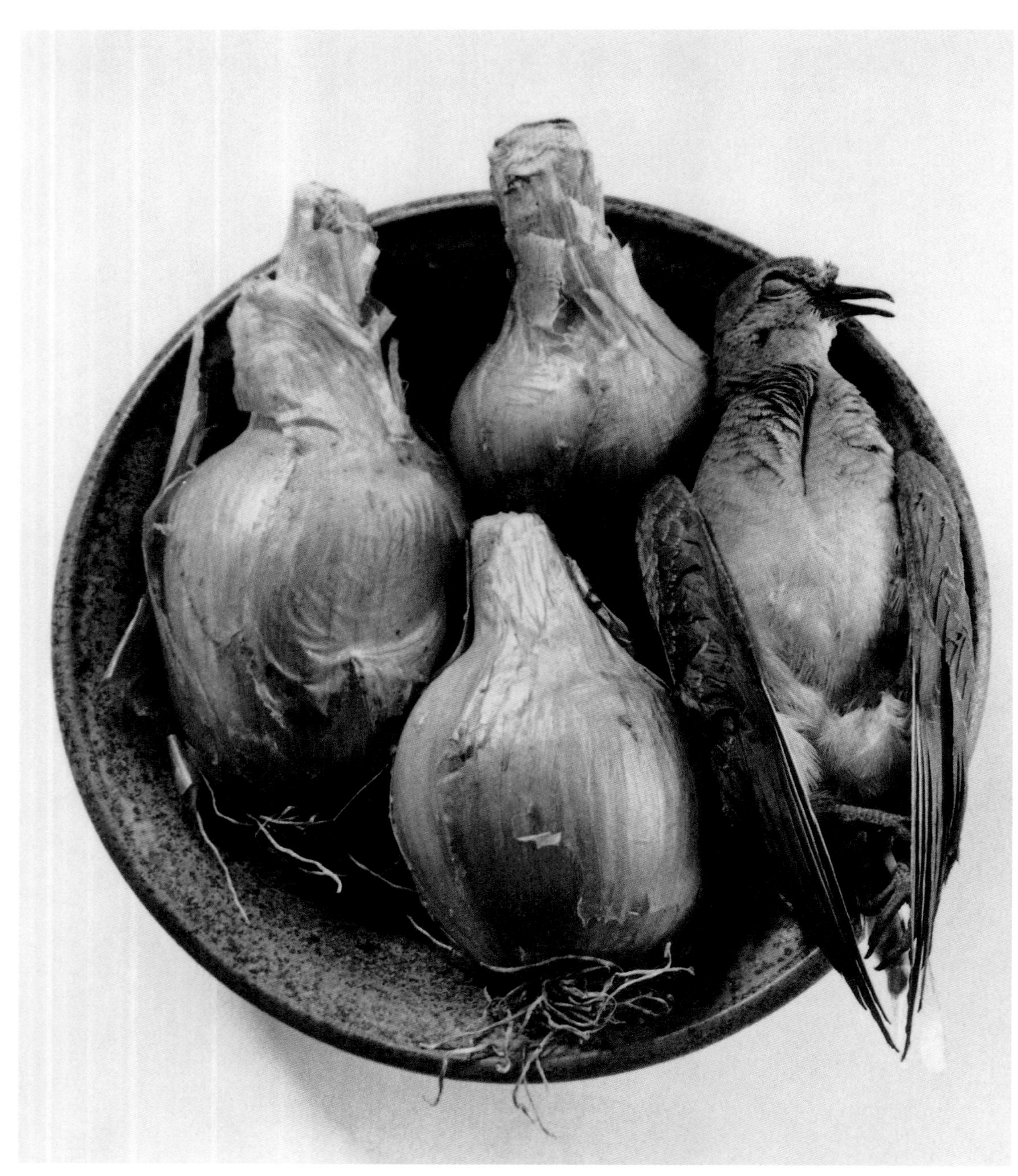

92 *Bird and Onions.* 1989

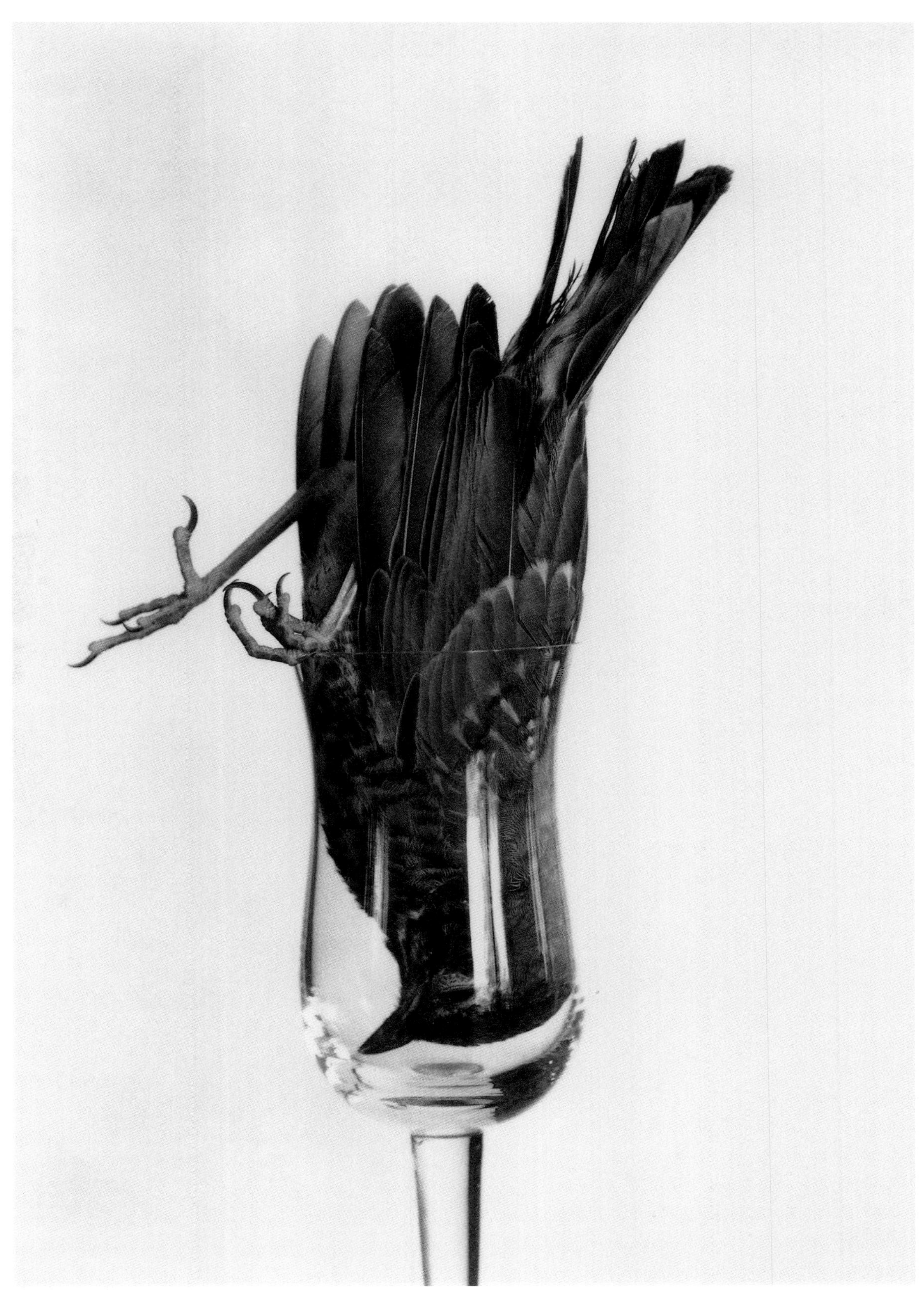

93 *Bird in Glass.* 1989

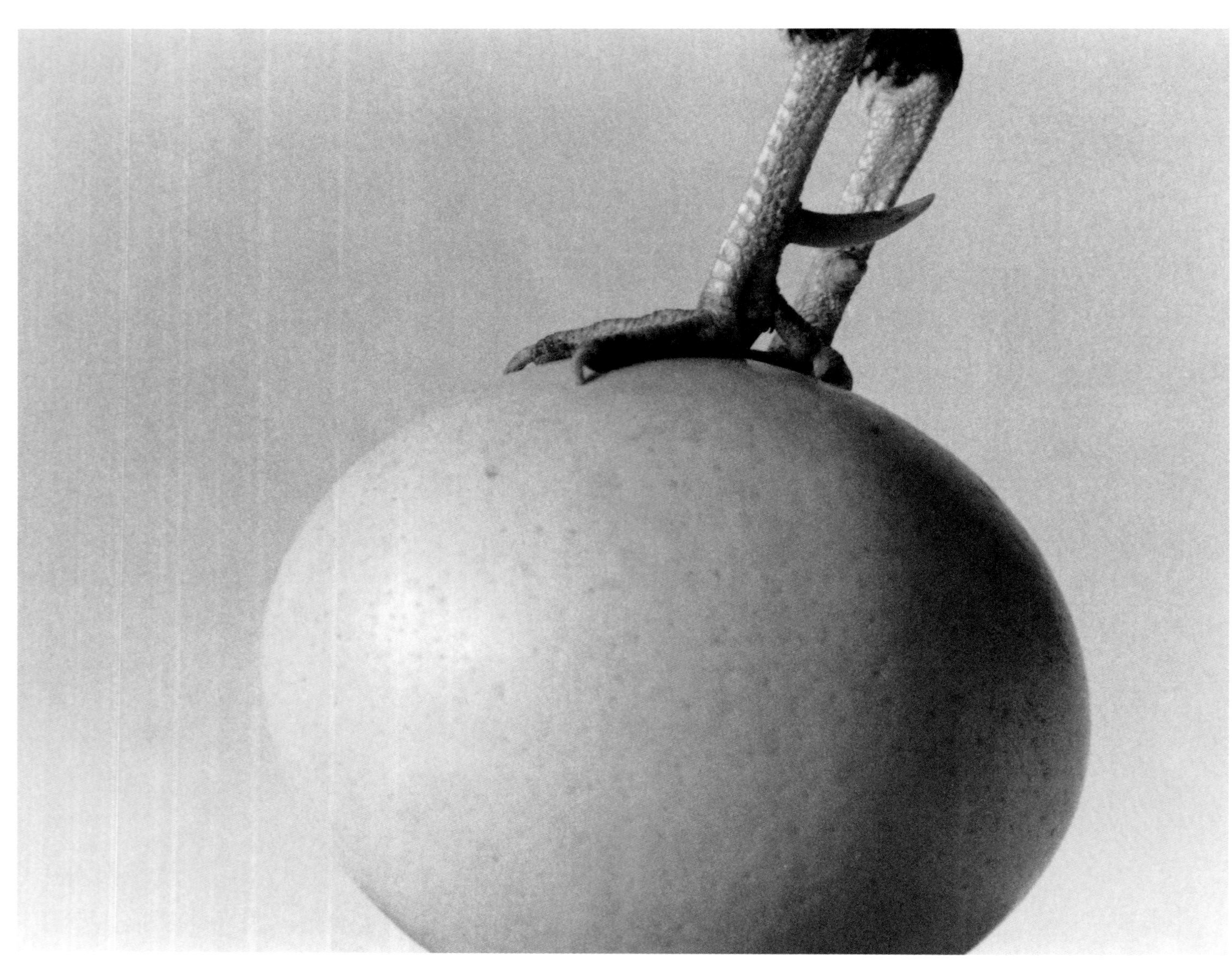

94 *Which Came First,* 1997

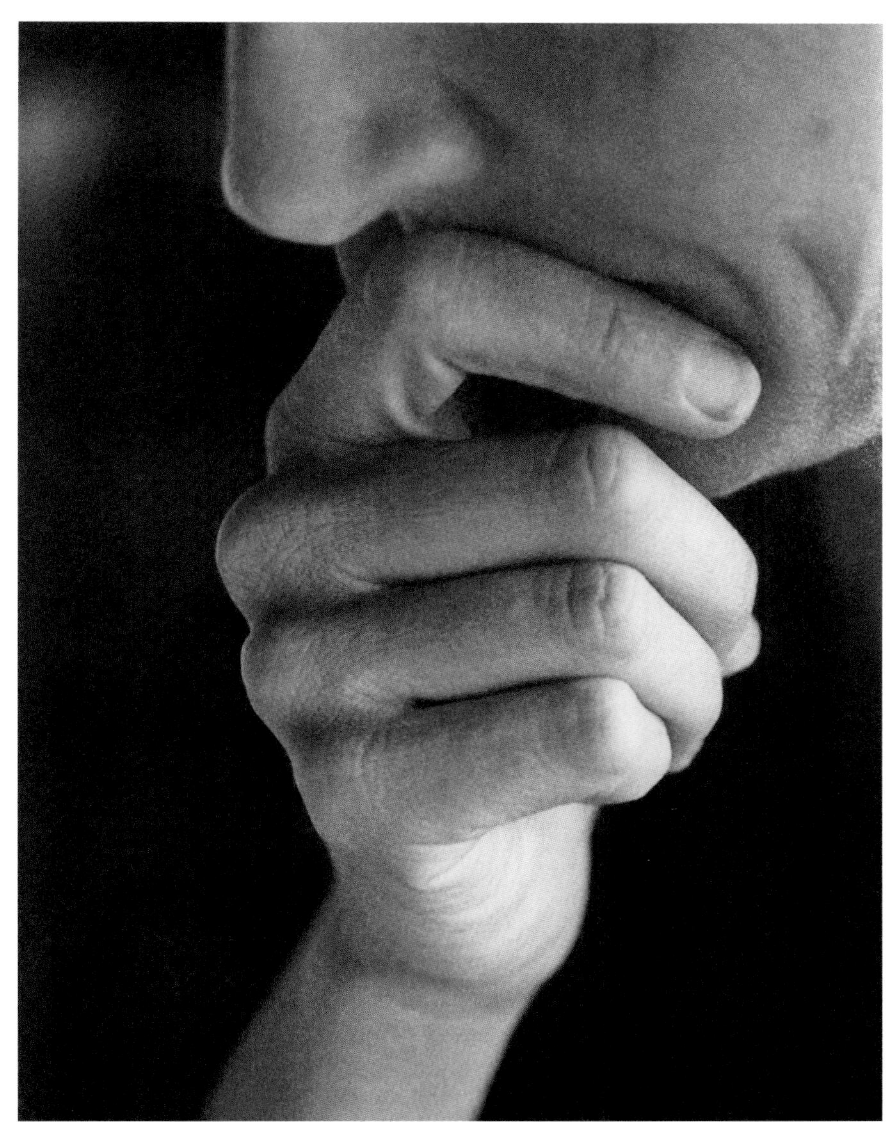

95   *Carole's Hand.* 1985

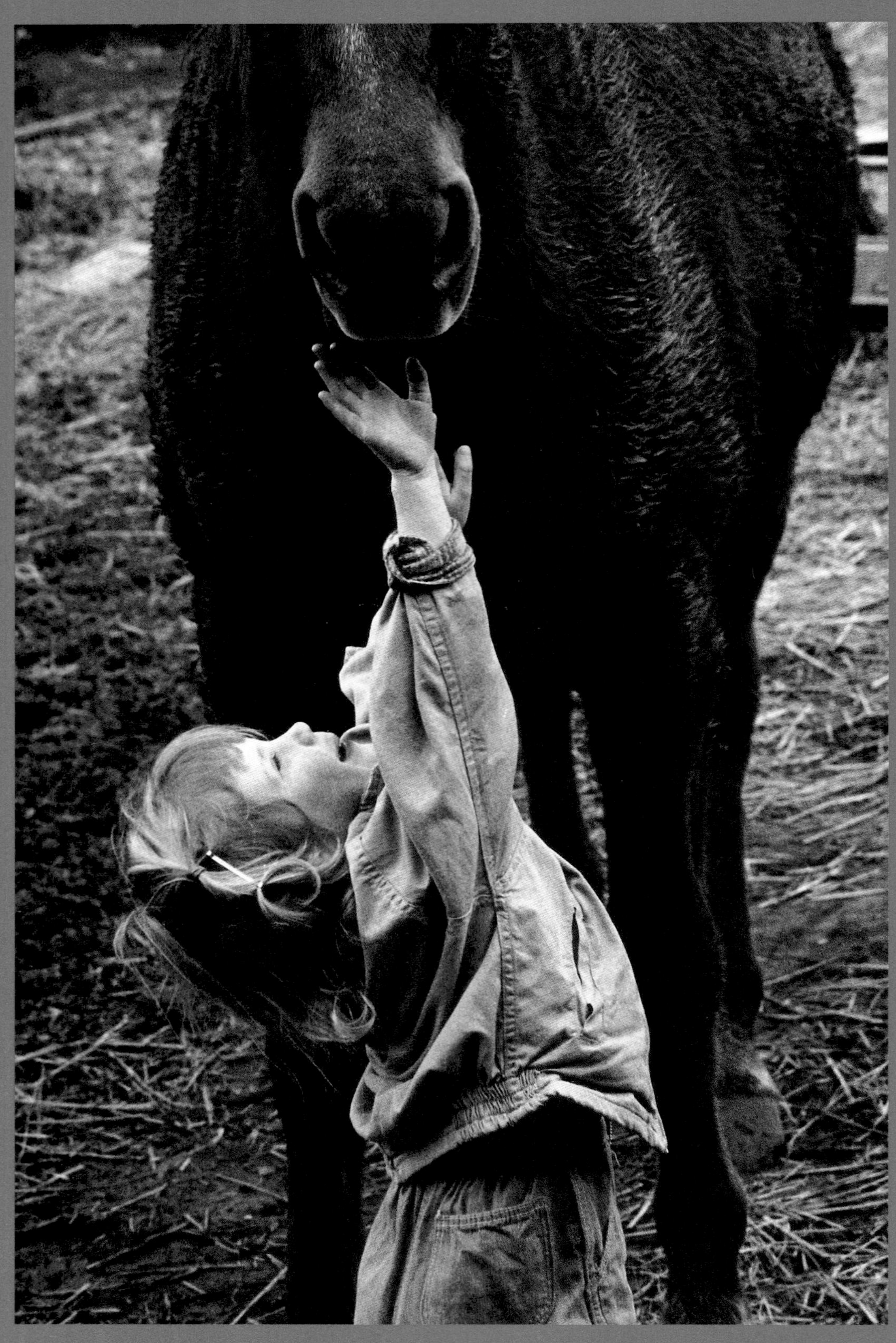

AFTERWORD | Dark and Light

My parents, Rondal and Elizabeth Partridge, had three inviolate rules when we were growing up: never leave the house without putting on cowboy boots, in case we came across a rattler; never scream unless we saw one; and always stay out of my father's light.

We lived on twelve grassy acres in the San Francisco Bay Area: close enough to the city for my father to take architectural photography jobs, but far away enough to give us all the freedom of the country. We had a little shack with just two bedrooms, a nearly dry well, and the world's leakiest roof. When I was about six, my father built his own studio, with a darkroom, a workroom, and a massive porch (Plate 30).

Whether on an architectural job or at home, Ron always had a camera hanging from a leather strap around his neck, ready to photograph at a moment's notice. His full concentration funneled through his lens to whatever he was shooting: a blue jay grabbing a treat from my sister's hand (fig. 1), or the elongated shadows of our horses cantering in the late afternoon sun. If we were careless enough to get between him and his light source, he'd bark, "Out of my light!" without even looking up. Something in the tone of his voice made us jump behind him, gazelle-like, to be sure we were in the clear.

In 1960, when I was nine, the water company claimed our land to build a reservoir. Our property was condemned just as my mother's great-aunt decided to sell her stately but run-down home in one of the nicest parts of Berkeley. My parents pulled together a down payment and we moved in. My mother thought it was perfect: with four kids and no money, my parents could look at UC Berkeley's landmark campanile and envision a good education for us—we could all live at home and go to college.

We moved into the posh neighborhood: four raggedy children, two dogs, a wild assortment of country cats, and my father's three Cadillac limousines, two from the forties and one early-fifties model—one to run and two to cannibalize for spare parts.

Meg Reaching, late 1950s

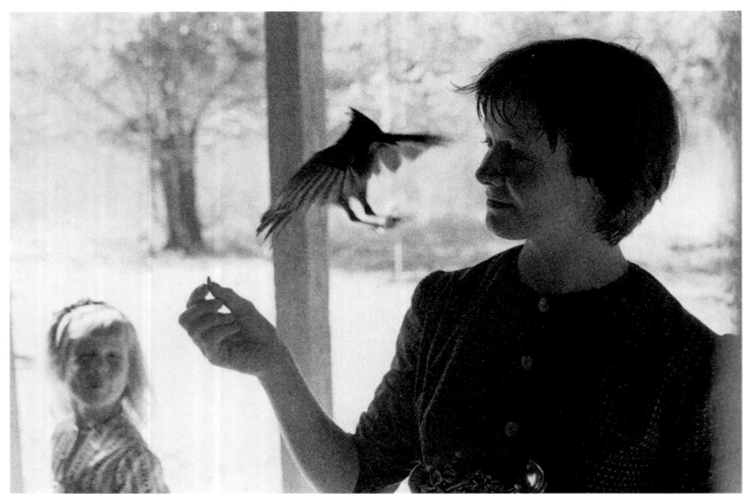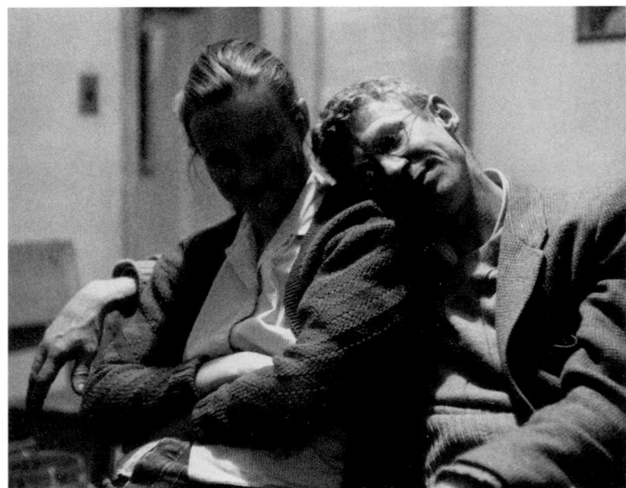

To say we stuck out would be putting it politely. The girls I met wore beautiful dresses and new Mary Janes. A strange hierarchy reigned on the asphalt-covered playground. It wasn't based on who could run fastest or throw the ball farthest, but on who had the most money and the nicest house. The fathers in this neighborhood put on suits every morning and headed out their doors for their important jobs in San Francisco. A part of me began to long for a father like these men, one with neatly cut brown hair who carried a briefcase, not a camera case. One who earned lots of money and bought a new Chevrolet station wagon for his wife every two years, and a new Pontiac Bonneville for himself every year.

I didn't realize that, in contrast to my dad cheerfully throwing open the front door and yelling, "I'm home!" other fathers often came home tired and drained, were short-tempered with their children, and took their frustrations out on their dogs.

Not Ron. He was around, in and out of our lives every day, gone for a few hours, then home again (fig. 2). He dropped his lanky frame onto our beds at night, playing a small, sweet guitar from Mexico and singing "Goodnight Irene" and "Fox Went Out on a Stormy Night." Then he headed to the darkroom to develop and print his day's work.

I used to pull my bedside light under my covers so no one would know I was still awake, then read until the house was quiet. Once my brother and sisters were asleep and my mother was working in her little office, I'd slip down the wide stairs to the first floor, run down the narrow basement stairs to my father's chaotic, messy workroom, and knock on the darkroom door.

"In the dark!" he'd usually yell, which meant I'd have to wait patiently, listening to the surge of water being turned off and on, pipes creaking, the tread of my father's feet as he walked back and forth in front of his sink. While I waited, I moved slowly around his workroom, searching the walls to see what had been pinned up lately. I'd find a strip of a photograph torn from a larger print, just someone's eyes; an image of a bride with her

1   *Joan's Blue Jay,* 1958

2   *Elizabeth and Ron: A Quiet Moment,*
late 1950s (Photograph by Phil Lewis)

hands tightly clenched in excitement; a small animal, made from putty by my little sister Meg, marching across the window shelf with her other animals.

Then Ron's footsteps would come toward the darkroom door, he'd give a shove, and the door would fly open.

Sometimes his hands held wet prints, water splattering around him in big drops. "Watch out!" he'd yell, and I'd jump back. Reaching up, he'd clip the prints to clothespins hanging from wires running across the ceiling.

I'd slip into the darkroom, the room damp, filled with the acrid smell of hypo. My father kept a tall, sturdy stool tucked under the table where the enlarger sat. I'd drag it to the far side of the darkroom, where my father wouldn't trip over it, and slide under the enlarger table, where my father wouldn't trip over me.

Ron would swing back into the darkroom, yank the door shut, and go back to work. He'd switch off the overhead light, leaving the room lit only by the deep yellow safety light and the soft hues coming from a small television directly across from the enlarger, its screen muted by a sheet of orange plastic gel.

While my father printed, I stayed quietly under the enlarger table, watching Red Skelton and Danny Kaye, feeling gentle puffs of air stirred by Ron's endless treading back and forth in front of the sink. Sometimes he'd call me out when he was ready to drop a print in the developing bath. Fingers splayed, his hand would trace lazy circles in the water, gently flip over the print, and rub the other side. I'd watch as the water made tiny waves in the tray, the reflection of the safety light dancing around like a demented moon, and try to guess which side the silvery grays of the image would appear on.

Back in the warm safety of my little nook under the enlarger, I resolved never to be self-employed. It took both my parents to keep my father's business running, my mother to do all the administrative work, my father the photography. He worked long days, out shooting buildings for architects during the week, weddings over the weekends, portraits whenever he could fit them in. His darkroom work often wasn't finished until midnight or later.

Despite how hard they both worked, money was painfully tight. There were periods of palpable tension in the house, my mother's movements tense, my father's whistling sharp and staccato. Bills piled up unpaid and my father, looking embarrassed and defeated, would have to go down to the bank to explain that he'd pay the mortgage soon, if they'd just give him a couple more weeks.

Fortunately, our family's freedom outweighed the money tensions.

With no boss and no regular job, my parents were always willing to head for the beach or take off on a camping trip. The summer of 1962, when I was eleven, my father arranged to photograph buildings across the United States. He spray-painted his 1941 Cadillac limousine a glittering, metallic gold and built a wooden platform from the back of the front seat across the back seat. He laid a double-bed mattress on top of the platform, and the four of us kids piled onto the mattress. My mother squeezed the new baby, Aaron, and his cot in with us, and the two dogs curled up next to the camera equipment in the cave under the mattress. Luggage, tools, and camping supplies were lashed on top.

Never able to be punctual, we finally left in mid-July, the sun glancing off the shiny gold car as we headed across the blazing hot Sacramento Valley. Afraid the head gasket would blow, my father carried a spare seal on the shelf behind the back seat, the copper gleaming around the four round holes meant for the pistons.

On the high Sonora Pass out of the Sierra Nevada, the air thin and the carburetors straining, we all piled out and walked the last steep mile. My mother anxiously led the way, Aaron in her arms, followed by the four of us and the two dogs, crunching through the gravel beside the road.

We zigzagged from state to state, photographing buildings as we went. My father carefully packed his exposed film in the camera cases tucked back in the cool darkness below the mattress, to be processed when we returned home. As we drove from city to city, Ron kept his eyes moving from side to side, always watchful, his camera hanging around his neck, reading glasses nestled in his curls. When he saw something interesting, he pulled off the road and leapt out of the car. I learned to watch him carefully as he sighted along his outstretched arm, forefinger and thumb extended. Squinting his left eye shut, he'd peer intently through the right angle formed by his finger and thumb. Down went his arm, up swung the camera, and he took his shot.

We made it to New York in late August (fig. 3) and started home, looping down through the South. Under the hot sun of Atlanta, Georgia, I danced ahead of my parents and siblings, heading for a drinking fountain. "What does 'Whites Only' mean?" I hollered back to my mother, whose disapproving look let me know this was a whispered truth, not a shouted truth.

I was surprised that my father, who has photographed hundreds of signs, didn't pull the camera up to his eye. "I never photographed a 'Whites Only' sign," he told me years later. "I was too embarrassed. I thought someone might mistake my photographing for approval."

Still in the Deep South, with his work nearly completed, my father asked an architect to wire him money at a local bank. We walked in to get the money, a relief after days of camping and eating peanut butter and drinking Tang. The clerk seemed to be unimpressed with my father's ID, or perhaps with my father himself, and decided to call the architect to verify that my dad was the authorized recipient. Ron never could stand any kind of authority and immediately began fidgeting nervously at the counter. I worried that we would be stuck with peanut butter, then I had the terrible thought that perhaps we wouldn't be able to pay for gas, and we'd be stuck for real.

Staring sternly at my father, the clerk made the call. After a few moments he laughed, hung up the phone, and counted out the money.

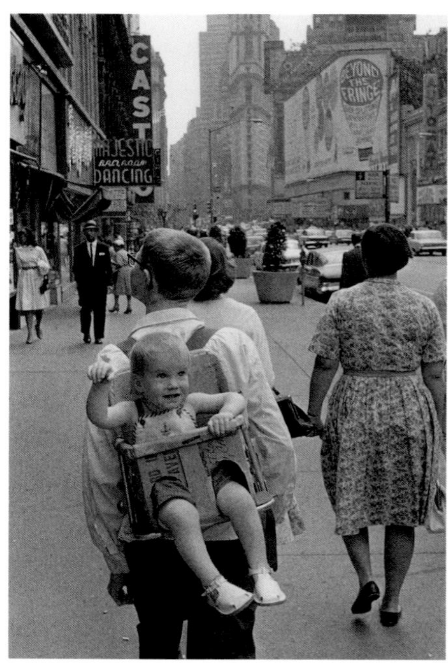

3 *Josh with Aaron in Homemade Backpack,* New York City, 1962

"What did he say?" my father asked, mystified and relieved all at once.

"He said you were tall, with red hair, glasses on top of your head, and a camera around your neck." He pushed the money across the counter.

We made it as far as the cornfields of Iowa for my birthday on October 1, when my mother realized that we were missing school. She sent a letter back to the Berkeley schools, asking them to save space for the four of us, assuring them we would be back soon.

We were home a few weeks later. I was half-sorry to leave the excitement of the road, where every day brought new adventures, and half-glad. Months of being stuck on a mattress with all my siblings had made me long for my own bed, a safe haven for reading long past lights-out. I was ready for my well-dressed classmates, ready to learn from books, and ready for quiet times in my father's darkroom late at night.

My father claims he was almost born in the darkroom, surely an exaggeration. But his mother, Imogen Cunningham, did have a darkroom in their home in Oakland, California, where her husband, Roi Partridge, taught art at Mills College. By the time he was five, Ron was curious about photography. Imogen set a wooden apple box in front of the darkroom sink so he could climb up and watch the exposed paper developing in the baths. "I was fascinated as the print slowly emerged as vaporous grays, then darkened and darkened," Ron said. "Right there I learned how to print."

For many years, Imogen proofed her negatives on printing-out paper (P.O.P.), which made proof sheets in shades of red rather than grays and blacks. Instead of being developed in the darkroom, the exposed paper was run outside into the sun and watched carefully for four or five minutes until it was perfect, then pulled out of the light. Imo began sending Ron outside with the printing frames, with instructions to come to her when he thought they were ready. She quickly discovered he had an unerring eye for when the prints were at their most luminous, and left it up to him to decide when to bring them in.

When he wasn't in the darkroom, Ron was often out roaming the neighborhood with his identical twin brother, Padraic. Nicknamed the "Partridge devils," Ron and Pad had unruly red hair, abundant kinetic energy, and mischief-filled souls. They seemed to be everywhere at once, and always in trouble.

Again and again, Ron returned to his mother's darkroom. What he learned from her about photography came not as technical instruction, but through osmosis. Technically sloppy, Imogen never used a timer to develop her film. Instead she lifted the negative out of the developer tray every few minutes and peered at it under a green light. When it "looked" like the right development, she pulled it out, which led to plenty of over- and under-developing. To make prints from these dubious negatives, Ron says Imogen "dodged, worried, and harried each negative into making some sort of satisfactory result."

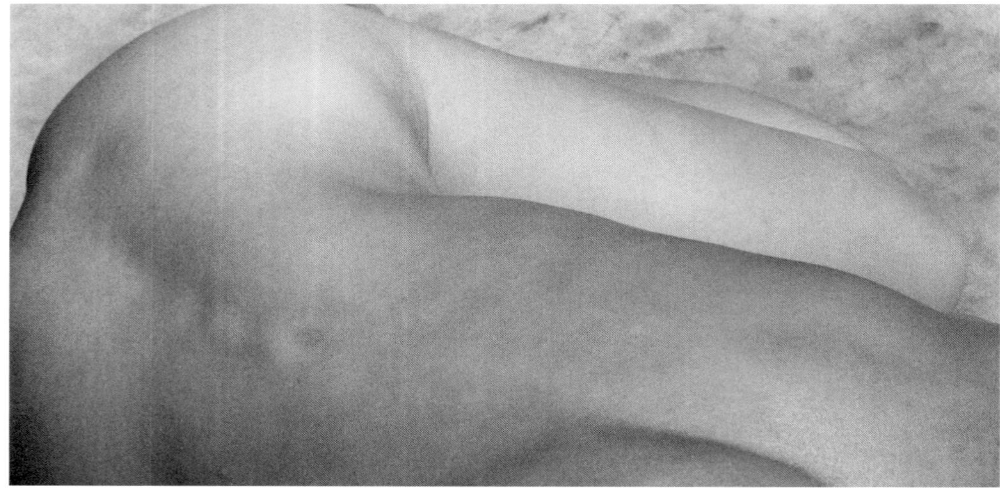

The dinner table was also a fertile learning area for Ron. Several times a week, Imogen and Roi had dinner parties, inviting over anyone they found interesting, including close friends like photographers Dorothea Lange and Ansel Adams.

By the time Ron was in high school, he was serious about his own photography. He began photographing his classmates and neighbors, and dancers at Mills College. On Ansel Adams' advice, he bought his own camera, a 35mm Zeiss Icon. Imogen began taking him on her shoots. Side by side with his mother, he took photographs of his first nude, the Olympic fencer Helena Meyer (fig. 4). He quickly picked up Imogen's deft way of doing portrait photography, putting her subjects at ease and catching them in moments of relaxed concentration.

After graduating from high school in January 1936, Ron packed up his camera and joined the rodeo circuit. It was a rough crowd, but a welcoming one, and the cowboys paid Ron a dollar for every print he made of them on the back of a bucking bull or a wild horse (fig. 5). Ron, standing right out in the middle of the ring with his 50mm lens, learned to shoot fast and to run even faster.

One of Ron's favorite cowboys was a man named Pete Knight. A skilled rider, by the early summer of 1937 he needed to win only one more event to make the final payment on a ranch of his own. When Pete's horse broke out of the gate, Ron was right in the middle of the ring, shooting. The horse bucked Pete off and threw a powerful sideways kick at his falling body, crushing Pete's ribs and killing him. Ron went back home to his darkroom to develop the film and threw up. He didn't last long with the rodeo after that. Nor would he ever choose to photograph people in dangerous situations. He didn't like to see others get hurt.

For the next few years, Ron divided his time between working for Dorothea Lange and Ansel Adams. Nominally paid as an assistant by each of them, he shuttled between two photographers whose photographic goals and techniques couldn't be more different.

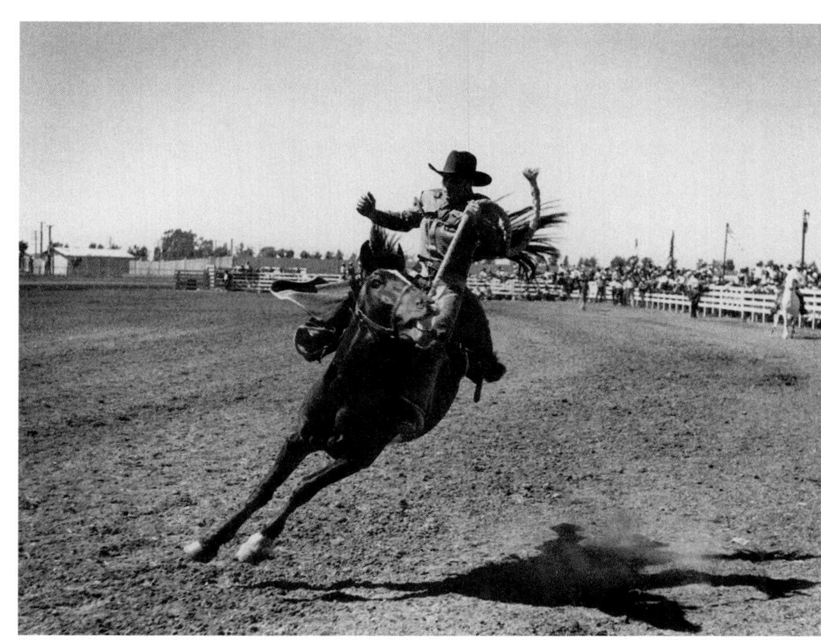

5   *Pete Knight's Last Ride*, 1936

During the summers of 1937 and 1938, Ron joined Ansel in Yosemite. Ansel's energy level was astonishing, and Ron's hyperkinetic state matched Ansel's. Up before dawn, they'd head into the mountains loaded with gear, ready to photograph just as light spread over the peaks. Back in Yosemite Valley by breakfast, Ansel and Ron flung themselves in the darkroom, developing film and making prints.

When Ansel decided to photograph Mount Ritter, he and Ron made the strenuous hike up to Electric Peak several days in a row, but the light was flat. Finally, on the fourth day, storm clouds rolled in, diffusing the light beautifully. Ansel ducked under his focusing cloth for last-minute adjustments, and Ron saw a clear streak of bluish light rise from the top of Ansel's camera. As Ansel popped out from under the cloth and pushed the trigger, Ron raised his own tripod. The blue streak snaked from the clouds down to Ron's tripod. A buzzing sound filled the air, like a swarm of bees. "Let's get the hell out of here!" Ansel yelled. They grabbed their equipment and ran. About seventy-five feet down the mountain they heard a terrific *boom* as lightning hit the place where they'd just been standing.

Besides shooting in the mountains, Ansel was busy with other tasks: putting together exhibitions, writing articles and books. "He could do three or four things at once," Ron said. "He'd type a letter with one hand, talk on the phone, and perfectly time things in the darkroom—and he never lost track of anything." As soon as the afternoon sun slanted across the sky, off they went, rushing toward another granite peak to catch the silvery evening light.

They got along best in the field, their energetic bodies pushing one another on. At Ansel's studio, Ron did the darkroom work when it pleased him, and he was annoyed by Ansel's insistence that the sinks be kept spotless, the floor free of dust. Ron liked to swing the radio dial to a jazz station, which drove Ansel, trained as a classical pianist, up

125

the wall. And anytime Ron thought the fish were biting, he grabbed a fishing pole and took off.

The second year, things hit the boiling point when Ansel was invited to a dinner at the Ahwahnee Hotel to receive an award for his photograph taken from Electric Peak. As Ansel's assistant, Ron felt he should be included, but Ansel said no.

Ansel went off alone and came home drunk and happy. "Great party, Ron, you should have been there," said Ansel, sitting on his bed. "Help me get my shoes off." Ron unlaced each boot, then tied the laces together in a strong sailor's knot. He swung Ansel's legs up on the bed and wished him good night.

In the morning Ansel rolled out of bed, fell flat on his face, and fired Ron.

Ansel had fired Ron before, but this time he really meant it. Though they remained lifelong friends, Ron and Ansel never worked together again. Their styles were just too different.

Ron headed into the Sierra with a burro for a last photographing trip, then returned to the Bay Area. In the fall of 1938 he went back to work as Dorothea Lange's assistant. She fed him, bought him cigarettes, and paid him a dollar a week. It was the beginning of a rich, complex relationship—part mentor and student, part mother and son, and eventually, part colleagues.

Dorothea had Ron drive her up and down the Depression-filled roads of California as she looked for migrant camps, a boss, a broken-down piece of farm equipment. Ron would maneuver her car over the rutted back roads at twenty miles an hour with Dorothea in the seat next to him. "Slow down, Ron, slow down," she often commanded.

When they saw an interesting situation they'd pull in, walk slowly up to the people, and introduce themselves. Seeing Dorothea's limp from childhood polio put people at ease. They knew she understood being slapped down by adversity. Ron noticed that she never took a "grab shot" and always enlisted the help of the people she wanted to photograph. Patiently, she explained that she was from the New Deal's Farm Security Administration and that she wanted the people back in Washington to see how things were. She let the children touch her equipment with their grubby hands, and then often asked one of them to pose in front of her 4x5 Graflex camera (Plate 11). It wasn't that she wanted a posed shot, it was part of her campaign to gain trust.

The work was hard, physically and emotionally (fig. 6). One Thanksgiving they were out shooting and were invited into a family's tent. The mother had managed dinner on meager resources: each child got one biscuit covered in white gravy, with a small square of green pepper for flavor. The father bowed his head, thanking God for His Grace. Dorothea and Ron backed out of the tent, unable even to photograph.

At the end of one long day of shooting, Dorothea and Ron pulled into one of the Central Valley's cheap motor courts and went into the office to register. The clerk looked over

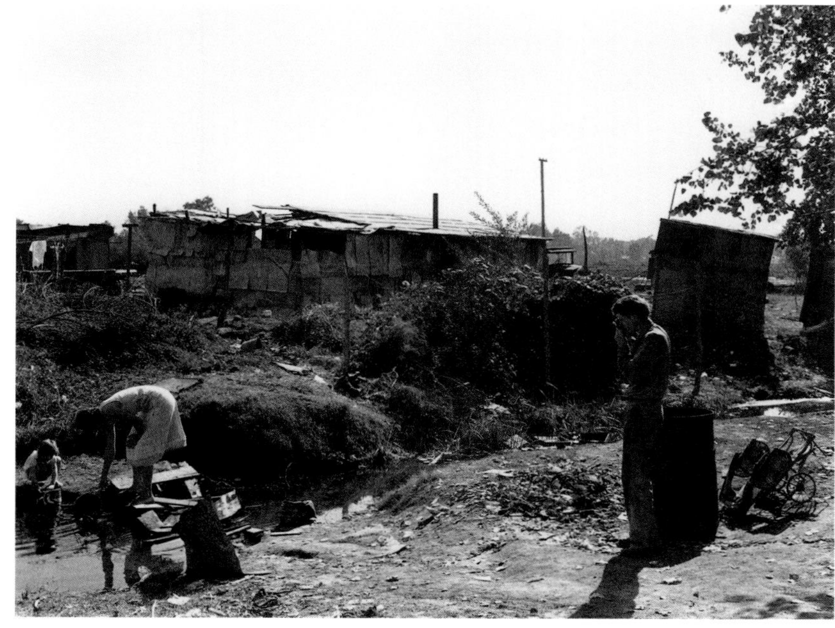

6 *Rondal Partridge Photographing at a Hooverville,* 1939 (Photograph by Dorothea Lange)

at Ron, twenty years younger than Dorothea, and his eyebrows shot up. Dorothea glanced at the clerk, then signed the guest book with a flourish: "Dorothea Lange and Fancy Man."

When they got back home from a trip, Ron would help Dorothea in her basement darkroom, working late into the night. Sometimes he left her house so late that the street-cars had stopped running. Not wanting to wake the household by going back inside, he'd curl up in the leaves in her yard or sleep on a pile of blankets at the moving business down the hill. In the morning, after coffee and a cigarette, he was ready to work again.

Dorothea saturated Ron with completely different values about photography than Ansel had. Ansel likened the negative to a musical score, and he considered the print to be the musical performance; a beautiful, resonant print was his object. Dorothea wanted people to look at one of her photographs and have it hit them in the solar plexus. The message conveyed by the photograph was all that mattered.

Dorothea taught Ron to focus on small details as well as vast landscapes: bare feet on a broken porch, a child's arm crossing her chest as she pledges allegiance. She insisted that he should be able to take a photograph from the back that revealed as much about a person as a photograph taken from the front (fig. 7). She encouraged him to make his prints so simple and clear that they could be read from across the room.

Only slightly older than Dorothea's two children and three stepchildren, Ron was drawn into her family. When Ron and Elizabeth Woolpert, married in 1941, had their first child, Dorothea designated Joan her godchild. One by one, the rest of us Partridge children entered this group, family and yet not quite family.

It was Dorothea's formidable will that held the family together, a bittersweet source of chafing for her children and stepchildren. When Dorothea went over her photographs, she would often mutter to herself, "Not good enough, Dorothea, not good enough." The same impossibly high standards applied to those close to her. Ron was just enough on the periphery of the family, and had just enough of an independent streak, to be invulnerable to her displeasure. He absorbed the best she had to offer and deflected the rest.

When I was young, Dorothea realized that Ron had the makings of a great photographer. She encouraged him to go back to New York to make it in the world of photojournalism. She pushed at him, sure that he could be successful.

Ron said no. He liked being in Berkeley with his family, making a living freelancing. He wanted to decide which jobs to take, and which to pass on—he didn't want someone else deciding for him. Pleasing a boss, processing his work at a photo lab, and traveling without his family didn't appeal to him. The big city life of the photojournalist wasn't for him.

Had he followed Dorothea's advice, I wouldn't have had a dad around the house with wild red hair and a camera case and no "real" job. I wouldn't have had the chance to sit quietly in the darkroom as Ron rattled around doing his printing. I wouldn't have seen him photographing all these years, carrying with him the knowledge of these California photographers, filtering it through his own inimitable sense of being.

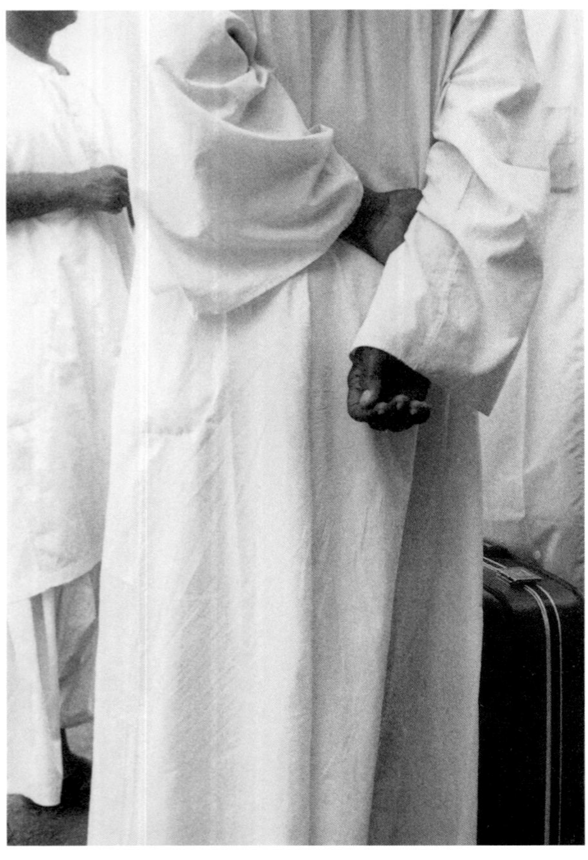

7 *Sudanese Muslim, 1980*

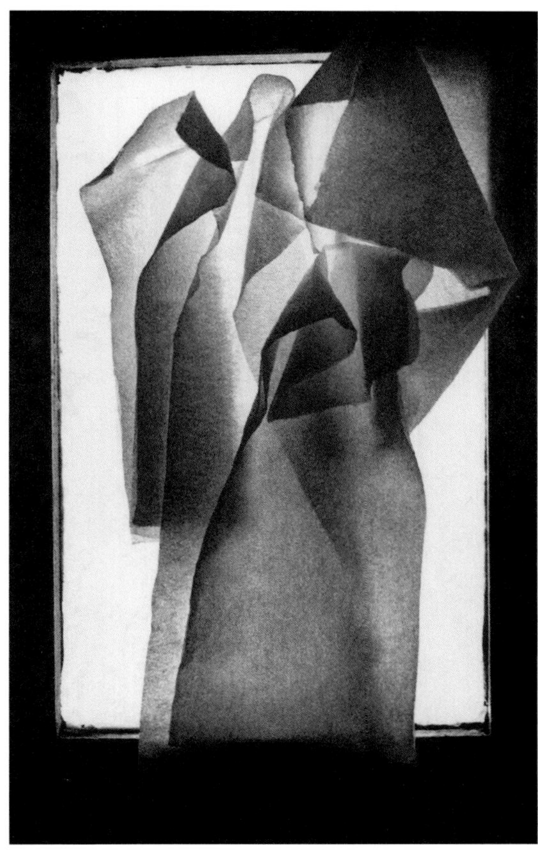

8 *Bathroom Window, 2002*

Ron would have lost something too. He's been a photographer on his own terms, making the images that appealed to him, not to someone else. At eighty-five years old, he has files containing seventy years of photographs (so far) and he still photographs nearly every day. If anything, he has a greater sense of urgency now. "I don't know how long I have left," he explains. Anything can trigger his photographic curiosity: braided cornrows on a woman's head, the diffuse light in his bathroom window (fig 8). He'll shoot off a roll, and head for the darkroom to see what he's got.

I haven't fit under the enlarger table for a long time, but I still enjoy wandering around his messy workroom, waiting for him to burst out of the darkroom. I always find treasures: the clean, white skull of a skunk, a small box of foreign coins chosen one by one at the flea market, and always, new prints hanging from wires running across the ceiling.

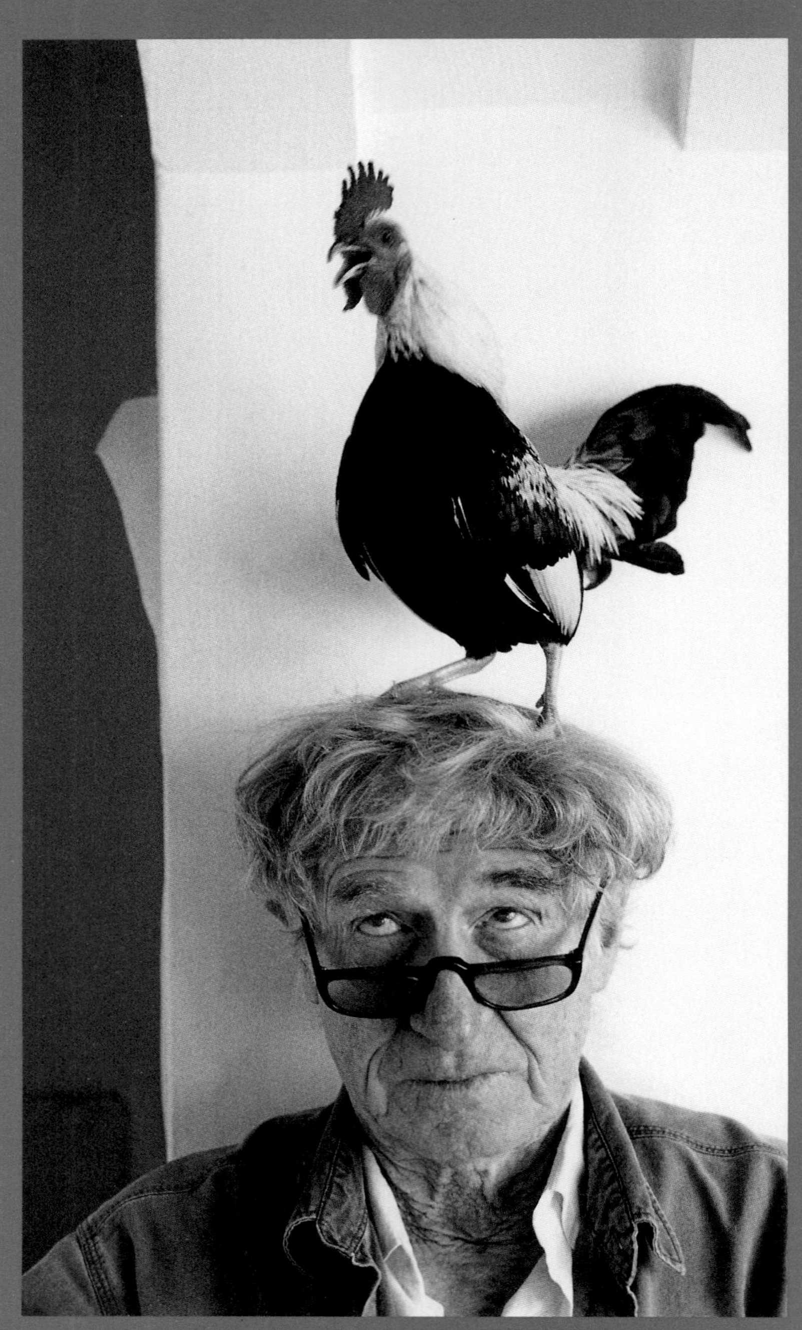

Notes on Plates

All comments by Rondal Partridge, interviewed by Elizabeth Partridge, 2002

1.   *Airplane Bathroom,* 1999
Whatever I'm doing, I convert what I see into a possible photograph in my mind. I have a camera with me most of the time, so I take the shot. I'm sort of like Boss Tweed: I see my opportunity and I take it.

2.   *Self-portrait in Bathroom Mirror,* 1953
I love mirrors. They double your vision.

3.   *Self-portrait in a Motel,* Anywhere, USA, mid-1980s
I took this photo because it defined all motels in its total loneliness.

4.   *Self-portrait with the Bride,* mid-1970s
That's a funny shot—I saw the sign and just took the picture. I'm always on the lookout for signs—the quirkier the better.

5.   *Old Photographers Never Die,* 1994
I took this photo in a twisted sheet of old Mylar that I found in a garbage can. Then I threw it away. I wish I hadn't—I can't find another one.

6.   *Ansel Adams in the Sierra,* late 1930s
I was assisting Ansel in Yosemite. While he was taking a picture with my Speed Graphic, I took this photo of him with his camera.

7.   *High Sierra,* late 1930s
I dove into one of these lakes through a hole in the ice about eighteen inches across. I don't know why I did that—I could have died! I looked up and I could see the trout sucking at the ice, going for the ice worms. Later I met a cowboy up there who told me that years ago the government paid him ten bucks for taking cans of golden trout up to stock lakes. He put one can in that little lake for his own larder.

Oscar Crowing, 1997
(Photograph by Joan Partridge)

8. *Devil's Postpile*, late 1930s

This was on a trip I took by myself into the mountains with a burro. I loaded my camping equipment and food and a brand-new climbing rope on the burro, but I didn't trust the burro to carry my camera.

9. *A Different View of Ansel*, late 1930s

We could get pretty grubby after we'd been out in the mountains photographing for a few days.

10. *Dorothea Lange and the Zeiss Jewell Camera*, 1937

We all respected Ansel and his knowledge of cameras. He convinced Dorothea to buy this view camera. She used it for years. Dorothea climbed up on top of that car with her camera so many times. It looks like she's up there to get a wide view, but she wants a precise view, free of ground-level obstructions.

11. *Dorothea Lange in the Field*, 1938

This photo is pure Dorothea. This was how she got her entrée at migrant camps—photographing children.

12. *Migrant Kids Jumping Rope*, Arvin camp, California, 1938

I took this photograph with Dorothea at Arvin camp, set up by the Farm Security Administration. When families came to Arvin, they came to a place where survival wasn't such a struggle. There was a school, and kids could learn and play instead of just working in the fields.

13. *Weighing Cotton*, Central Valley, California, late 1930s

Dorothea and I were in a field where the workers were picking cotton. It began raining, so they weighed up and went home. You can't bale wet cotton.

14. *Entering California 1*, late 1930s

15. *Entering California 2*, late 1930s

This family had been picking crops in Arizona and were moving on to California. They had some kind of car trouble they were trying to fix.

16. *Hymn Singing*, Arvin camp, California, 1938

At Arvin camp, Dorothea and I photographed a meeting of the Mothers' Club. They started with hymns and prayers. The migrants all brought their religion with them. But there was a real difference between the preachers who said everyone would get their reward in heaven and the communists organizing in the field.

17. *Asparagus Worker*, Sacramento River Delta, California, 1940

Elizabeth and I were driving up the River Road in the Delta, on our way to Nevada to get married. I saw people harvesting and stopped to photograph.

18. *Potato Field Madonna*, Kern County, California, 1940
This girl came from Oklahoma. She never finished high school. She was beautiful, but she didn't have a chance. She was bound to get exploited, pregnant, and wrinkled under the sun.

19. *April Peace Strike*, University of California, Berkeley, 1940
This was a demonstration at Cal sponsored by the "Yanks Are Not Coming" committee as the U.S. prepared to enter the war. The photo is part of my National Youth Administration work now held in the National Archives. I photographed the demonstration, then I went over to the ROTC and photographed them drilling.

20. *Riding the Freights*, Yuba County, California, 1940
Riding the freights was rough stuff. You had to watch out for the railroad guards and the small-town police. Everywhere were signs saying "Keep Moving." This guy had just been fired from a kitchen job in Los Angeles. He was carrying a clean white shirt, heading north and looking for work.

21. *Falling Ice*, New York City, 1940
I took this for Black Star [photography agency] to show the aftereffects of an ice storm.

22. *Taking Down the Sixth Avenue El Train Tracks*, New York City, 1940
Seeing the elevated train be deconstructed had a great influence on me. It was very, very powerful. I didn't *see* that New York was my subject, but I did see the trains as my subject. The elevated destroyed the life and the light on the street and substituted blackness and noise. They took it down to get light on the street. Decades later, I worked to underground the Bay Area Rapid Transit system in Berkeley, California.

23. *Preparing Sheets of Steel to Make Battleships*, Pennsylvania, 1940
This was one of the naval shipyards in Pennsylvania. They had great big sheds with cranes. It was dirty and dusty and noisy. I climbed up the scaffolding to photograph. The photos in this series were used in *Fortune* magazine for an essay on preparing for the war.

24. *Installing a Periscope*, Pearl Harbor, 1945
I was in the Navy as a chief photographer's mate for nearly five years. I went in as a chief, came out as a chief. I never advanced, was never reprimanded or court-martialed. I used to salute with my left hand. It drove them crazy, but it was legal.

25. *Sailors in Central Park*, New York City, 1940
They had to dance with each other—there were no women around.

26. *Couple in Central Park*, New York City, 1940
They were lying on the grass, listening to the radio. The Zenith radio was an all-wave battery radio that ran on tubes. People love radios, they still take them to the park.

27. *Testing an Overhauled Submarine*, Midway Island, 1945
I had a job photographing subs from a submarine chaser. I was up the mast about
seventy-five feet, strapped in, with a big aerial camera that weighed about twenty pounds.
Every bomber pilot would get pictures of our subs, so they'd see what the sub looked
like, what the wake looked like, so our pilots wouldn't shoot them.

28. *Loading a Machine Gun Belt*, near Hawaii, 1945
I was never on a war patrol. I was only on subs that were testing after a retrofit. Serving
on a sub was the most dangerous job during the war. A good day was getting on deck
and taking off your shirt in the warm sun.

29. *Gambling in the Galley*, near Hawaii, 1945
On submarines, blacks and whites served together. The majority of people underwater
were young and very self-disciplined. There were no freak-outs, no crazies. Because the
guys were always so close to dying, money meant nothing. They gambled their money
away to each other.

30. *View from My Studio*, Bear Creek, California, late 1950s
I don't have any preconception of what is valuable as a photographic subject. A view,
a snake—I never know what will catch my eye. I shoot it, print it, and wait for fashion
to catch up with my eyes. Some photographs get accepted after a long period of time.

31. *Snake in a Box*, Bear Creek, California, 1953
Our house in the country was surrounded by hills. The rattlesnakes came down out
of the hills and slithered into gopher holes, looking for food. This snake was near the
house, just resting in the box. I cut a hole in a big piece of cardboard and stuck my lens
through it so I could get close enough to photograph without the snake being able to
strike at me.

32. *Waiting*, 1953

33. *Nursing*, 1953

34. *Thirsty*, 1953

35. *The Eye*, 1953
This was the birth of our daughter. I did a photo essay for *Look* magazine (Decem-
ber 29, 1953) called "The Birth of Margaret." All my skills as a photographer came
together when I shot this essay. I finally knew what I was doing. It took me a long time
to learn photography.

36. *Odetta*, mid-1950s
Odetta was about twenty years old when I met her. Her voice was pure Odetta. She'd just
moved to Sausalito from Los Angeles. Clayton Lewis organized a storefront concert. I took
photos of her and tacked them up on telephone poles with news of the upcoming concert.
We charged $1.25 and filled the place. Odetta made enough to get by for three months.

37. *Me Too*, 1948

Elizabeth was handing our new baby, Josh, to her grandmother. I heard the back door
open and knew Joan was coming in. I had a camera around my neck. I didn't have time
to focus, just pulled the camera up and pushed the trigger—a lucky shot. I was totally
surprised it came out. But you always have to try.

38. *Cat's Cradle*, 1952

That's our daughter Joan, amusing herself with a piece of string. It's just a quiet moment
of a kid being a kid.

39. *Anna Halprin*, mid-1950s

Anna Halprin was a great innovator of modern dance, and a great teacher.

40. *Joan Dancing*, mid-1950s

Joan took classes from Anna Halprin, and she used to wrap herself in scarves and dance
for hours. In the country, kids have to find ways to entertain themselves.

41. *Fossil Hunting*, late 1950s

The art of photographing bodies—or anything else in motion—is the art of anticipating
where they'll be by the time you get the trigger pushed and the negative exposed. You
have to be a fraction of a second ahead of yourself. If you wait to see the shot, by the
time you take it, you'll be too late.

42-47. *Reading 1-6*, late 1950s

Sometimes a series of photographs says much more than just one.

48. *Ruth Asawa in Her Studio*, San Francisco, 1969

I met Ruth's husband, Albert Lanier, when I was photographing for Mario Corbett, the
architect. Al was so interesting. I thought he and Imogen ought to meet. He and Ruth
went over to Imogen's for dinner, and we all became good friends.

49. *Ruth Asawa's Living Room*, San Francisco, 1969

Ruth could work anywhere. She had a studio, but she would work at the dining room
table as well, with the kids all around doing their own art projects. She made these
little sculptures out of salt and flour and water and then put them all together and
made them into huge brass fountains by burning out the flour mixture. She took a lot
of criticism for making little flour-and-salt figures, but the sculptures are incredible.

50. *Shop Carpenter*, Berkeley, California, late 1980s

This man was an old finish carpenter, too old to do any hard work. He'd been hired to
manage a contractor's shop. He sharpened saws, put things away, cleaned up. This sort
of employment was frequently used to give old workers a job, especially before Social
Security. The pay was low, but people could hold themselves together.

51. *John Warneke*, San Francisco, early 1960s

I was photographing the house that the architect John Warneke had just built, and
he said he needed a photograph of himself, quick, for publicity. I had just bought

an antique camera from the 1880s at a secondhand store. I had a holder with film,
guessed the f-stop and the speed, and took two shots straight on.

52. *Ratcliff House*, Berkeley, California, 1951

53. *Corbett House*, Tiburon, California, n.d.
I photographed architecture in natural light without changing anything. If the room
was too dark, that's what I photographed. I refused to add light.

54. *The Secretariat*, Chandigarh, India, 1962

55. *Assembly Building*, Chandigarh, India, 1962
Architectural Forum magazine gave me the assignment to photograph the parliament
building in Chandigarh, designed by Le Corbusier. He was really hard on photographers—
he thought they distorted things. He liked my photos, though. He wrote me twice in
French thanking me.

56. *Brickyard Worker*, New Delhi, 1962
I was at a work site where women handle all the bricks. They live in workers' villages
you couldn't believe, in small huts about four feet high. They do all their cooking out-
doors, over dung fires. That's a tough life. This Rajasthani lady was so beautiful. She stood
for several photographs, then she must have felt she was being exploited by a westerner.
I didn't take any more photos of her, but I love her hand. Hands are as important as
faces, sometimes more.

57. *Dorothea Lange*, early 1960s
The essential difference between me and other people photographing is that I don't go
in with a preconceived notion of what I want. But sometimes when I *do* see what I like,
I say "hold it." It gives me time to get the camera in position and focused. That's what
happened here. Dorothea rubbed her face and then looked at me through her hands,
and I said, "Hold it."

58. *Pave It and Paint It Green*, Yosemite National Park, mid-1960s
I went to Yosemite with a producer from KQED to make a film. All he saw was falling
water, tall cliffs, and happy people. He wanted to do a story on how Yosemite was discovered. I saw congestion, destruction, erosion. I got up on the top of the car and took
the shot and was blasted by a bullhorn from a ranger. He demanded I get off the car.
He wanted to arrest me, and I said I refused to be arrested. I convinced his supervisor
that I had obtained permission to photograph, and that I could shoot from wherever
I wanted.

59. *New Chevy*, Emeryville, California, 1964
Look at that billboard rising up from the junkyard! In ten years that car will be in the
junkyard, not on the billboard.

60. *Airport Parking*, San Francisco, 1965
Automobiles are a main concern of mine. They'll cover the world ten feet deep in the next fifty years. I have dozens of photographs of parking lots.

61. *Freeway*, San Francisco, late 1960s

62. *Housing*, Daly City, California, late 1960s
In California we build freeways that encourage subdivisions that encourage more freeways. It will end with California smothered in houses and freeways and parking lots.

63. *Rolling Hills*, Danville, California, 1958
I took this after Dorothea said that Danville was bound to be the fastest growing place in California because all the freeways went through there. I wanted to show what we were going to lose.

64. *Power Grid*, Southern California, early 1970s
I was fascinated by the fact that underfoot and overhead we were inundated with stuff. We don't even notice it.

65. *Modern Midden*, Albany, California, 1965
I wanted to show that all pollution ends up in the ocean sooner or later.

66. *Tire Marks*, Pismo Beach, California, late 1960s
Pismo Beach used to be world famous for clams. Now they've gone—pounded into the sand by recreational vehicles.

67. *Bayfill*, San Leandro, California, 1960
This was taken in the days when it was acceptable to dump everything into the bay. That's just a huge mound of garbage. Then they'd cover it with dirt, plant grass, and call it a park.

68-71. *Shadow as Substance* 1-4, Oakland, California, late 1990s
I love flea markets, just love them. I love bargains. There is a certain joy in buying something you wouldn't think of buying unless you saw it and got it cheap. I buy cameras at the flea market and give them away. I've found exquisite lenses, marvelous old tools, and all kinds of things that I wouldn't find anywhere else.

72. *Poultry Shears*, 1997

73. *Handle of a Keyhole Saw*, 1996
The flea market led me into focusing my eyes on things I would never have looked at except at a flea market.

74. *Judy Dater*, 1978
Judy came to photograph me for the book she wrote on Imogen. I was sitting in front of her and I had a camera, and I took a portrait of her.

75. *Pregnant and Proud,* 1976
Isn't she beautiful? She was so happy to be pregnant.

76. *Being Who They Are,* n.d.
Photographs are enhanced by having two things in the image. A mother and daughter,
two hands, two plants. They play off each other.

77. *Annie at Steep Ravine,* Marin County, California, 1972
I love photographing in natural light. In the city, I don't even like street trees. I like open
streets. I feel at home with the light filling in the shadows.

78. *Dorothea Lange,* early 1960s
Dorothea was the best photographer of the twentieth century, the best. Really look at
her photographs, and you'll see what I mean. Look at the images of any of the world's
greatest photographers, and you'll learn something. You can ask questions of great
photographs, and great photographs ask questions of you.

79. *Sisters,* 2000
Two sisters, one mirror. A few weeks later they had their babies, side by side in the
hospital, the babies coming just two hours apart.

80. *Queen of Tarts,* late 1960s
This is my mother, the tart-tongued photographer, Imogen Cunningham. She was legend-
ary for her stinging remarks. But they were a badge of honor in the San Francisco art
community—people gleefully traded stories of what she had said to them.

81. *Two Right Hands,* 1988
My identical twin and I each put our right hand down on the table.

82. *Aaron's Silicon Valley Pants,* 1994
My son, Aaron. I wanted to show that he spent too much time in his chair in front of a
computer. Look at all those wrinkles!

83. *My Fingers,* 1996
The smaller the subject, the more mysterious it becomes when enlarged. That's why I
love using macro lenses.

84. *Shell Shadows,* 1989
This is one photo of a shell, printed twice. If you turn the image upside down, it will still
look the same. Our minds do that with light and shadow. Try it!

85-87. *Chester 1-3,* 1982
I took two or three rolls of Chester while he slept. I was exploring texture and design.
There must be a thousand photos in one Weimaraner.

88. *Anise Quartet, 1995*

Everything is grist for the photographic mill. You just have to grind it fine—that is, look carefully. Look, see, and shoot. Simple.

89. *Decaying Leaf, 1995*

I found this leaf on the ground and brought it home just to record the extraordinary beauty of decay.

90. *Leek and Squash Tendrils, 1995*

I photograph with the light that's there. I rarely use anything else. Part of my philosophy of photography is that if you add light, you change the subject. You distort it. I have my light stand set up by a window, and I just wait till I think the light is right, then I shoot.

91. *Industrial Bulb, 1995*

I picked up this lightbulb at the flea market. I wanted to see if I could shoot those filaments. I like to solve problems, go at things in a different way. It wouldn't matter if I were a mathematician, an astronomer, or a photographer—I just like to challenge myself.

92. *Bird and Onions, 1989*

I was photographing onions, and the dead bird appeared on the sidewalk in front of my house. The breast of the bird looked like the smooth skin of the onions.

93. *Bird in Glass, 1989*

I photograph all the dead animals that come by. I don't know why.

94. *Which Came First, 1997*

I got my rooster, Oscar, to stand on an egg. I wanted to see if he would recognize it as an egg. I have a whole roll of him peering at the egg sideways, tipping his head back and forth.

95. *Carole's Hand, 1985*

Every once in a while there are things that only you see, there is a photo that only you could make. It's simple—a hand, a chin. But only this one hand and chin at this one moment.

Chronology

<table>
<tr><td>1917</td><td>Born September 4, 1917, in San Francisco to photographer Imogen Cunningham and etcher Roi Partridge.</td></tr>
<tr><td>1920-36</td><td>Raised near Mills College in Oakland, California, where his father teaches art.</td></tr>
<tr><td>1922</td><td>Begins to spend time in the darkroom with Imogen. Learns to develop film and make sun prints.</td></tr>
<tr><td>1932</td><td>Borrows a camera from Imogen and begins taking photographs and developing, printing, and selling them to his classmates and neighbors.</td></tr>
<tr><td>1934</td><td>Parents divorce. Partridge begins to assist Dorothea Lange occasionally.</td></tr>
<tr><td>1936</td><td>Graduates from high school in January and follows the California rodeo circuit, photographing the cowboys. Returns to Berkeley and assists Dorothea Lange for wages of one dollar a week, food, and cigarette money.</td></tr>
<tr><td>1937-39</td><td>Assistant to Ansel Adams in Yosemite National Park and to Horace Bristol, a San Francisco photographer working on magazine assignments. Continues to work with Dorothea Lange.</td></tr>
<tr><td>1940</td><td>Works for the National Youth Administration, photographing in the western part of the United States. Photographs archived in the National Archives in Washington, D.C. Works as a photojournalist for Black Star Publishing in New York.</td></tr>
<tr><td>1941</td><td>Marries Elizabeth Woolpert, a University of California law student. Joins the Navy in October and begins service in Navy Intelligence as a photographer.</td></tr>
<tr><td>1945</td><td>Daughter, Joan, is born. Partridge, discharged from the Navy in the fall, establishes freelance photographic business, primarily magazine and architectural photography. Extensively photographs his family and the urbanization of California.</td></tr>
</table>

1947   Son, Joshua John, is born.

1951   Daughter, Elizabeth, is born.

1953   Daughter, Margaret, is born.

1962   Son, Aaron, is born.

1963-75   Produces and directs films on painter Wayne Thiebaud; Yosemite National Park,
            Pave It and Paint It Green; education, *They're Your Kids;* and water reflections,
            The Water Movie. Assembles *The Magic Lantern,* a multi-projector presentation of
            hand-painted slides for the Oakland Museum of California. Photographs Califor-
            nia's growing pollution problems.

1972-73   Lecturer on photography and film at University of California, Santa Barbara.

1973-74   Lecturer on photography and film at California State University, Hayward.

1976
to present Continues with his own work, appointed trustee for the Imogen Cunningham
            Trust.

1980
to present Master printer for the Imogen Cunningham Trust.

1987
to present Develops an interest in platinum printing. Gradually shifts his focus from silver
            printing to platinum.

SELECT PUBLICATIONS AND EXHIBITIONS

Rondal Partridge's photographs have been published in *Life, Time, Fortune, Harper's Bazaar,
Look, Collier's, Scientific American, House Beautiful, House and Home, Ladies' Home Journal,
Architectural Forum, Architectural Record, Progressive Architecture, American Heritage, Sunset,
Horizon, Think, Audubon, Cry California, Sierra,* and *Educational Facilities Laboratory* publica-
tions. Many of his photographs are included in Peter Blake's *God's Own Junkyard,* William
Bronson's *How to Kill a Golden State,* and Thomas D. Church's *Gardens Are for People.*

Partridge's photographs appear in exhibitions and collections, including the *Golden Gate Expo-
sition, 1939;* Edward Steichen's *Family of Man;* the Museum of Modern Art; the San Francisco
Museum of Modern Art; the Santa Barbara Museum of Art; the California Academy of Sciences;
the Louvre; the National Archives; Fotografie Forum International; the Oakland Museum of
California; and the California Historical Society.

Authors

Son of etcher Roi Partridge and photographer Imogen Cunningham, RONDAL PARTRIDGE (b. 1917) took to photography as a teen and before he was twenty had begun working seriously with both Ansel Adams and Dorothea Lange. Moving to New York in the early 1940s under contract with Black Star, he gained experience in photojournalism as practiced by such major magazines as *Life* and *Fortune*. After serving as a Navy photographer in the Pacific during World War II, he returned to the Bay Area to raise a family. For more than five decades since, he has juggled freelance commercial work with his own passionate commitment to documenting the changing environment of California, all the time continuing to chronicle his expansive circle of friends, family, dogs, chickens, and nearly all other forms of flora and fauna that engage his free spirit.

ELIZABETH PARTRIDGE grew up in the San Francisco Bay Area in a large, eccentric family filled with photographers: her grandmother, Imogen Cunningham; her godmother, Dorothea Lange; and her father, Rondal Partridge. She has been an acupuncturist for over twenty years and writes books for both adults and children. Her most recent biographies are *Restless Spirit: The Life and Work of Dorothea Lange* (Viking, 1999) and *This Land Was Made for You and Me: The Life and Music of Woody Guthrie* (Viking, 2002).

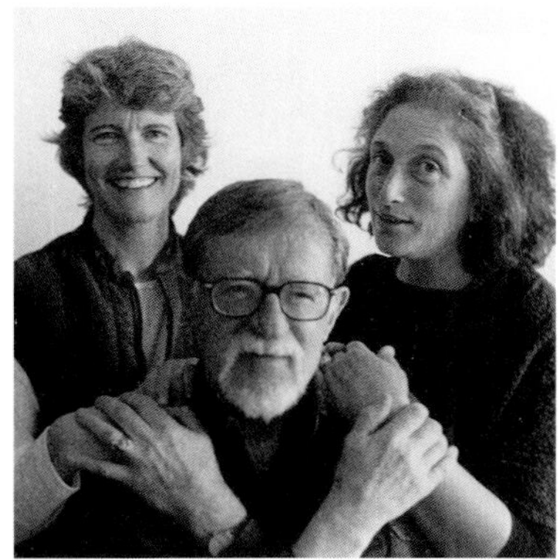

Elizabeth Partridge, Daniel Dixon, and Sally Stein, photograph by Rondal Partridge, 2002

SALLY STEIN lives in Los Angeles, teaches art history and visual studies at the University of California, Irvine, and writes about the history of photography, especially American photography and mass media in the Great Depression. Stein co-authored and co-curated *Official Images: New Deal Photography* (Smithsonian, 1988) and *Montage and Modern Life* (ICA/MIT, 1992). She is currently at work on a volume of essays on Dorothea Lange, the first of which, "Peculiar Grace: Dorothea Lange and the Testimony of the Body," was published in *Dorothea Lange: A Visual Life* (Smithsonian, 1994).

DANIEL DIXON has been an advertising executive, a political consultant, and a newspaper columnist. His articles have appeared in *Life, Cosmopolitan, Esquire, House & Garden*, and many other magazines. He's also the author of *The Thunderbird Remembered*, a memoir of his father, artist Maynard Dixon. His mother was Dorothea Lange.